# SOLIDARITY

*Selected Essays*

by Dan Gallin

A LabourStart Book

Published by LabourStart

www.labourstart.org

Copyright 2014 by the Global Labour Institute

All rights reserved

ISBN: 1497345618

ISBN-13: 978-1497345614

# Table of Contents

Preface ................................................................... 5
What the Third Camp Meant To Me, And To Some Others . 7
Summer days on Utøya [2011] ............................................ 27
The state of the French Left [1958] .................................... 31
Colonial revolution [1961] ................................................ 48
Revolutionary at Large [1963] ........................................... 53
Inside the New World Order: Drawing the Battle Lines [1994] ................................................................... 58
Labour Strategies: Options and Perspectives [2002] ....... 88
The WEA & the Future of International Workers' Education: Rebuilding the Movement [2003] ..................... 93
The International Labour Movement: History and Ideologies [2003] ............................................................. 98
Political Education and Globalization [2004] ................... 111
Not With a Bang But With a Whimper [2004] ................... 121
Organizing in the Global Informal Economy [2004] ........ 126
Organizing: Means and Ends [2006] ............................... 137
International Framework Agreements: A Reassessment [2006] ................................................................... 150
Looking for the Quick Fix: Reviewing Andy Stern [2007] ................................................................... 185
Bureaucratism: Labour's Enemy Within [2009] ............... 213
Informal economy workers and the international trade union movement: an overview [2012] .............................. 234

Our Crisis [2013].................................................................. 253

The Future of the Domestic Workers' Movement [2013] 260

# Preface

**LabourStart is very proud to publish this collection of essays by Dan Gallin, the former general secretary of the International Union of Foodworkers (IUF).**

Gallin's writings over the course of the last six decades are an important contribution to thinking about the labour movement and, we hope, will reach a wider audience through the publication of this book.

The nineteen essays which follow are in chronological order except for the first two.

The first is the closest thing to a memoir that you'll find in this book, as Dan recounts the story of his progression from student socialist in the USA to general secretary of the IUF. Many of the issues Dan raises here are touched on again in much greater detail later in the book.

The second, "Summer days in Utøya," was published in 2011 and is a short, and very touching, account of a visit Dan paid to the Norwegian island back in 1955, more than a half-century before it became the scene of carnage. His reflections on Scandinavian social democracy, and on the rise of the fascist Right, offer valuable insights.

The next three essays -- about the post-war French Left, the Algerian revolution, and Victor Serge, were published in small socialist journals in the USA and Britain in the late 1950s and early 1960s and are worth re-reading more than a half-century after they were first written.

Serge is an author who is periodically "re-discovered" and then forgotten again, and Dan's essay reminds us of his lasting importance. For those interested in alternative histories, Dan's essay on Algeria reminds us that another revolution had been possible. One cannot help but think of the "Arab Spring" of recent years when reading this powerful account. The ups and downs (mostly downs) of the French Left today have their origins in the fate of the post-war Socialist Party, whose decline Dan relates in detail.

And then there's a thirty year gap – roughly the period when Dan was playing a leading role in the international labour movement. Dan wrote a great deal during this period too and perhaps in a future volume, we'll be able to share some of these articles.

The next essay in this ("Inside the New World Order") was written in 1994 and all the remaining essays are from the last two decades. In fact all of them except one are from the period following Dan's "retirement" from the international labour movement -- a time when he moved from being general secretary of the IUF to other arenas, such as establishing the Global Labour Institute, attempting to revitalize the International Federation of Workers Education Associations (IFWEA), building a global network of unions and others working with the informal sector, and finally his work with the first-ever global union led by women workers, which was founded in 2013 in Montevideo.

In the course of these essays you will learn much about the history and the future of the labour movement, and the principles and values that must be at the core of its existence.

Dan's criticisms of the labour movement, from a movement insider, are often sharp. I expect that some of you reading this will find parts of this book difficult going. For Dan, there are no sacred cows. He says what he thinks.

The independent, democratic labour movement has nothing to fear from sharp criticism. Indeed, we thrive on it.

*Eric Lee*
*London, 2014*

# What the Third Camp Meant To Me, And To Some Others

**I was not your typical recruit to the Independent Socialist League (ISL) or its youth organization, the Socialist Youth League (SYL).**

My family came from Czernowitz, as it was known in the Austro-Hungarian Empire (Cernăuți in Romania after 1918, Chernivtsi in the Ukraine after 1939). My father was a senior civil servant in the Romanian foreign service, a conservative nationalist but a democrat, who saw himself as a servant of the nation, by which he meant the people. My mother had no time for Romanian nationalism, or any other nationalism for that matter, she grieved over the collapse of the Austro-Hungarian Empire. Emperor Franz-Joseph, who died when she was sixteen, remained her father figure. Later she became enthusiastic about the early Pan-European movement.

In 1943 my father was stationed in Berlin and my parents sent me to Switzerland to get me out of the way of the war. In the summer of 1944, my mother had joined me in Switzerland and my father, through an unbelievable piece of luck (nobody ever believed he hadn't received advance notice, but he hadn't) came to join us for a week's vacation in the week where Romania changed sides in the war. There was no way he was going to go back to Germany (later we heard that the Gestapo had been waiting for him). So my father was reassigned by the Romanian foreign service to Bern and Switzerland became our home.

I finished high school in Switzerland in a cadre school for the kids of the ruling class. My family had destined me to follow my father in the Romanian foreign service but history decided otherwise. In 1945/7 Stalinism took control of Romania. My father resigned from the Romanian foreign service in December 1947, was called back and refused to return. In 1949 he and his family lost the Romanian citizenship (as well as his income, which led to an existential crisis for my parents, of which I was blissfully unaware until much later).

So here I was, young, stateless and without family pressures. I may have been the only person in the world who experienced the Stalinist take-over in Romania as a liberation, even without realizing it. Meanwhile, I had developed other interests. I had been brought up as a highly political person in an unpolitical sort of way, aware of world politics through my father's bedtime stories about the Balkan wars (of the early 20$^{th}$ century) and his own experiences as a commander of an armoured train in the Romanian army during the first world war.

By the time I was eighteen I had come to the conclusion that the only worthy aim in life was to serve the community and the only struggle worth fighting was the fight for justice. Exactly how to do this I had no idea, the socialist parties seemed boring, Stalinism was out of the question (although some of Gletkin's arguments in Koestler's "Darkness at Noon" seemed uncomfortably cogent). I had discovered surrealism and was enthralled by the radical revolt it expressed, in literature and in painting. I had also discovered existentialism, and devoured Camus, Sartre, de Beauvoir, as well as Malraux and Koestler (later Sperber, Serge, Orwell).

In my last year in high school I had a brilliant philosophy teacher, a Frenchman, who once dropped in passing a reference to La Vérité, the French Trotskyist journal. That registered. Here was an unknown shore yet to be explored (in the event, much later).

After high school, I did not really know what to do with myself but, through an accidental meeting, I got a scholarship at the University of Kansas, in Lawrence, where I arrived in August 1949. After a while, I found my milieu: it was the student co-ops, mostly inhabited at this time by veterans on the GI-Bill some of whom had been active in the Progressive Party campaign of 1948 to get Henry Wallace elected president. There was also an Italian who had been with the socialist resistance movement Giustizia e Libertà. Contrary to the other student housing, the co-ops were integrated: in ours, the only Black was a lone member of the Socialist Party.

I had been co-opted to the editorial board of *upstream* a small student magazine with literary ambitions and liberal-left politics. Through exchanges between student publications in different universities, I came across *Anvil & Student Partisan*, the student magazine of the SYL, which looked really interesting, so much so that I decided I wanted to meet the editor. A trip to New York, in the summer of 1950, gave me the opportunity to do so. This was my first meeting with Julie Jacobson. We talked at length; he also introduced me to Hal Draper and Gordon Haskell, the *Labor Action* team, at the Long Island office, as they were packing crates for moving to 14$^{th}$ Street.

This was a vision of socialism, at the same time revolutionary and democratic, that I could accept. My world view suddenly clarified, history was falling into place. There was only one thing I couldn't accept, I told Julie, and that was the theory of the Third Camp. It seemed obvious to me that a liberal democracy like the United States was preferable in every respect to a totalitarian police State like the Soviet Union, and should therefore be supported in the global power struggle, albeit critically. We talked some more and finally Julie said: "OK, why don't you write an article for *Anvil* explaining your position, I'll write an answer setting out our position, and we'll have a discussion." Fair enough, I thought, and went back to Kansas.

Back in front of my desk, a remarkable thing happened: I found I could not write that article. My arguments seemed shallow, not thought through. I began to have an inkling of what I later fully realized: actually, there is no Third Camp, only two camps, "them" and "us". The "Third Camp" was a slogan for a world polarized between two super-powers, but its profound meaning was different. Later, when I started to give courses in the trade union movement, I explained it this way: the fundamental line of cleavage in today's world is not the vertical one separating the two blocs, it is the horizontal one separating the working class from its rulers, and that one runs across both blocs. We are not "East" or "West", I would add, we are "below", where the workers are.

In the event, I wrote Julie that I could not write that article and that I was joining the SYL.

The following months were hectic. I threw myself into activity with the zeal of the recent convert, stopped studying and flunked the university, became very visible and attracted the attention of the authorities (FBI and Immigration) who arrested me and released me on bail on condition that I should show up at the Immigration headquarters in New York and "show cause why I should not be deported."

Being stateless, with an expired student visa, having flunked university and no money, my bargaining position was not as strong as I could have wished, so I went to New York, with Liz, a Chicago SYL comrade who was to become my wife.

We stayed in New York about six months waiting for my hearing. In the meantime we had both found jobs at the New York Public

Library and organized a local of the CIO Government and Public Employees Organizing Committee (which in 1955 merged with an AFL union to become AFCSME). This AFCSME local still exists and it is the only union I ever organized directly so I feel sentimental about it. When we left New York, another SYL comrade took a job at the Library and continued organizing.

Eventually I got my hearing at Immigration and the officer in charge had a stack of reports in front of him documenting my subversive activities. He had a long look at me, no doubt figured that I was less of a threat to the security of the US than I had hoped and the FBI believed, and said, after joining his fingertips in an almost prayer-like gesture and a moment of silence, that he was "granting me the privilege of voluntary departure" – a more lenient measure than deportation, which would have made it nearly impossible to return to the US.

So in March 1953 I was back in Switzerland, with Liz. I thought there were two ways I could help the ISL I had left behind: by reporting on European developments for its press and by strengthening its network of international relations. After consulting with Hal Draper, that is what I did.

Meanwhile, we had to organize our new life in Geneva. We stayed with my parents, and relations were tense. Nothing in their life had prepared them for a return of the prodigal son as a Trotskyist activist, with a wife they hadn't vetted (they thought she was my "control"). Eventually Liz got a job, we were able to move out and life became more normal. I was looking for an apprenticeship as a printer, to join the proletariat.

Then, through ISL German contacts, I met Henry Jacoby and his wife Frieda, they had been close comrades of Otto Rühle, the leader of the German council communists, and had escaped to the US through Czechoslovakia and France, in 1940. They had become US citizens and were living in Geneva where Henry was director of a FAO office at the UN. He knew everything I knew and much, much more, and became my mentor. Don't be silly, he told me, finish your university studies and get a degree, you will need it. After I got my MA in 1958 he hired me in his office in the Geneva UN.

Henry Jacoby wrote as Sebastian Franck for *Funken*. a small review published in Frankfurt by survivors of various revolutionary Marxist organizations sharing the Luxemburgist tradition. It was one of a number of groups and individuals that I contacted throughout

Europe, corresponded with and worked with to build an international network of the independent socialist Left, between 1953 and 1958.

Some were old ISL contacts with a long history of relations going back to the London Bureau, such as the British ILP, the POUM, Marceau Pivert, who was again active on the left of the French SFIO, the syndicalists of *Révolution prolétarienne*, Dimitri Yotopoulos of the Greek Archeo-Marxists. Others were new contacts, like the Danish syndicalist Carl Heinrich Petersen, the Norwegian *Orientering* group, an anti-NATO left split from the Labour Party, the Italian Unione Socialista Indipendente, which originated in a Titoist split in the Italian CP in 1951, *Socialist Review*, which became the International Socialists, where Bernard Dix was already writing for *Labor Action*, and Walter Kendall of the *Voice* publications, in Britain. There were many others – broadly speaking, the Third Camp constituency in Europe.

I also reached out to the "official" Trotskyist groups in Belgium, France, Italy, the Netherlands and Switzerland, but they had of course a different agenda and were allied to the American SWP, sectarian and hostile to "centrism". Nothing came of any of these contacts.

My networking activities did not lead to any form of permanent co-ordination, the differences of political cultures and traditions were too great and the organizations too weak to sustain a major international joint effort. What emerged was a more active co-operation between publications and some lasting bilateral relations.

In May 1960, an International Conference of Socialist Publications and Reviews was convened in Brussels by the Imre Nagy Institute, a center of political research founded by exiled Hungarian socialists who were associated with the "revisionist" tendencies in the Hungarian Communist Party before 1956. Fourteen publications were represented, from France, Britain, Germany, Italy, Spain (in exile) and the US. I represented *New Politics*. Mike Kidron represented *International Socialism*, Wilebaldo Solano represented *Tribuna Socialista*, the review of the POUM.

The conference adopted two resolutions: in one, the participating reviews stated their intention to extend all possible practical assistance to each other, in the form of exchanging articles, addresses, publicity, distribution facilities, information on the working program and activities of each participating review. It was also decided to publish a liaison bulletin twice a year. In another resolution, the conference singled out two themes: the independence of the working class was one, and the nature and perspectives of the Cuban revolution was the other.

Although its outcome was modest, this conference was the high water mark of co-operation of the independent Left milieu in that decade. Unfortunately, it was also decided that the follow-up would be the responsibility of the Imre Nagy Institute, which proved too frail a vessel to carry that load: it folded in 1963 for lack of funding. No other international meetings were convened and the upheavals of 1968 created a new situation for the independent Left.

From 1953 I had started writing for *Labor Action*, mostly as André Giacometti, and reporting most of the time on developments in France. Why "Giacometti"? – because I was, and still am, an admirer of the great Swiss sculptor and painter Alberto Giacometti (his most famous sculpture, the "Man Walking" can be seen on the Swiss 100 Franc bill).I contributed to *Labor Action* until it ceased publication in 1958, when the ISL dissolved into the Socialist Party. I also contributed to *The New International,* in particular "The Working Class Movement in Tropical Africa", a survey of the African labour movement South of the Sahara, which appeared in 1956 and 1957 in three instalments, at a time when virtually nothing was known about Africa and its unions in the American Left. After the ISL disappeared, I kept contact with Hal Draper and with Julie and Phyllis Jacobson who had started publishing *New Politics,* to which I also contributed, and later, when the Socialist Party split in 1972 over the Vietnam War, with comrades from DSOC.

I contributed to *The New International Review* which Eric Lee was editing at the time, kept in touch with Bogdan Denitch and others. In 1955 I joined the Swiss Social-Democratic Party (called Socialist Party in the French and Italian language regions), where I am still a member.

In 1954 the Algerian war broke out and most of my reporting had to do with this war. My position, which became the ISL position, was of course for the independence movement, but not for the winning side. I supported the Algerian National Movement (MNA) led by Messali Hadj. I had met Messali, and I was impressed by the modest dignity of the founder of the Algerian independence movement, but my main contacts were the trade unionists of the Messalist Union of Algerian Workers (USTA), founded in February 1956, and I recognized in them the revolutionary determination, the internationalism and the spirit of independence that is always what is best in the labour movement. These were the qualities that ensured their destruction.

The uprising which started the Algerian war was initated by a group of dissidents from Messali's party who called themselves the National Liberation Front (FLN) and immediately challenged his authority, including by military means. A civil war developed within the Algerian independence movement. The FLN had the support of Nasserist Egypt, Morocco and Tunisia, of the French CP and, among others, of the Fourth International. Within a week of the USTA having registered, the FLN had registered the General Union of Algerian Workers (UGTA).

The MNA and the USTA had the support of one of the three branches of French Trotskyism (Pierre Lambert's PCI), the *Révolution prolétarienne* group, the anarcho-syndicalists in Force Ouvrière, the POUM, the anarchists, some scattered socialists - and of course the support of at least one hundred thousand Algerian workers in France, where the UGTA and the FLN represented nothing. But they had their bases in the municipalities controlled by the CP, and their had their killer teams.

In Algeria, the FLN had a military superiority and quickly wiped out the MNA partisan units. In France, where the MNA had a massive working class constituency, this was not so easy, but the MNA was facing at the same time repression by the French State and a terror campaign by FLN death squads supported by the infrastructure of the CP municipalities, to which it was unable to respond on the same scale. The casualties of the civil war of the Algerian independence movement in France are estimated at approximately 6,000 dead. By 1961, most of the USTA leadership had been assassinated or was in jail and the FLN had established its hegemony.

The campaign of assassinations was accompanied, in the best Stalinist tradition, by a campaign of slander, representing Messali and his followers as collaborators of the French State – a very effective campaign since even experienced comrades like Jim Higgins of IS, who should have known better, were taken in by it.[1]

---

[1]

More Years For the Locust, Chapter 5

The last general secretary of the USTA, Abderrahmane Bensid, sought refuge in Switzerland in 1961, with his wife and young son. They stayed for six months in my home, then returned to his home town of Tlemcen. By then, he was seriously ill with a neurological disorder. He died in Tlemcen, in 1978, at the age of 46.

In 1960 my life had taken another turn. In 1956 I had been sent by the Sociology Department of the University of Geneva to participate in a conference of the European Productivity Agency in Rome, a technocratic exercise, boring in the extreme.

There I had met another bored and rebellious participant, Charles Levinson, then Assistant General Secretary of the International Metalworkers Federation.

We remained friends, and in 1960 Levinson told me that Juul Poulsen, the general secretary of the food workers' international, the IUF, was looking for an assistant.

I jumped at it. My job at the UN was well-paid and convenient, with plenty of free time for political work, but it was a dead-end. Meanwhile I had also decided that between the political and trade union wings of the labour movement, the last one was my preferred option. I had no interest in a political career and I saw the trade unions as the first and last line of resistance of the working class under attack, and that's where I wanted to be. In fact, not long before Julie Jacobson had darkly accused me of syndicalist deviations, not without reason. So in August 1960 I started work in the secretariat of the IUF as chief cook and bottle washer.

All went well for a while. At that time the IUF, like most other International Trade Secretariats, was little more than a contact point of the leadership of the affiliated unions and its main function was organizing the exchange of information. Juul Poulsen, the general secretary, thought that an international trade union federation could do better than that. He was a solid social-democrat and, even though this was the heyday of social partnership in the industrialized capitalist world, he sensed that future trade union struggles would inevitably be international, and that therefore building the International had to be a priority. Such skills and experience I had acquired by this time proved useful. Through research and correspondence I started the expansion of the IUF into Asia and the Pacific, edited a monthly bulletin, etc.

In 1962 I was contacted by Dan Benedict, who had been appointed

Assistant General Secretary of the IMF and moved to Geneva. Benedict had been a member of the Workers' Party, then of the ISL. In the IMF, his field of activity encompassed mainly Latin America and the Mediterranean Region. We soon became close friends and comrades.

The following year Benedict warned me that we had been infiltrated by the CIA in Latin America. What had happened was that in 1959 the IUF Managing Committee (the smaller governing body, composed at the time entirely of European members) had accepted an offer by the AFL-CIO to provide an Inter-American regional representative free of charge, to help build IUF presence in Latin America. This regional representative, who took control of IUF Latin American activities in 1960, turned out to be Andrew McLellan, an operator without a serious trade union background who co-operated closely with American government agencies (the CIA and perhaps military intelligence) and used the IUF as a cover to build a network of agents, mostly in Central America, who were reporting to him, not to the IUF secretariat.

Poulsen and I did not immediately realize what was happening, we only noticed increasing difficulties in relations with the Interamerican Office. Its activities and priorities did not reflect IUF policies, queries and instructions from the general secretary were ignored, activities were initiated that made no trade union sense, etc. There were also Latin American reactions. The Mexican Sugar Workers' Union, our major Latin American affiliate, had stopped co-operating with the IUF. When Poulsen enquired what the problem was, the answer came: its either that lot, or us, you can't have both.

When Benedict gave me the background and told me what was happening all over Latin America, it all fell into place. I went to Poulsen and briefed him. In fact, the IUF had lost control over its regional work in Latin America, with regard to staffing, policy objectives and activities.

We realized then that there was no alternative: we had to end this operation to protect the integrity of the organization. We also realized that this could not be done without a major conflict with the AFL-CIO.

The IUF was lucky: its two largest American affiliates were left-wing unions: the Amalgamated Meat Cutters and Butcher Workmen were headed by Pat Gorman, an old-time socialist who despised George Meany, the president of the AFL-CIO, and his policies; the United

Packinghouse Workers' president was Ralph Helstein, a knowledgeable and tough radical trade unionist without a specific affiliation, mainly to be able to arbitrate between factions. Both unions had executive committees with strong radical representation, ranging from the CP to the IWW. So at least we had the backing of our two largest US affiliates for what we had to do.

When Poulsen made a quick trip to Chicago to explain the situation to Gorman and Helstein and to ask for their advice, their reaction was immediate and unanimous: kill that operation! So my next assignment was to prepare a position paper for the IUF Managing Committee that was to meet in Hamburg in October 1965. The Committee studied the paper carefully and, without much discussion, unanimously decided that by the end of the year all regional offices had to be closed down and all regional staff dismissed. When we proceeded to implement that decision, we found that we were firing more people we even knew about: in Colombia, we thought we were firing two people and in fact fired twenty-three we didn't know existed.

The next question we had to deal with was how to continue. We had to find a way to rebuild our activities in Latin America in a way that would guarantee that it could never again be hijacked by an outside operation. The solution to this problem was simple: give democracy a chance. Poulsen convened a regional conference in 1966 with a proposal: the IUF would create a Latin American region (no more "Interamerican" with North American domination); all affiliates in that region would elect a regional committee which would be the de-facto governing body of the regional organization; they would also elect a regional secretary (no more pro-consuls appointed from Washington or Geneva or anywhere else).

The proposal was accepted with enthusiasm and relief (at long last the IUF got it) and implemented immediately. There were two candidates for regional secretary. The conference elected Enildo Iglesias, from the Tobacco Workers' Union of Uruguay, the son of a Spanish immigrant who had been a member of the CNT. Enildo's approach to trade unionism was in the same spirit.

This regional organization became the model of all other regional organizations of the IUF: Asia/Pacific, Africa, Europe and, for a time, North America. In Latin America, it successfully fought on three fronts: the CIA and its trade union fronts, the WFTU and the CPs, the CLAT (the regional organization of the WCL). And of course the transnationals. And of course, worse than anyone could have imagined, the military dictatorships in Argentina, Brazil, Chile and Uruguay. The regional organization resisted, fought and ultimately prevailed in every one of these trials, because it was and remains rooted democratically in its affiliates, much deeper than the leadership level. It commands a level of loyalty and support I have rarely seen in any labour organization.

But of course the Empire would strike back. The drastic action the IUF had taken to terminate a program previously agreed with the AFL-CIO had stunned the AFL-CIO International Department, headed at the time by Jay Lovestone and his main enforcer Irving Brown. How could something like that happen? (This was before the exposure of CIA operations in civil society organizations by *Ramparts* and the *New York Times* in 1966 and 1967). There had to be an enemy at work. Eventually they found my FBI file and then they knew who the enemy was.

The crunch came in 1967, at the IUF congress held in Dublin. Poulsen had reached retirement age and a successor had to be elected. I was at that point the natural successor and I was a candidate.

But at the congress, Max Greenberg, president of the Retail, Wholesale and Department Store Union, speaking for the American unions, and popping tranquillizer pills as he was speaking, declared that I was unacceptable and if I was elected the American unions would disaffiliate.

Congress had a problem. After Greenberg's statement, a German and a Swiss candidate appeared, but Congress would not have them. The Scottish Bakers' Union advised me to fight, the Turkish Food Workers came to me and said: "Fear not, the Turks are with you". I took a gamble, and to the disappointment of my supporters, I agreed that the decision should be taken out of Congress and referred back to the Executive Committee of 1968; in the meantime, Poulsen would continue another year. I thought I needed to play for time.

The rest of 1967 was a strange year. I had come down with a bad case of sciatica, requiring a month in extension. Back home, I received the visits of people who had obviously been sent to profile me. There was this professor from Michigan State University, who had conducted anthropological studies in Chile, who wanted to know what I thought of General De Gaulle. I just laughed at him and told him: "Look, we are just a small organization, and we cannot change the world by ourselves, but there is one thing I can tell you: wherever and whenever we find the CIA in our organization, we will throw them out at once."

In the IUF office, I had the visit of a Pole from the Carnegie Foundation who put his attaché case on my desk and then asked me why I was never to be seen at parties of the international set. He was doing a survey of the social habits of Geneva international civil servants. When he left my office he noticed a portrait of Andreu Nin, turned to me and said: "Pretty controversial, this?" (he knew) - to which I replied: "Like so many things" and closed the door.

Meanwhile, Pat Gorman had woken up to what was going on, so when the Executive Committee met in 1968 they had before them a lengthy telex praising my qualities and stating that if I was not going to be elected, the Amalgamated would disaffiliate. The Europeans got the message and the Executive elected me as Acting General Secretary with only Greenberg dissenting.

The next IUF congress met in Zurich in 1970. At that point I was the only candidate for general secretary, but the candidate for president was Dan Conway, the president of the American Bakers' Union. Before the congress, Conway invited me for lunch in Geneva and said: "You will probably be elected general secretary and I might be elected president, we will have to work together. What have you got against the CIA?" I knew he had been organizer for his union in the Western States and I asked him: "When you get to a new town to organize a bakery, what is your first obstacle?" and he said: "The sheriff". I said: "Exactly. The CIA is the world sheriff. And I don't like cops". After that, we got along perfectly. Conway was not a left-winger, and in fact not very political, but he was a totally honest trade unionist and a decent human being.

The 1970 IUF congress unanimously confirmed my election as general secretary (the year before I had been granted Swiss citizenship) and the election of Dan Conway as president (after the US caucus had decided to propose Conway rather than Max Greenberg who was also a candidate, as I later found out). When Conway returned to Washington he got a call from Jay Lovestone who told him that now that he had been elected IUF president he had to "clean up the place". Conway told him he was not going to do any such thing and consequently was never offered a seat on the AFL-CIO Executive Board.

The AFL-CIO International Department and its allies continued to make war on the IUF in Latin America through another International Trade Secretariat where they had some influence, the

International Federation of Commercial and Clerical Workers, known by its French acronym FIET, which had cobbled together a food and allied workers' department from a half-dozen small unions with leaders who were hoping to be properly rewarded for their loyalty to the "free world".

That operation never got anywhere and became an embarrassment to the United Food and Commercial Workers' Union (UFCW), a big union which had been formed through the merger of the Amalgamated Meat Cutters and the Retail Clerks in 1979 (the Retail Clerks International Association, very supportive of the AFL-CIO's international policies, eventually got tired of being called the "Retail CIA" and renamed itself Retail Clerks International Union). The UFCW had continued both the FIET and the IUF affiliation and wanted to end the conflict. Its Vice President Tom Whaley called a meeting of all parties concerned in Brasilia which ended with an agreement by which FIET gave up all its claims to the food and allied industries, including hotels and restaurants, and disbanded its food department in Latin America. In exchange, the IUF agreed to stop calling it a CIA front.

FIET disappeared in 2000 through a merger with the internationals of communication workers, graphical workers and media and entertainment workers to form Union Network International (UNI), where its tradition lives on.

I have not said much so far about the WFTU and the WCL although I said that the IUF, in Latin America, had to fight on three fronts, of which these were two. The reason for this is that there is not much to say. The WFTU regional organization CPUSTAL, with Cuba as its main affiliate, and its food workers' department, functioned as an amplifier of international Stalinist policies but was totally incompetent as a trade union organization, not to be seen on the ground, much less in any conflict with a transnational company. They were never a serious competitor nor ever a potential ally, just a time-waster. Much the same can be said of the WCL and its regional organization CLAT, which had plenty of money from European Catholic institutions, but no members, conservative policies cloaked in radical rhetoric. Time wasters.

Another battle, not in the IUF this time, was looming in the 1970s. At the IMF Congress in Stockholm in 1974, Benedict was a candidate to succeed Ivar Norén as General Secretary. He was opposed by Herman Rebhan, an official of the United Automobile Workers (UAW) in Chicago, who had done a stint in the IMF as co-ordinator of world councils in the automobile industry before returning to the US. Rebhan, like Benedict, had been a member of the ISL, but by that time had gone much further right than even Shachtman, becoming a co-opted member of the Lovestone/Brown team. I took very publicly Benedict's side.

Rebhan had the active support of President George Meany and Director of International Affairs Jay Lovestone of the AFL-CIO, who organized a campaign without precedent in the international trade union movement, combining threats, blandishments and flattery to get Rebhan elected. Even though they managed to line up only three major countries (all US affiliates except the IUE, the German IG Metall and the Japanese affiliates), these, plus a few lesser client unions, tallied 7 million votes at congress. The rest of the world, voting for Benedict, only reached 4 million votes.

The fight between Benedict and Rebhan was a fight between two ex-ISLers: a socialist who was acting on the principles of what the ISL had always stood for, and a cynical renegade. The sense of the Rebhan campaign was to line up the IMF in the US Cold War camp, but mostly and principally to prevent Benedict becoming general secretary and moving the IMF towards a radical agenda, perhaps in alliance with the IUF and ICF. In the event, Rebhan was not able to do his worst: the IMF remained basically honest through organizational inertia. What he was able to do, was to create a culture of political conformism which continued after his retirement with new general secretaries. Neutralizing the IMF as a progressive force was no mean achievement.

Benedict remained IMF Assistant General Secretary but it became quickly apparent that he would be unable to exercise his function under the Rebhan regime. In 1977 he left the IMF and moved to Canada to join the United Auto Workers (UAW-Canada, later CAW) education department. In 1981 Benedict became a Canadian citizen, and felt "very comfortable" as such. He formally retired from the CAW in 1982 but remained active in the labor movement until his death in 2003.

Charles Levinson, my other ally, had become general secretary of the International Chemical Workers (ICF) in 1964, fought memorable and pioneering battles with transnationals, and had written several brilliant books about international trade unionism[2].

---

[2] Principally: Capital, Inflation and the Multinationals (1967); International Trade Unionsm (1972); The Multinational Pharmaceutical Industry (1973); Industry's Democratic Revolution (1974); Vodka-Cola (1980)

One of his historical merits was to destroy the International Federation of Petroleum and Chemical Workers (IFPCW). Unlike nearly all other ITSs which had a social-democratic identity and a history going back to the 19th century – and some of which had been infiltrated by the CIA – the IFPCW was a total creation of the CIA from its inception. Founded in 1954, it established its headquarters in Denver, with the Oil, Chemical and Atomic Workers' Union (OCAW) of the AFL-CIO. Its first president (O.A. Knight) and its general secretary (Loyd A. Haskins) were OCAW officials.

Any trade union activity it was able to develop until its demise in 1975 was incidental to its true mission: to line up oil workers' unions, mainly in the Middle East and in Latin America, with the US bloc in the Cold War. The disclosures in 1967 about the covert CIA funding of civil society organizations blew the IFPCW's cover: several of the CIA conduits appeared in the IFPCW's public audit records and it became clear that the organization was entirely dependent on these subsidies for its existence.

In 1963 the then IFPW had decided to expand its jurisdiction to the chemical industry, thus becoming IFPCW, and creating a jurisdictional conflict with the ICF. After 1967, Levinson became unrelenting in his attacks. As long as Lovestone was still director of the AFL-CIO International Department, the IFPCW continued to receive funding through the AFL-CIO regional institutes (themselves also funded by US government agencies including the CIA) but it gradually lost support.

In 1973 the IFPCW opened merger talks with the ICF, proposing that the ICF become the European regional organization of the merged International – a deal not unlike that which the International Federation of Plantation Workers (founded 1957) proposed to the mainly European-based International Landworkers' Federation (founded 1920), which led to the creation of the International Federation of Plantation, Agricultural and Allied Workers (IFPAAW) in 1959. The IFPAAW was from the start as dependent on external funding as the IFPCW and collapsed, as the IFPCW had, when the principal source of its external funding was withdrawn (in this case, the ICFTU). The remnants of IFPAAW merged with the IUF in 1994.

In the case of the IFPCW, the merger talks failed when the ICF demanded that it cease accepting financial aid from the AFL-CIO. However, in July 1974 Ernest Lee had replaced Lovestone as director of the International Department and the AFL-CIO on its own initiative stopped supporting the IFPCW, advising its affiliates in February 1975 to join the ICF. The same month the OCAW, under a new leadership, disaffiliated and ceased funding the IFPCW. In September, the IFPCW Executive Board dissolved the organization.

The ICEF, as it had become, was now a powerful organization, but Levinson lost it by a stupid mistake. He had to retire in 1983 under pressure, after having improved his pension plan without going through the approved procedure. Bad luck: a foolish leftist on the staff thought of himself as a whistle-blowing hero, the German pharmaceutical industry was watching, and pounced. The president of the German Chemical Workers' Union, later also president of the ICEF, Hermann Rappe, a strong believer in "social partnership" and a reliable defender of the interests of the German transnationals, made sure Levinson had to resign. He was succeeded by several general secretaries who were unable to stabilize the organization and to preserve it as the effective fighting force it had become under his watch.

Meanwhile, as from 1980, the IUF had become involved in one of its major battles, getting Coca-Cola to use its enormous influence to stop its Guatemalan franchise from assassinating union organizers and to recognize the union. No one believed we could do it, but we did. By 1984, the plant had a new owner, a new contract and union recognition. This story has been told elsewhere (see GLI website: www.global-labour.org) and does not need to be told again here. Suffice it to say that beyond and aside of the ideological and political battles internal to the international trade union movement, the IUF was of course principally focused on building an effective fighting machine to take on even the biggest transnational corporations. The two-stage campaign against Coca-Cola in 1980 and 1982 proved that we had in fact reached that point.

There was, however, one more defining political battle which started in the 1970s, this time in Europe. The obvious issue was European separatism, but the fundamental, underlying issue was no different from that we had to deal with in Latin America: the independence and the integrity of the trade union movement as the independent movement of the working class.

The creation of the European Economic Community (the Common Market) in 1957 led to the establishment of committees of trade unions from the six EEC member States, also in the IUF. Such committees were accepted everywhere because it was recognised that within the EEC trade unions had special concerns that required mutual consultation and co-ordination. The situation changed as the EEC became the EU with increasing powers and ambitions. At that point the EU became intent in building a "European" identity at all levels, including civil society, and where such institutions did not exist, they had to be created. Thus, the European Trade Union Confederation (ETUC) was created in 1973, leading to the dissolution of the European Regional Organization of the ICFTU.

The ETUC defined itself from the outset as independent of any international trade union organization. It included all European affiliates of the ICFTU and of the WCL, without any institutional links to either International. It was not, however, to be independent of the EU: on the contrary, rather than being a trade union lobby in the EU, it quickly became a EU lobby in the labour movement, with 70% of its budget coming from EU subsidies.

At the industrial branch level, it created European Trade Union Federations which were an integral part of its structures, but not necessarily linked to the International Trade Secretariats (ITS) of their branch. Where the ITS had had a European regional organization, it became, in some cases, the European TUF, but where no regional organization had previously existed the ITS were suddenly confronted with an independent European body created out of their own affillates with EU subsidies. This was the case in the International Transport Workers' Federation and in the IUF, where the former EEC committee (now the ETUCF) declared itself to be an ETUF with exclusive authority over all European matters. In their view, the IUF could henceforth deal with Asia, the Americas and Africa, whereas they alone would be responsible for Europe.

There was no way, as IUF general secretary, I could accept this. I was shocked at the staggering arrogance of the leadership of this European faction (at that time, the German, Belgian and Dutch affiliates), at their contempt for the concept of an international interest and identity of the world working class and their readiness to commit themselves instead to what I saw as a grubby little club of European nationalists.

Since the CIA operation in the 1960s, the IUF had not faced such a fundamental threat to its integrity. There were three obvious threats: the threat to the organization's independence as EU funding would start weighing in; the exclusion of the IUF from dealing with the European-based transnationals (as happened in the IMF); the longer term threat to the financial stability of the IUF and to its ability to support its weaker members in other parts of the world.

Fortunately not all European affiliates subscribed to this new wisdom of EU-funded trade unionism. Some because their countries were not part of the EU, some because, even though they were in the EU, they were not prepared to abandon an internationalist perspective and their commitment to the IUF and to all its members, and some for both reasons. The non-European members were of course appalled at what was happening in Europe.

There was only one way to stop this: create a European regional organization of the IUF, under IUF rules, and declare this to be the legitimate representation of the European affiliates of the IUF. The Executive Committee of the IUF decided (by a large majority) to do this by creating the Euro-IUF, running in parallel with the existing ETUCF. The Euro-IUF now applied for recognition as a food workers' ETUF, as the ETUCF had already done, with the result that neither received recognition from the ETUC. Stalemate.

What followed was a seven-year civil war in the IUF in Europe, with shifting line-ups. Because this was largely bureaucratic infighting, we were able to keep it at the margins, with the serious IUF activities developing anyway. It came eventually to an end by a change in the leadership of the German union: the new president believed that the IUF interest had to be safeguarded over European regional concerns, and the other Europeans fell into line.

The result was a merger of the ETUCF and the Euro-IUF to create the European Committee of Food, Catering and Allied Workers' Unions within the IUF (ECF-IUF), both a European regional organisation under the IUF rules and an ETUF of the European Trade Union Confederation. Much the same had happened, more or less at the same time, in the ITF.

That was pretty much the end of the story in Europe, although traces of European separatism linger on: the organization changed its name once again, to European Federation of Food, Agriculture and Tourism Trade Unions (EFFAT) with a new logo, effacing any reminder of an IUF connection, and continues to work in a bureaucratic style, heavily influenced by a "social partnership" ideology that the IUF does not share. However, these are now irrelevancies. That story is over.

My final years in the IUF were dominated by the need to deal with the fall-out from the collapse of the Soviet empire, for which we were theoretically well prepared, but practically not at all. That is another story.

So what about Third Camp Socialism?

I do not know whether, had I not joined the ISL, absorbed its political culture and understood its insights and its specific brand of socialism, I would have been able to contribute to the international labour movement in the way I did for over fifty years. What I do know, is that I was able to do this thanks to comrades like Hal and Ann Draper, Julius and Phyllis Jacobson, others like Max Shachtman, Al Glotzer, Herman Benson, Gordon Haskell, Ernest Rice McKinney, Saul Mendelson, Debbie Meier, Don Chenoweth, Al Davidson, Sam Bottone, others yet I hardly knew, like Joe Friedman (Carter), Paul Bernick, Jack Rader, Carl Shier, or only knew through their writings, like Lewis Coser, Ernest Erber, Stanley Plastrick, Irving Howe, B.J. Widick - and many others.

To all of them, I owe many hours of conversations, correspondence and reading. What I learned was that the "Third Camp" was really another name for the world's working class in the broadest sense of the term, including the informal workers, mostly women, the landless peasants of the "Third World", itself another outmoded term since the two other worlds have gone the way of the two other camps. In contemporary terms, what was our "Third Camp" is now the 99% of the Occupy movement.

As I see it, the core of the 99% is the organized working class, and our duty, overriding all other considerations, has to be to defend the integrity and the independence of the movement of the organized working class: the trade union movement or, more generally, the labour movement, against all threats, from anywhere, regardless of their many guises. At any rate, that's what I thought it meant to be an independent socialist in the labour movement in the last half century. Or, the way Marx put it in his time: "Considering, That the emancipation of the working classes must be conquered by the working classes themselves ..."[3]

The ISL's brand of socialism also provided me with a very useful theoretical framework to help me understand my contempt of Stalinism and, for that matter, of any brand of authoritarianism, including those which were not actual criminal conspiracies like Stalin's operation. The ISL was not blind to the dangers of the various brands of Third World authoritarianism, and none of us

---

[3] **Address and Provisional Rules of the Working Men's International Association, London, 1864**

ever went on those ridiculous quests for a promised land which would proclaim any tin-pot dictator with a radical discourse as the latest shining beacon of socialism.

Nor was the ISL blind to the bureaucratic and authoritarian traditions in social-democracy which, combined with opportunism, cowardice and obtuse stupidity – never to be underestimated - would inflict enormous damage on the labour movement, leading to its worst historical defeats. Even at the best of times, those traditions would cultivate conformity and passivity, wear down the activists, lead the movement into blind alleys. The ISL taught me, and others, to resist all this.

Finally, the ISL taught me to take the long view. It never proclaimed a terminal crisis of capitalism, nor declared a revolutionary situation every five or ten years. Most of us knew we were in for the long haul, and that we would not live to see our long-term goals. All we can ever do is the best we can, where we are, while we are there.

# Summer days on Utøya [2011]

*This article appeared in the Global Labour Column, which is managed by the Corporate Strategy and Industrial Development (CSID) research programme at the University of the Witwatersrand, South Africa, and is part of the Global Labour University (GLU).*

**I shall never forget the summer days I spent in 1955 on Utøya, the small island near Oslo that the Norwegian trade unions had given to the Labour Youth League as a study and leisure centre.**

I had arrived in Europe in March 1953, back from the United States where, as a student, I had discovered socialism in the shape of a Trotskyist dissidence. The brilliant explanation of the world, the heroic and tragic story of the "Old Man" and his movement, had taken hold of my imagination and my emotions. So much so that I drew the attention of the authorities, who gave me one month to leave the country.

So there we were, my companion and I, in Europe and needing to find our bearings. She was a member of the same group. By the summer of 1955, we were ready to discover Scandinavia, the bastion of a social democracy that we viewed with suspicion.

In Oslo, we found the Labour Youth League in the phone book. We turned up unannounced at the office of the man in charge, who was the General Secretary, and told him we were members of the American Socialist Youth League and we were looking for Norwegian socialists to discuss socialism with. The Norwegian comrade looked at us for what seemed a long time, then said, "Good timing.

Our summer course has just started. Later on, we can take you over there. You can spend a week with us. It's on Utøya, a little island near Oslo. You'll see."

On Utøya, there is a central building for the logistics (meals, showers, course rooms) and the participants were living in tents pitched all over the place, but mainly in a meadow in front of the building. We were assigned a tent, but we spent most of our time with the young Norwegians. I spent a whole night discussing with Reiulf Steen, who was later to become the Minister of Foreign Affairs and the Prime Minister, very much involved in assisting the resistance movements against the dictatorships in Latin America. We discussed the USSR, its social and political nature, and Stalinism. One night was not enough.

We met many of the hundreds of young socialists who were full of energy, joy, humour and determination, sons and daughters of the midnight sun which, during the Norwegian summer, never sets. They were ordinary young people, citizens like all others in a social democracy. No professional revolutionaries, but determined to change the world. There were as many of them on this little island, maybe even more, than in the whole of our American grouplet. The American comrades whom we had left behind were no less committed and courageous, but we had now discovered something we had not experienced before – a mass movement of young socialists.

This was the movement that Anders Behring Breivik, a fascist activist, attacked on 22 July 2011. After setting off a bomb in the government quarter of Oslo, killing eight people, he landed on the island disguised as a policeman, called together the young people there and started gunning down defenceless youngsters who had not had the slightest inkling of what was about to happen to them. On Utøya, Breivik killed 69 people in the space of an hour and a half.

Norway's Prime Minister Jens Stoltenberg, who is also the leader of the Labour Party, declared that the massacre was an assault on democracy and the open society, and pledged that Norway would not cave in to it. More precisely, though, it was an attack on the Norwegian labour movement. Breivik was quite explicit: the labour movement, guilty of "cultural Marxism", had to be targeted – and what had to be hit was labour's most precious asset, its youth, to punish it for betraying the nation by promoting its "islamisation". If the shooting had happened a few hours earlier, Stoltenberg himself and former Prime Minister Gro Harlem Brundtland might well have been among the victims. They had visited Utøya that day, to take part in the debates.

We socialists ought to be more concerned about what is happening to us in Northern Europe. On 28 February 1986, Sweden's Prime Minister Olof Palme was assassinated. He had been to the cinema with his wife Lisbet, and as usual they had no bodyguards. At 11.20

p.m., while they were walking home, a man stepped up from behind and fired two pistol shots. The first one mortally wounded Palme. The second one injured Lisbet, who survived. The assassin fled and was never found. A man was arrested and sentenced, but was later released upon appeal. The motives for the assassination, and those who may have ordered it, were never identified. The police investigation, which went on for years, led nowhere.

Stemming from the upper reaches of the bourgeoisie, Palme was a "traitor to his class" and the Swedish Right harboured an intense hatred for him. In government since 1965, twice Prime Minister (1969-1976 and 1982-1986), and Chairman of the Social Democratic Workers' Party (SAP) from 1969 to 1986, he strengthened the Social State even further, as well as the trade unions' power vis-à-vis the employers. As regards foreign policy, he was the only leader of a western government to oppose the Vietnam War. He also opposed the invasion of Czechoslovakia in 1968, the Pinochet coup in 1973 and more generally, throughout his career, the military dictatorships in Latin America, the fascist dictatorships in Europe and the apartheid regime in South Africa. Although never really on the Left of the Party, he has often been described as a "revolutionary reformist".

Palme's assassination was a turning point in the history of our movement. None of his successors have had his charisma, political intelligence and daring. The SAP lowered its profile. In fact, its moderation probably pushed it out of office. It has lost two parliamentary elections in a row since 2006. It has less of an international presence now, and as a result the Socialist International has lost some more of what little influence remained to it. Had Palme lived, the capitulation of social democracy to neoliberalism and the "third way" buffoonery of Blair and Schröder would have been more difficult. If Palme's assassination had been the result of a right-wing conspiracy, that plot would have achieved its aims.

It could all have gone differently. In 1998, Swedish Social-Democracy had somewhat recovered. It had a rising star: born in 1957, Anna Lindh was the brilliant chairperson of the Social-Democratic Youth from 1984 to 1990, a Member of Parliament from 1982 onwards, Environment Minister in 1994, and Foreign Minister in 1998. She was cast in the Palme mould, and the intention was that she would succeed the dull bureaucrat Göran Persson as head of government and of the Party.

But the assassin was lying in wait. On the afternoon of 10 September 2003, Anna Lindh was shopping in a Stockholm department store, without any bodyguards of course, when a man knifed her in the chest, stomach and arm. Despite the doctors' efforts, at 5.29 the next morning she was dead.

The assassin was caught on 24 September. He was Mihailo Mihailovič, born in Sweden of Serb parents, angry with the Swedish government because it had supported NATO in Kosovo. Following various judicial bouts, and his certification as psychologically deranged, he was sentenced to life imprisonment.

After Sweden, that historical bastion of Nordic socialism, it is now the turn of Norway, the only remaining Nordic country with a social democratic government that defends progressive causes at the international level as well as defending the social State. Yet again, a lone madman has struck.

A lone madman? That claim is made mainly by the extreme Right. Because, of course, if the ideas of the extreme Right are to be safeguarded, it is vital to put as much distance as possible between the ideology vehiculated by its parties and the criminal acts their ideology inspires. The belief has to be fostered that fascism is an opinion, not a crime, and that the organisations of the extreme right are made up of normal, ordinary citizens. Whereas in fact, they are nurseries for Breiviks who can emerge anytime, anywhere, armed to the teeth and ready to sow death.

Shortly after the Norwegian drama, Oskar Freysinger, an extreme right-wing Swiss politician famous for opposing the construction of minarets and for stating that abortion has caused an "invisible genocide", gave the following reply to a journalist who pointed out that a number of Breivik's standpoints matched Freysinger's own and those of his party, the Swiss People's Party: "Do you think there will be fewer terrorist attacks and madmen if I'm forced into silence? It will be worse!" That answer should be taken as a threat.

# The state of the French Left [1958]

*This article was published in International Socialism (UK) No. 1, Summer 1958, and also in The New International, under the name "André Giacometti". Thanks to Ted Crawford & the late Will Fancy. Transcribed and marked up by Einde O'Callaghan for ETOL.*

The victory of de Gaulle has harshly spotlighted the weakness of the French Left. The following excellent article written some months before the coup shows clearly the causes of the lefts weakness – the betrayal of the "Socialist" and "Communist" leaderships. In this article Comrade Giacometti deals mainly with the Socialist Party of France. We hope to publish another article dealing with the French Stalinist Party ... Editor

**To describe and analyze the French Left today is a difficult and unrewarding task. Where to begin? The concept itself has been elusive and ambiguous. It is not, as many have said, that the terms "Left" and "Right" have become meaningless. For us who continue to view the working-class as a sociological fact, as a community of action with specific interests, tasks, historical aims and perspectives, the terms have never lost their clarity. To us, the "Left" is the broad, historical movement of the working-class, the movement which represents its interests, seeks to fulfil its tasks and purposes. To spell it out: the "Left" is the movement which seeks to establish a society based on the common ownership and democratic control of production. In all countries there are organisations which, each in their own way, represent this historical movement: socialist parties, labour parties, revolutionary nationalist movements, trade-unions.**

But if we turn to France today, we are faced with the fact that no such movement exists, at least not in organised form. There are, to be sure, the traditional organisations of the working-class: two large parties, the Communist Party and the Socialist Party (SFIO); three important trade-unions: CGT, CFTC and FO. What these institutions have in common, is their lack of real content. Of the parties, it can be said today that they do not even represent the historical movement of the working-class implicitly and in spite of themselves. The trade-unions only represent a minority of the working-class, and not necessarily its most active and conscious part. The bulk of the workers is unorganized, and the real life of the working-class takes place outside of their scope.

The two major mass movements in recent years – the strikes of 1953 and 1955 – were initiated spontaneously, outside the trade-unions, and they were carried forward to a large extent by the unorganized. Figures of actual union membership are difficult to obtain, but it seems doubtful that the number of paid-up members for the three major federations exceeds 1.8 millions (1 million for CGT, 500,000 for the CFTC and 300,000 for FO) [1*] According to a well-informed union official, the total number of union members at the Renault auto works does not exceed 2,000 – out of a total labor force of 40,000.

Union elections also give an indication: in the union elections at Renault of May 1947, abstentions ran up to 41.5%; at Citroen, the average percentage of abstentions is 50%. [1]

In the political elections, the disaffection of the working-class is even more evident. According to an analysis of the 1951 elections by the French Institute for Public Opinion Research (IFOP) 1.9 million workers voted for the CP (38% of the total CP vote) 576,000 voted for the SFIO (21% of the total SFIO vote) and 450,000 voted for the christian-democratic MRP (19% of the MRP vote) while approximately 5 million did not vote at all. [2]

The country is ruled by an omnipotent and irresponsible bureaucratic apparatus, while the people elects an irresponsible Parliament, which spawns one impotent government after another. The mechanism of official political life has not broken down but functions in a void; the mass of the people has withdrawn its interest from it and seeks to express itself by other means.

Both communist and socialist parties have become deeply involved in this shadow life of official politics: they are indeed among its main supports, and share many of its features. They are included, with reason, in the disaffection and mistrust the people, and particularly the working-class, feels towards "politics" in general.

Some will object that these parties, after all, exist. It is true, there are party organizations, a party opinion, a party press. Voters continue to cast their ballots for the party tickets. But if one looks at the role these organizations play, at their real function in society, it becomes clear that they are important only by virtue of their inert bulk, in a purely negative way. From the point of view of the historical working-class movement, they are nothing more than obstacles. Since this has not always been the case, and since large numbers of workers and socialists still do not see it that way, it is necessary to explain. In what way. are they obstacles? How and when did this come about? Who do these parties represent and what do they want? When these questions are answered, the perspectives of the real labor movement in France will become clearer too.

The decline of the SFIO

Since the end of the war, the history of the French Socialist Party (SFIO) has been one of steady and rapid decline.

This decline of the SFIO is equally striking on all levels: in terms of numerical strength, of organizational structure, of social composition, of age composition, of political, cultural and theoretical vitality. The statistical facts of the decline have been assembled by scholars such as Raymond Fusilier, Pierre Rimbert, Maurice Duverger and others, who have devoted well-known studies to this problem. It is useful to summarize these data here, as they save a lot of explaining. At first, the decline in membership is perhaps the most striking fact [3]:

>     1938 .... 275.526
>
>     1939 .... 180,219
>
>     1945 .... 338,625
>
>     1946 .... 353,742
>
>     1947 .... 322,881
>
>     1948 .... 222,781
>
>     1949 .... 150,627

1950 .... 135,809

1951 .... 115,025

1952 .... 108,437

1953 .... 105,760  )

1954 .... 107,670  ) approx.

1957 ....  97,000  )

A glance at these figures shows that since 1945 the SFIO has lost over two thirds of its membership. After having been the strongest ever in its history in 1945, it is now at the lowest ebb since 1927. Moreover, the departure of the old members is coupled with a failure to recruit new ones. In his essay on the SFIO, Maurice Duverger remarked [4]:

"in the years 1925-1928, when the party's strength was about equal to its strength today, many new members joined it every year (between 20,000 and 50,000 each year). People left, but others came to take their place. When the total number dropped, as in 1932-34, it meant that the number of the former was greater than that of the latter, but the recruitment remained significant: about 19,000 new members joined in 1933, almost 15,000 in 1934. Today this turn-over no longer exists. The sources of recruitment have practically dried up. Old members leave, nobody takes their place; only 708 new members in 1948, for a total number of approximately 285,000! In 1950, the party claimed 5,000 new members, but the rounded and vague figure leaves room for every kind of doubt, Since 1951 the party leadership no longer dares to publish figures, which is symptomatic."

The nature of this decline is different from that of previous crises. Since the founding of the unified party in 1905, four significant drops in membership occurred. All these drops are short in time (none lasts longer than three years) and can be attributed to specific causes: World War I and its consequences, the split which gave birth to the Communist Party, the departure of the "neo-socialist" right wing in 1933, the expulsion of the left wing – the future PSOP – in 1938.

The present drop in membership is a continuous process of almost ten years, if one excepts the short-lived recovery of 1954-56. It is not the result of one or several splits, as before the war, but of a general decline, although small groups have left the party in 1948 and in late 1956. Very few of the former members left to join or to form other organizations: there is no amputation, only a wasting-away. Splits assume political vitality, energy, fighting; a wasting-away may mean many things, but excludes all of the above.

It could be pointed out that the drop in membership is not a phenomenon confined to the SFIO, but one which has affected all French parties since 194-5. The Communist Party, for instance, has dropped from 1 million members at the end of the war to 430,000 members today, while the circulation of L'Humanité has shrunk from 601,000 copies in 1945-46 to 173,000 copies in 1954. The general process of de-politization does not account, however, for the extent of the drop. Moreover, the popular vote of the SFIO has also shrunk considerably during the same period [5]:

| date | number of votes | percentage |
| --- | --- | --- |
| 1945 | 4,561,411 | 23.2 |
| 1946 (June) | 4,187,818 | 21,6 |
| 1946 (Nov.) | 3,431,954 | 17.9 |
| 1951 | 2,661,686 | 13.9 |

In 1932 and 1936 the SFIO represented approximately 20% of the voters; thus, even if one discounts the effects of the general turn to the Left at the end of the war, the decline remains substantial.

The party's Paris daily, Le Populaire, dropped from a circulation of 278,000 copies in 1945-46 to the level of a miserable one-sheet bulletin today, with a circulation of 27,000 copies in 1954, of which only 35% were actually sold. It has declined further since.

Why this unprecedented drop in membership and influence? There are general political reasons which we mentioned above: the withdrawal of the French people from political life. But the specific reasons weigh more heavily in the balance. In the immediate post-war years, where the French working-class and, for that matter, most other people, were looking for radical solutions, a party that took the main responsibility for prosecuting the war in Indo-China, repressing the nationalist movements in Algeria and Madagascar, freezing the wages, stabilizing the political regime and turning the country into a pawn of US foreign policy could not help but disappoint its working-class and left wing supporters. In fact, the consequences of a conservative policy at that particular time turned out to be more serious than a passing disappointment: it was during these years that the party shifted its social base and changed its political nature. It was not until the government of Guy Mollet that the full impact of these changes was revealed.

It is true that between 1954 and 1956 the downward trend was slightly reversed. For one thing, the party was getting close to rock-bottom and those oppositionists that remained in spite of their disagreement with the leadership represented a selection of case-hardened people, determined to stay in the party even under very difficult circumstances, On the other hand, the party had undergone a long "opposition cure". Its role in the Indo-Chinese war and Jules Moch's activities as a Minister of the Interior were far enough removed in time to be forgotten by many. The statements of the party leaders seemed to show a genuine desire for reform, and their strong support of "Mendesism" led many people to view the SFIO once again as a party of reform with potentialities for growth and, perhaps, radical developments. Although the party did not grow nearly as much as the "Mendesist" wing of the Radical Party, it also benefited from the general trend towards liberalism and reform.

In the election of January 1956, which brought the "Republican Front" coalition into power, the SFIO polled 3,171,985 votes, an increase of roughly 500,000, representing 15% of the total vote. It is interesting to note that in these elections the number of abstentions also decreased from 19.8% to 17.2%. [6]

Within three months, however, the party plunged once more downward, this time to hitherto unfathomed depths. By its policy in Algeria and in the Middle East, and by its brutal suppression of the opposition within the party, the party leadership created a situation where, for the first time since 1947, compact groups were leaving the party, the "Action socialiste" group, led by Andrée Vienot of the

Ardennes Federation, being the most important. The loss of party members resumed and increased with every new sanction against militants of the opposition: the expulsion of Weitz, the sanctions against Pivert, Philip and others, the dissolution of the student organization, etc. In July 1957, Maurice Duverger estimated the party membership at 96,000; it has doubtlessly gone down since. [7]

In terms of popular vote, on the other hand, the party has held its own since 1951: this is shown by the various local elections which have taken place since 1956, and it has remained so even after Suez. An analysis of these votes shows the reason: the party of Mollet and Lacoste has won the support of right-wing voters, who have come to view it as a solid bastion for their ideas and interests.

This brings us to the center of the problem: more important than the numerical decline itself, is the change that has occurred in the party during this decline. Its recent political evolution cannot be understood without reference to the changes in social composition, geographical distribution, age composition and organizational set-up within the SFIO. The partial recovery of 1954 – 56 then appears as the result of a misunderstanding that was rapidly and decisively cleared up during the government of Guy Mollet.

The most recent data on the party's social composition go back to 1955. They concern the party membership as a whole (based on a sample of 15,000 members), the cadres (i.e. the members of the Executive Committees of the Departmental Federations, the members of the parliamentary groups and the members of the Directing Committee) and the voters. The figures concerning the election candidates refer to the 1951 elections, "No profession" means mostly housewives. [8]

| social group | members | cadres | election cand. | voters | general pop. |
|---|---|---|---|---|---|
| workers (industrial) | 24.3 | ) | ) | 21 | 19 |
|  |  | 11.4 | 7 |  |  |
| workers (agriculture) | * | ) | ) | 6 | 3 |
| civil servants | 24.9 | 37.4 |  | 13 | 5 |

| | | | | | |
|---|---|---|---|---|---|
| office workers | 8.8 | 13.5 | | 6 | 6 |
| pensioned and ret. | 12.8 | 7.7 | | 10 | 6 |
| farmers | 7.4 | 6.8 | 12 | 8 | 16 |
| shopkeepers artis. | 12.3 | 10.6 ) | | ) | |
| | | | 19 | 10 | 15 |
| professionals | 2.6 | 10.1 ) | | ) | |
| no profession | 6.9 | 2.5 | | 26 | 30 |
| prop. of women | 12,1 | 5.6 | | 41 | |

* included under "farmers"

Among the party membership, 58% are wage-earners, and 30-35% are probably workers: the figure for "civil servants" includes probably one third or more workers in the public services (railways, city transport, electric power and gas), who have a special statute, and the figure for "farmers" includes a small number of agricultural workers. Nevertheless, the specific weight of the working-class in the party is small. If one combines the results of political elections and of union elections, it appears that the SFIO has no working-class following in any of the basic industries nor, as we shall see, in the main industrial concentrations; very little in mining, next to nothing in the metal industries, in steel, in maritime transport, in the building trades. The workers of the SFIO are mostly scattered in small enterprises, and work for the most part in secondary industries; leather, ceramics, textile.

On the other hand, the "new middle class" (civil servants and office workers) represents about 25% of the membership; the "old middle class" (shopkeepers, artisans, professional) about 20%. These categories are relevant because under the present circumstances the political behaviour of most civil servants and office workers is determined not so much by the fact that they live by selling their labor power than by their bourgeois aspirations, There are notable exceptions: the bank-clerks in Paris, for instance, and the post-office workers, but in general the "white collar" groups have remained conservative.

The change in the social composition of the SFIO parallels a geographical shift of the basis of its support from North-East to South-West and from the industrial to rural regions. This is the phenomenon that Duverger called the "radicalization" of the SFIO, that is, the tendency of the party to adopt the features of the Radical Party and to replace the latter on the political spectrum.

Before 1919, the SFIO was mostly a northern party, based on the industrial regions of Paris and of North Eastern France (steel and mining). After the split leading to the founding of the Communist Party, the movement towards the South begins. By 1928 and 1932 the SFIO began to replace the increasingly conservative Radical Party in its traditional strongholds in the South-West and in the West, In 1946, the SFIO weakens in the North, East and Center Regions, and again gains in the South. Duverger concludes: "except for the mining departments of the North, the SFIO has become more a southern than a northern party; it occupies the position of the old "republican left" of pre-1900 days, which had no specific socialist characteristic. It thus inherits the Radical traditions." [9]

Today, the two "industrial" departments of the Nord and Pas-de-Calais represent about a quarter of the party's membership. The second largest group is the Paris region (Seine and Seine-et-Oise) representing about a tenth. The Marseille region (Bouches-du-Rhone) represents another tenth. The rest of the membership (over half) is distributed in the provincial federations, most of which are Southern.

The shift from North-East to South-West also involves a shift from the industrial to the rural regions: in the elections of 1951, the votes of the SFIO were composed as follows:

| from communities | under 2,000 inhabitants: | 42% |
| --- | --- | --- |
| | between 2,000 and 5,000: | 11% |
| | between 5,000 and 20,000: | 22% |
| | between 20,000 and 100,000: | 15% |

over 100,000 inhabit.: 10%

This does not mean, however, that the party has succeeded in gaining significant support among the farmers, like the CP has been able to do: as we have seen, only 8% of the SFIO voters are farmers. The SFIO tends to become less a rural party than a party of the small provincial towns. [10]

The political consequences, of this shift have not been either immediate or direct. The two large federations of the North, with a working-class majority, have been so far among the most steady supporters of the Mollet apparatus, while several southern federations have voted for minority resolutions. The geographical shift has reflected more directly on the psychological climate within the party, and on its organizational habits. Like all parties in the Marxist tradition, the SFIO was originally organized as a centralized and disciplined mass party, based on an active membership of hundreds of thousands, welded together by a system of sections and federations. This structure is now being increasingly replaced by another type of organization, characteristic of bourgeois parties; the party comes alive only at election time, and is held together between elections by a committee or bureau of party functionaries. The membership hardly participates in the life of the party, nor is the party relevant to the lives of the members. Often, the local committees claim a membership that exists on paper only and whose dues are paid by generous donors. These paper members then become some of the most reliable supporters of administrative majorities at party congresses.

In other places, the local party section becomes a club where old-timers meet to cultivate memories of the Popular Front or Liberation period. It is easy to see how difficult it would be to spoil the atmosphere of the club by suggesting action on the issues of the day.

These organizational habits and practices bring the SFIO close to Saragat's Italian Social-Democratic Party, which is in every respect more degenerate than its French counterpart and perhaps represents the image of the latter's future.

The evolution from mass-party to electoral machine is also shown in the "membership ratio", i.e. the proportion of party members to voters. In left-wing mass-parties, the ratio ought to be high: the higher the ratio, the more intense the participation of the ranks in the party's life, the stronger the roots of the party in the population. For the social-democratic labor parties of Britain and Austria the ratio is about 40%, in Sweden and Denmark it is about 35%, in Norway 25% and in Switzerland over 20%. In France, the "membership ratio" of the SFIO exceeded 10% only once, in 1936, but hardly ever dropped below 7%. In 1946, it was 9%. In 1955, however, it had dropped to 4%. [11] Today it is even lower, since the party membership has decreased much faster than the popular vote.

Finally, the party has grown old. The sampling of 1955 indicated the following proportions for each age group (in percent) [12]:

| | |
|---|---|
| under 25 years | : 2.6 |
| from 25–30 years | : 7.4 |
| from 30–40 years | : 20.6 |
| from 40–50 years | : 32.3 |
| over 50 years | : 37.1 |

Another sampling of 1952, by the French Institute for Public Opinion Research, among the party's electorate, confirmed these results: [13]

| | SFIO | CP | Average in tot. pop. |
|---|---|---|---|
| under 35 years | 30 | 42 | 34 |
| from 50–60 years | 22 | 19 | 20 |
| over 65 years | 15 | 4 | 14 |

These proportions grow worse as one gets closer to the top leadership. Although the SFIO is not strictly speaking a party of old people (the average age of the members and voters is higher in the right-wing parties, and the proportion of pensioned and retired voters is highest in the Radical Party) it is a party on the older side of middle age, with an insignificant proportion of youth and more important, with an inability to recruit among the youth. Among its top leaders and parliamentarians, it has its generous share of the ancient French politicians "who never resign and rarely die."

The high proportion of older people in the age-structure of the party has had a double effect: first it determines the psychological atmosphere: slow reactions to new situations, a world made up of pious recollections, of small, rigidly observed routine habits. Secondly, it reinforces the conservative tendencies of apparatus rule: advancement is slow and based on seniority alone. Creative intelligence, drive, outstanding abilities are not an asset but a handicap in this kind of organization.

From another point of view, the social composition has also contributed to strengthening these tendencies: the high proportion of civil servants has undoubtedly favored the bureaucratization of the party and the rule of the General Secretariat. The habits of discipline, of obedience to authority, the acceptance of administrative hierarchy and dependence are always present in a large group of civil servants and office workers, and assert themselves with particular force in a conservative social climate.

The rule of the apparatus is also favored by the heterogeneity of the party's class composition: in the absence of a dynamic policy, the apparatus is the principal force which keeps together the contradictory interests that have sought shelter in the party.

One of the most important consequences of this situation has been the disappearance of the party ideology: the apparatus shuns theory, as it necessarily involves critical thinking. For ten years now, any interest for theory has been confined to the isolated minorities on the Left, mostly composed of individuals who have learnt to think in other organizations before joining the party.

In actual practice, the ideology has been replaced at best with liberal empiricism (as in the case of the "center" faction led by Defferre) or with a vague feeling of solidarity with the "little man", at worst with the kind of party patriotism in which the organisation has become and end in itself. The effect achieved is not unlike that of Stalinism in the CP: the party can do no wrong, the leaders of the party must not be criticized lest the criticism be used aginst the party by its enemies, etc. This is what André Philip refers to when he says that the parly "seems to have lost the very notion of truth" and that an action "is held to be good or evil not on its own merits but according to the party affiliation of the men responsible for it." [14]

The reaction of Mollet to the capture of the Moroccan plane carrying the leaders of the FLN is typical in this respect: anger when he received the news, then acceptance and endorsement in order to cover up for Lacoste. The responsibility of the left minority in this situation should not be hidden: during the electoral campaign in Paris in January 1957, the left-winger Mirelle Osmin defended the official party policy in spite of her well-known opposition to the party leadership, contributing only to the discredit of the opposition and to the confusion of party members and sympathizers.

One may summarize the preceding point by quoting Duverger's description of the present state of the party [15]:

"Without doctrine or program, the party confines itself to the defense of immediate interests, supporting in a day-by-day fashion the demands of the interest groups under its protection without relating them to each other or to the general situation, without even analyzing their chances of success. It agrees to wage-raises, but without undertaking the fiscal and social reforms that would enable it to limit profits; it agrees to lower the prices of foodstuffs but without ceasing to support useless agricultural products; it is all in favor of economic expansion, but without touching marginal enterprises: all those are themes which the SFIO holds in common with all other French parties, each insisting on one or the other aspect, according to the weight of the different interest groups within the party. The Radicalized SFIO is becoming increasingly assimilated to French conservatism: a conservatism of little people, nicer than the other kind from a sentimental point of view, actually much worse since it involves the acceptance by the victims of their condition as victims. The verbal reference to socialism only exists for the sake of a good conscience; in this country of ours, the conservatives insist on seeming revolutionary to others and, most of all, to themselves."

We have seen in the preceding sections of this survey the ways in which the sociological degeneration of the SFIO has determined the shift towards an inferior kind of bourgeois politics. It is necessary at this point to turn to the other aspect of this process, and to assess the part that policy has played in the degeneration of the party. This, in turn, raises other questions: to what extent can a change in policy by the party leadership or by sections of the party modify or reverse the present process of decline? What are the forces that make policy in the SFIO of today, and what forces could be expected to change it?

It should be clear that as complex a process as the complete sociological and political transformation of a mass-party cannot simply be explained by a "mistaken" policy of its leadership, nor can it be said that the adoption of a "correct" policy by this leadership would annul that process. One could also express the wish that the left wing of the party should adopt a militant yet realistic policy which might, even under the present circumstances, neutralize the right wing and change the party all over again. But such wishes remain empty speculations when the forces don't exist that could create such a policy and act upon it.

It is probably true that the presence in the party of a strong and homogenous Left in 1944-5 would have determined an entirely different evolution. The sociological base for an independent and militant labor party does exist in France: the social-democratic workers of tho Northern and Eastern departments, a large part of the Communist workers, the Catholic workers of the West. As late as January 1956 the leader of the CFTC; in Nantes pointed put to the SFIO that its electoral victory in that region was due to the votes of the Catholic workers, and urged the party – ironically – to follow a more militant course in order to cement this alliance. [16] By that time, however, the SFIO was no longer in a position to turn itself into the basis for a political regroupment of the working-class. In 1945, when hundreds of thousand of young men and women from the Resistance movement felt attracted to socialist solutions, the operation could have been successful had it been carried out by the Left – the only section of the party capable of implementing such a perspective. But in 1945 the Left was neither strong nor homogeneous, not even to the extent of keeping itself together. The historical reasons for this cannot be discussed within the framework of this article[3*]; suffice it to say that a conquest of the party by the Left had become a pious wish by 1948. [4*]

Above all other things, the recent history of the SFIO teaches the lesson that good intentions, and even policies, that are good in themselves, are inevitably defeated when working at cross-purposes with the fundamental trends of an institution. The failure to face this fact accounts for the quiet and thorough defeat of the SFIO's left wing.

Institutions have their own logic; the political history of the SFIO since the end of the war has been the history of men who, by the logic of that particular institution, have been compelled to transgress every principle of socialism, or have been forced out of positions of influence. It is important to remember that the present leadership of the party came to power in 1947 as a left-wing caucus (with Mollet as General Secretary and Dechezelles as Assistant Secretary) and that it came to power by defeating a right-wing led by Daniel Mayer, who today opposes Mollet's policy – from the Left? Within one year, the party had returned to the bourgeois politics which the left wing had fought: war in Indo-China, "Third Force" coalitions, support of US foreign policy and opposition to the economic demands of the working-class. Then, as today, the party has acted as a machine to produce conservative politicians.

As in the case of Stalinism, the institution has not only transformed the men, but also the meaning of words and ideas: "party discipline" now means blind obedience to the Secretariat, anti-"clericalism" is a pretext for fighting the Catholic Left, "internationalism" has become a pretext for opposing the right of the Algerian people to self-determination.

Footnotes

1*. There are about 10 million potential union members in France: 1.2 million agricultural workers, 6,5 industrial workers and 2 million office workers. There are also about 400,000 teachers but their case is different: almost all belong to unions, most of which are federated in an independent organization, the Federation de l'Education Nationale. Their unions are outstanding for their militancy, their high degree of internal democracy and their high standards of organization.

2*. André Philip defines this policy as "practical conservatism", thinly disguised by a general ideology of the defense of the "little man" against the "big man".

3*. They have been explained in two valuable studies by Saul Berg in The New International, February and March 1947.

4*. In March 1949, the former National Secretary of the SFIO Youth wrote: "The few attempts of some cadre elements, mostly former left oppositionists, to modify the structure of the party and to give a political education to its members remained without results. The failure of the socialist factory groups illustrate very well the lack of real basis for the efforts of certain militants who intend to organize the workings-class with a party that has neither the social composition nor the policy necessary for such work." [17]

References

1. Le Monde, May 9, 1957.

2. Jean-Daniel Reynaud and Alain Touraine, La representation politique du monde ouvrier in Partis politiques et classes sociales en France, Colin, Paris 1955.

3. Raymond Fusilier, La situation actuelle du Parti socialiste francais, L'Observateur, June 18, 1953 and Maurice Duverger, SFIO: mort ou transfiguration?, Les Temps Modernes, Nr.112-113, 1955.

4. Duverger, ibid., p.1865

5. Fusilier, ibid.

6. Le Monde, January 5, 1956.

7. Duverger, Demagogie de bureaucrates, Le Monde, July 12, 1957.

8. Pierre Rimbert, Le Parti socialiste SFIO in Partis politiques et classes sociales en France; Sondages, review of the IFOP, Nr.1952; Maurice Duverger, op. cit., Les Temps Modernes, p.1869.

9. Duverger, op. cit., Les Temps Modernes, p.1868.

10. Sondages, 1952, Nr.3.

11. Duverger, op. cit., Les Temps Modernes, p.1870.

12. Rimbert, op. cit.

13. Sondages, 1952, Nr.3.

14. Andre Philip, Le Socialistic trahi, Plon, Paris 1957. p.205/6.

15. Duverger, op. cit., Les Temps Modernes, p.1873.

16. Gilbert Declerq, Questions posées au Parti socialiste, Tenoignage

Chretien, Jan, 20, 1956.

17. Marcel Rousseau, Sur la crise de la SFIO, Confrontation Internationale, March-April 1949.

# Colonial revolution [1961]

*This article by "André Giacometti" was published in International Socialism (1st series), No.6, Autumn 1961, pp.28-29. Thanks to Ted Crawford & the late Will Fancy. Transcribed & marked up by Einde O'Callaghan for ETOL.*

Algeria, Rebellion and Revolution
Joan Gillespie
Ernest Benn, 27s.

**Surprisingly little has as yet been written about the war and the revolution in Algeria, considering that almost seven years have passed since the first military battles were fought, considering also the far-reaching political and ideological implications of the conflict, and the strong commitments it has called forth.**

Several types of literature have begun to emerge, it is true. As is natural, polemical and apologetic writing prevails. On the French side, Les rebelles algeriens by the Figaro journalist Serge Bromberger is a classic of its type. Its main concern is to rake up as much dirt as possible on the military leaders of the Algerian revolution. But, thanks to the easy access the author enjoyed to the French police and army archives, it contains interesting information that may prove valuable when checked and sifted by future historians.

On the Algerian side, the bulk of political writing has so far been produced by French supporters of the FLN. It ranges from the passionate and sometimes dishonest polemics of the Jeansons – L'Algerie hors la loi and Notre guerre – to the testimonials of soldiers who refused to fight the dirty war – Maschino's Le Refits. These latter are the first writings by actual participants; they describe a lived experience of the war and express a moral choice, and they are valuable as such. Others, like Davezies in Le Front, have reported on the FLN in interview form.

Documentation on various aspects of the repression conducted by the French army are another valuable source. Henri Alleg's La Question, Keramane's La Pacification and the pamphlets by the lawyers defending FLN prisoners before French courts fall into this category. Most recently, the main documents relating to the Manifesto of the 121, advocating civil disobedience in France, have been added to this documentation.

Finally, there are the books by liberal politicians pleading the neo-colonialist case, and the case of the right wing of the FLN. Jacques Chevallier's Nous Algeriens and Jean-Jacques Servan-Schreiber's Lieutenant en Algerie are typical.

Joan Gillespie's book reflects a very different kind of approach from any of the above. It is not an uncommitted book: the writer is clearly sympathetic with the Algerian nationalists. The difference is in the aim of the book: its primary purpose is not to plead a case, but to analyze the background of the conflict, and to describe the social forces involved. It is the first time this has been attempted by a serious writer.

The book begins with the beginning, that is, with the colonization of Algeria in the middle of the last century. The European settler is described in detail, as is the destruction of Algerian society, the Algerian economy as an object of exploitation, the property relationships and their consequences, the mass migration of Algerian workers to France, the gradual recovery from the shock of colonization among Moslem intellectuals, the policies of the successive French governments and the always abortive attempts at reform.

In a second part, Joan Gillespie examines the beginnings of nationalism: the North African Star, the Algerian People's Party, the Ulemas, then the development of nationalism during World War II, the revolt of 1945 and its repression, the main Algerian political parties in the post-war period.

Part III is a history of the actual war, as of November 1954. The political, military and international aspects of the war are all discussed; much space is given to a description of the structure and the policies of the FLN. The book ends with the first months of 1959; a post-script brings it up to 1960.

To understand the nature of the book, something must be said about its author. Joan Gillespie, who died suddenly in Tunis in 1959, was an American journalist with a special interest in African affairs.

She was a New Englander, and studied political science and international law in the United States and in France. She worked for two years in the American foreign service, then worked as a journalist and wrote a series of magazine and newspaper articles on

Africa, as well as the book under review. Her last trip to Africa, in the summer and autumn of 1959, was to have provided material for a book on the leaders of the nationalist movements in sub-Saharan Africa. In his introduction to her book, her brother writes that

'her great love was for ideas, particularly the idea of freedom. Similarly, her great hate was for those ideas which denied freedom. She was an idealist par excellence, and the love of her ideas, although intellectually conditioned, was a profoundly emotional thing. Above all, she was a person of action, bound and determined to do what she could in furthering the aims for which she stood.'

It may seem paradoxical, but it is actually not too surprising, that a person of this cast, an American liberal, that is a person who could never become directly involved in this fight, from the inside, should have been the first to attempt to place the Algerian conflict in its historical context. The main value of the book lies in this approach, supported by an undeniable journalistic competence.

Its weaknesses are those of the liberal point of view, that is, the inability to sympathize with or fully understand those who believe that the fulfilment of liberal values can never take place within the framework of formal democracy controlled by the native bourgeoisie. Within the nationalist camp, Joan Gillespie's sympathies unmistakeably gravitate towards the 'moderates' and away from the 'extremists'. When she writes about the early proletarian nationalism of the North African Star, she seems to blame the movement for formulating demands the French government would be likely to reject:

'In 1933, the ENA (North African Star) again reappeared and held an important General Assembly meeting in France. Messali and his followers passed a long resolution containing demands for measures to be taken both before and after independence. Their wide scope reflected not only the Communist influence upon the movement, but also the quite utopian and theoretical framework of the few devoted militants in the early 1930s. If total independence was not startling enough for the French, the provision concerning eventual confiscation of large properties in Algeria made it almost certain that the authorities would reject the ENA demands outright.'

However, characteristically, the entire program of the ENA is reprinted in the references and is available to the reader to judge for himself.

She also quotes with approval, from Lacheraf's article Le nationalisme algerien, that 'the early militants of the ENA had only a vague doctrine, which has been described as "a surface Marxism, a nostalgic and sentimental Algerianism, a summary Islamism",' little realizing that this description is not so much the product of a historical judgement, but that of a present polemic against the ENA's successor, the MNA, by one of the leaders of the rival FLN, and that it is meant to serve, retroactively, present-day purposes.

In the third part, dealing with the actual war, the author, understandably, seems somewhat overwhelmed by her subject.

The account is hurried, as if telescoped. Insufficient cross-checking on the available evidence may account for the fact that Gillespie fell for the official versions of the death of the leader of the FLN 'left wing' of 1957, Abane Ramdane ('killed outright in a French ambush'), although it has been known for some time now that he became a victim of an FLN purge. She also writes that 'mystery still surrounds the circumstances of the death of the 'Father of the Aurès (Ben Boulaid)', although in this case too it is known that he was killed by the explosion of a booby-trapped radio transmitter, following his declaration of loyalty to the MNA after his famous escape from prison. Predictably enough, she also plumps for the lie of 'collusion between the MNA and the police in France', one of the most infamous slanders spread during the whole period.

On the Bellounis question, however, she succeeds in largely sticking to the facts. She stresses that, although he took arms from them, 'Bellounis did not make a political agreement with the French, and refused to rally to the cause in May 1958, when the French Army called for closer cooperation between Muslims .and Frenchmen in Algeria. Bellounis became a casualty of the colon-Army coup of 13 May. The French later claimed to have executed him.' In actual fact, Bellounis died in battle with the paratroopers of the fascist colonel Trinquier, of subsequent Katanga fame.

The liberal point of view is also, no doubt, responsible for the insufficient attention given to the labour movement. All that is said, is that

'In late February (1956), stimulated somewhat by the formation of a MNA labour union, the FLN founded the Union Générale des Travailleurs Algeriens (UGTA) – General Union of Algerian Workers. Up to this time, those Algerian workers who were organized had been members of unions affiliated with French unions, notably the Communist-dominated CGT. The UGTA had considerable initial success, and by the end of May, claimed 110,000 members. The UGTA asked for better working conditions for Algerians, and its political programme resembled that of the FLN. It was admitted to the ICFTU in July, and established close relations with the stronger organized unions in Tunisia and Morocco. But the UGTA has suffered severely from French repressive measures.

'Its leaders have been arrested several times, and its activity brought to a virtual standstill. It now maintains a training centre in Tunisia and carries on social welfare work for Algerian worker refugees.'

This is a little bit thin, considering the prominent role which working-class militants have played in the Algerian nationalist movement, from its formative period up to today. It ignores, among other things, the role played by the MNA-oriented trade union centre, the USTA, which is the only organization that has so far actually succeeded in carrying out trade union functions, and which has already two congresses behind it (Paris 1957 and Lille 1960).

Small mistakes in translation from the French occur in a few places. The FLN Central Committee did not condemn Berberism as a 'communistic' but as a 'communal' deviation, and the MTLD Congress of 1953 did not reaffirm its will to follow a 'sane' political line, but a 'sound' one. These are details.

The 'classic' about the Algerian war has yet to be written. Neither the Harold Isaacs, nor the George Orwell of the Algerian war have so far appeared. In the meantime, Joan Gillespie's book will be a good guide as to what actually happened. It contains the basic background information, and most of its facts are straight. It has served, above all, to mark out the field which future historians will have to cover in greater detail, armed with the wisdom of hindsight.

# Revolutionary at Large [1963]

*This article by "André Giacometti" was published in International Socialism, Winter 1963/4 No.15, Winter 1963/4, p.38. Transcribed & marked up by Einde O'Callaghan for ETOL.*

Memoirs of a Revolutionary
Victor Serge
translated and edited by Peter Sedgwick
Oxford University Press, 1963, 426 pp., 42s.

**The publication of Victor Serge's autobiography at the present time is a public service. Never have people like him been more needed, and never have they seemed as scarce. Fortunately, some write and leave books.**

Victor Serge, born Victor Lvovich Kibalchich, is one of the most important witnesses of the European revolutionary movement in the period between the two world wars, and his autobiography, hitherto unavailable in English, is an essential contribution to the 'dossier' of this period. Serge, son of an exiled Russian revolutionary, was born in Brussels in 1890, lived in Belgium and France and spent his youth in the anarchist movement. In October 1917 he was working with the syndicalist trade unions in Barcelona; by 1919, he had made his way to Petrograd, where he immediately took up service as a propagandist and functionary of the Third International. In 1922, he went on mission to Germany and Austria, then returned to Russia in 1926 where he joined the Left Opposition and witnessed the beginning of the purges. He was imprisoned himself, deported to Siberia, saved from execution by his French connections, then released and allowed to return to Belgium in 1936. He arrived in France soon afterwards, witnessed the Popular Front, the Spanish Civil War and the defeat of the Spanish revolution, deeply involved in all these events, fighting at the same time against the Moscow Trials, the assassination campaign of the GPU against oppositionists (Ignace Reiss, Andres Nin, Marc Rein, Kurt Landau, Rudolf Klement, Walter Krivitsky – the best known among many). When France collapsed before the German army, he fled south and succeeded in escaping to Mexico in 1941, in the company of a small band of revolutionary socialists of various origins (Gustav Regler, Marceau Pivert, Julian Gorkin and others). He died in Mexico in

1947, still fighting; 'his upturned shoes had holes in them, his suit was threadbare, his shirt coarse. Really he might have been some vagabond or other picked up from the streets. Victor Serge's face was stiffened in an expression of ironic protest and, by means of a bandage of cloth, the State had at last closed his mouth.'

Victor Serge wrote a great deal. His novel The Case of Comrade Tulayev is, without doubt, the best novel on the Moscow Trials and the Stalinist purges, although less well known than Darkness at Noon. Another novel translated into English, The Long Dusk, is a record of how revolutionary refugees in Southern France were attempting to escape from the Gestapo and various other political police. Among his other writings, Russia Twenty Years After, From Lenin to Stalin, and various fragments published in radical reviews (mostly The New International and Politics) are alone available in English. All of these are relevant today, but none so much as his Memoirs, which are particularly important in the context of the deep changes the Communist movement is undergoing at present.

The ideological and political breakdown of the Stalinist system has led not only to the rehabilitation of people, but also to the rehabilitation of facts. There is wide acceptance in Communist circles of notions which were dangerous heresies in Serge's time: that Stalin not only made mistakes, but also committed crimes; that the world Communist movement need not necessarily be directed from a single centre: that more than one form of artistic and literary expression is compatible with a commitment to socialism: that the Bolshevik old guard were not paid agents of foreign capitalist powers and that the Moscow Trials were a frame-up. In Serge's time people were murdered all over the world for asserting these same things, which today are admitted by official spokesmen for Communist governments. Is there a victory for truth and justice in this? If so, why does it so often leave a bitter taste? Working with Communists in certain situations – nuclear disarmament, trade unions – one has occasion to see a Communist rise to speak on one subject or another, in the smooth, well-behaved fashion that most of them have today, and irresistibly other thoughts crowd in on the mind: here is a man who accepted Khrushchev's denunciations of Stalin as unflinchingly as he accepted any of Stalin's crimes, and as unquestionably as he will accept other crimes tomorrow. He has understood nothing. He is no more destalinized than Globke and Oberlander are denazified. This is altogether too easy. Clearly, the lesson has not sunk in. The lesson has not been assimilated because the 'errors' of the Stalin period are not a mere matter for rehabilitation. Rehabilitation of people, and of facts, is useless when it is not coupled with an understanding of the pattern which produced the 'errors', and with an altogether different approach to politics. Hearing a Communist talk about Stalin and the great purges today, one is rather reminded of the repentant Nazi who regrets the uncritical acceptance of Hitler by his party because Hitler made the mistake that lost the war.

If a certain view of politics is not destroyed, nothing has really changed. To drive this lesson home, a discussion of ideas and of theoretical differences is not enough: it is necessary to produce object lessons, that is, the facts of the period and, more important perhaps, the feeling and the flavour of these facts, and the nature of the personalities that made them. Only then does the overall pattern and the explanation emerge. Serge's autobiography does all of this. It is largely a record of what actually happened in Russia and in the European Communist movement in the 1920's and 1930's, and of the way in which it happened. In this sense, it is a testimony, like Orwell's Homage to Catalonia, or Alfred Rosmer's Moscou sous Lenine (still not translated into English), or John Reed's Ten Days That Shook the World, and it says more about different approaches to the problems of socialism and of revolution than any number of theses and programmes. Not that theses and programmes did not mean anything to Serge. He was an intensely political person, and there is hardly any issue that is central to socialism that does not come up in his memoirs. His libertarian and syndicalist background made him particularly sensitive to the dangers of bureaucratic degeneration within the revolutionary movement, and issues such as workers' control, the unavoidable and the avoidable factors in the degeneration of revolutions, pluralism of tendencies in the labour movement, are continuously present in his writing. His approach to these problems, and his description on how they were regarded in the revolutionary movement of his time, provide a welcome standard of comparison between the Stalinists of all tendencies of today and the revolutionaries of yesterday and of tomorrow. By these standards, the counterfeit article becomes easily recognizable.

Dolores Ibarruri, the leader and figurehead of the Spanish Communist Party, has just published her own memoirs entitled (guess what?): Memoirs of A Revolutionary, where she repeats the slanders against the POUM and the anarchists which were used as a political cover for the assassination of Nin, Berneri and others. There is no better example of a literary confrontation between lie and truth, degradation and integrity, than in these two books, issued accidentally at the same time under the same title.

Serge was incapable of cynicism, whether born from pessimism and despair or from smug conceit. His description of the 'soggy left' of his time, paralysed as today by lack of intelligence and courage, makes instructive reading, although there is very little polemic, just confrontation with the facts.

Brecht, another sensitive and intelligent man, wrote a poem in 1938 called To the Coming Generations. It is a moving testimony by a man who stood in the Stalinist camp when Serge was fighting against the crimes later denounced by Khrushchev. Brecht, who 'slept among murderers', wrote:

'You, who shall emerge from the flood
In which we are sinking
Think –
When you speak of our weaknesses –
Also of the dark time
That brought them forth.'

and also

'... when at last it comes to pass
That man can help his fellow-men
Do not judge us
Too harshly.'

This is a misdirected appeal. The only people qualified to judge were Serge and his companions. They are all dead now, Stalin the butcher, Brecht the apologist, Serge the witness, and the many thousand victims. But this fact cannot obscure that other fact, that these were right and these others were wrong, that this inescapable contradiction is still true today and will still be true tomorrow.

Although Serge had every reason to, he did not 'judge too harshly'. He was a man who sought to understand before he sought to condemn, and his description of people always shows compassion, rarely tinged with contempt. He had qualities of which there is a great dearth in the radical left of today: compassion, sanity, a sense of humour, optimism. He did not move like an enemy agent in the midst of ordinary humanity: to him, to be a revolutionary meant to participate in every aspect of the life of ordinary people, and he never allowed himself to forget that this is where socialism must come from if it is to come at all. There is a paradox here, perhaps only an apparent paradox, that this man, who was a genuine professional revolutionary, should have been least deformed in his personality by his 'profession'. Perhaps the real revolutionaries do not conform to some of the ideas of what constitutes 'Bolshevik hardness'? A comforting thought.

Peter Sedgwick deserves our thanks for an intelligent, informed and readable translation. The footnotes, providing extensive information on persons mentioned by Serge, and extremely useful, now that many of the actors are forgotten. I cannot resist indulging in the small pleasures of the critic by pointing out the one small mistake I found: Marceau Pivert (p.339) was never expelled from the SFIO after he rejoined it after the war. He was still a member of the SFIO when he died in the night of June 2 to 3, 1958, some 3 months before the founding of the Autonomous Socialist Party (PSA). However, Sedgwick is right in substance. On May 28, 1958, Pivert wrote in his last article: 'The traitor Mollet must be unmasked within the Party. It is no longer possible to coexist with a man who has chosen to serve so cynically the bourgeois class, preparing its military dictatorship, whilst at the same time officially representing a working class party.'

The book also includes a bibliography of Serge's writings, an index of names and many illustrations, most of which are not generally known.

# Inside the New World Order: Drawing the Battle Lines [1994]

*The following article first appeared in the American socialist review New Politics, Vol. V, Nr. 1, Summer 1994.*

**Expectations of prosperity, peace and freedom following the collapse of communism have given way to unprecedented levels of permanent unemployment and, in many countries, deep poverty for which no one seems to have any cure; a multitude of incredibly barbaric wars in Europe, Africa and Asia which have destroyed the lives of millions and the continued threat of nuclear conflict. The New World Order has turned into a nightmare for all but a small elite. We are witnessing the catastrophic failure of really existing capitalism as a world system at the end of the 20th century.**

What to do? Parties of the Left have demoralized their members by failing to defend them against the policies of their enemies or, worse, adopting them as their own; they have run out of steam, out of fire, out of ideas. It sometimes seems they have run out of a future.

But this is not the first time in history that wrenching change has thrown societies into seemingly uncontrollable turmoil. It is not the first time that the values of justice and solidarity, of equal rights for all, of cooperation and mutual responsibility, are held in contempt by those in power who dictate fashions, not the first time that the people have seemed powerless.

Let us start by trying to understand what is happening to us, then think about what needs to be done, what can be done and how to do it.

The Global Economy

A good place to start is the economy. In a recent issue, Business Week asked: "What's Wrong?" and echoed the general perplexity: these should be "the best of times," brought about by the end of the

Cold War and the spread of "free market" economies. Instead, we have a deep recession in the advanced industrialized countries and "everywhere you look, fear is pitting those profiting from the global economy against those losing their jobs to overseas rivals."

Indeed. And *Business Week* itself gives the answer: "A new, brutally competitive world economic order is emerging with the demise of the Cold War. ... The fundamental force behind this new order is the integration into the global economy of the new capitalist nations and much of the developing world," representing some 3,000 million people.

Transnational corporations (TNCs) are the driving force of this integration. There are now approximately 37,000 TNCs, with more than 170,000 subsidiaries outside their country of origin; because of non-equity arrangements like licensing and franchising (typical for the hotel and fast-food industry, among others) their true influence extends even further than these figures would indicate. According to a recent report by the United Nations Commission on Trade and Development (UNCTAD), sales generated by TNCs outside their country of origin totalled $5.5 trillion (million million) in 1992, thereby exceeding the total value of world exports ($4 trillion). TNCs now control one-third of the world's private sector productive assets. The stock of foreign investment world-wide totals $2 trillion. The biggest group of owners are the TNCs based in the U.S. with $474 billion; those based in Britain come second with $259 billion, followed closely by the Japanese TNCs with $251 billion.

Growth in foreign investment will continue in the foreseeable future, the report predicts and goes on to say that "international production has become a central structural characteristic of the world economy," partly as a result of the revolution in communications and transport systems which allows companies to integrate more fully with their subsidiaries abroad. Privatization is helping the trend, and TNCs have been particularly active in taking advantage of the selling off of public assets in Latin America and in Eastern and Central Europe. The strategies of TNCs are fostering world-wide economic integration, the report says. Companies are locating central functions in whichever country is most cost-effective. Such activities, the report points out, cause integration between national economies even in the absence of formal agreements, such as the European single market. Asian economies have been more closely integrated by the production strategies of Japanese companies, while U.S. companies were establishing links with Mexican companies even before the NAFTA negotiations. "The traditional division between integration at the corporate and country levels begins to break down," the report says. "TNCs ... encroach on areas over which sovereignty and responsibilities have traditionally been reserved for national governments."

In 1990, according to the U.S. Department of Commerce, U.S. companies employed 2 million people in Western Europe (up 4% from the previous year), 1.5 million in Asia (up 2%) and 1.3 million in Latin America (up 2%). Japanese companies are building more plants overseas even as unemployment increases at home. For example, Nissan's $800 million expansion of its Mexican plant is intended to produce not only for the Mexican market but also for export to Japan, Canada and the rest of Latin America. French transnationals employ approximately two million workers outside of France.

The Global Labor Market

We all now live in a borderless global economy made possible by new communicationand transport technologies. This global economy has created a global labor market where European, North American, Japanese or Australian labor is in direct competition with the labor force of countries where labor costs are kept 10 to 20 times lower, with *both* rising unemployment and falling wage levels in the old industrialized countries.

A British economic consultant, Douglas McWilliams, predicts that in the global labor market a combination of population growth and spreading literacy will expand the world's labor force from 600 million, at present, to about 4,000 million in 25 years, with real hourly labor costs in Europe declining by over 1% per year over the same period.

As early as the 1970s and 1980s, a massive transfer of production started taking place to take advantage of cheaper labor costs in the poorer countries and of the newly industrializing countries, particularly the Asian "tigers." As a result, entire industrial sectors virtually disappeared from northwestern Europe and North America: basic steel, shipbuilding, textiles, footwear, electronics. Today's relocations of production affect not only traditional industries in search of cheap labor, but sophisticated manufacturing and service operations, as well.

Airlines like Swissair and Lufthansa have moved all their accounting to India and KLM is considering a similar move. A software programming center in Bangalore services some 30 transnational corporations, including Microsoft, Digital, Fujitsu, Bull, Olivetti, Oracle, IBM, Motorola, Texas Instruments, 3M, Hewlett-Packard and Siemens at half the price the same work would cost in the U.S. or in Western Europe.

Between April and September 1993, Indian exports in electronic services increased by over 20%, for software over 30%. The projection is that in the next three or four years such exports will triple to reach $1,500 million, of which half will be for software alone.

Infosys, an Indian software company which works for General Electric, among others, does "some of the best work in the world" according to the president of Siemens' U.S. subsidiary. The managing director of Texas Instruments in India, quoted by *Fortune* magazine, says that "as designs and software get more complex, the cost advantage of India becomes greater. We have only scratched the surface of what could happen here." Tata Consultancy Services (TCS) has sold INR1, $800 million worth of electronic services worldwide in the past business year; it opened a subsidiary in Germany two years ago which services a major bank and the German subsidiary of Hewlett-Packard among others, and has established a joint venture with IBM which will further expand its business.

Since the mid-1980s, TCS has been leasing out teams of computer specialists by the week or by the month to software laboratories or computer firms in industrialized countries. This "body-shopping" is the up-market end of the new international slave trade; the down-market end is the leasing by the Chinese or the Burmese governments of entire crews for construction projects or for the merchant marine of foreign countries for monthly wages which are a fraction of international minimum standards, not all of which is paid to the worker but withheld by the government.

Siemens Information Systems Ltd. (SISL), which was established in July 1992 after three years' preparation, now employs 250 software specialists in Delhi, Bombay and Bangalore. In 1993 and 1994, Siemens is planning to permanently lay off 5,100 employees — 3,900 in Germany alone — in its loss-making computer business in the industrialized world. Indian wages for the same jobs amount to less than $7,000 per year. There are virtually no social costs; working hours are generally 48 per week. In Jamaica, 3,500 people work at office parks connected to the U.S. by satellite dishes, processing airline reservations, tickets, calls to toll-free numbers, data entries, credit card applications, etc.

The lesser developed fringe countries of Europe are also targets for relocation. Ireland has a telecommunication-based service sector servicing U.S. computer programming for insurance companies such as Metropolitan Life, which employs 150 workers in County Cork to examine medical claims from all over the world. Operating costs in Ireland are 30-35% cheaper than in the U.S., the Irish Development Authority provides generous tax and other incentives and "there appears to be a strong work ethic intensified by a serious shortage of jobs in Ireland."

The former Communist states are playing the same role as Third World countries with a high-tech capability: *Business Week* quotes the case of Polish programmers in Gdansk working for a U.S. communications equipment maker at "a fraction of the pay for a comparable U.S. worker" and Siemens reports that it is receiving offers for Russian computer specialists at $5 per day.

To understand these figures in their context it must be kept in mind that the Russian official minimum wage today stands at $7 per month, which represents 20% of the income needed for "physiological survival," according to a recent report of the International Labor Office (ILO). In the Ukraine, the minimum wage is even lower than in Russia; in Bulgaria, it represents about 60% of the subsistence level, in Albania 24%, in Romania less than 50%, in Estonia 61%, in Hungary 64% and in Poland 70%.

The minimum wage has also fallen drastically in relation to average wages, which have themselves been falling rapidly. In 1993, wages in Russia grew by 12%, but after falls of 45%, 38% and 60% in the preceding three years. Hungary had the lowest drop, with wages stable in 1990, falling 6% in 1991 and 3% in each of the succeeding two years. Percy Barnevik, of ABB, quoted in *Fortune*, foresees "a massive move from the Western world. We [ABB] already have 25,000 employees in former Communist countries. They will do the job that was done in Western Europe before." More jobs will also shift to Asia: ABB, which employed only 100 workers in Thailand in 1980, has 2,000 there now and plans on 7,000 at the end of the century. Barnevik forecasts a drastic and permanent drop in employment: "Western European and American employment will just shrink and shrink in an orderly way. Like farming at the turn of the century."

Transfers of production are not the full story. Less well-known is the internationalization of services believed to be inherently domestic: several countries in Europe have household garbage collected by a U.S.-based transnational, the streets of London suburbs are being cleaned by a French transnational and a Danish transnational is a leading building cleaning and maintenance company in Europe and in North America. In general, this subcontracting of public services to private transnationals has involved job losses. The important point, however, is not only that production is being massively transferred, but that it is being transferred not only in manufacturing but also in services, including high-tech services, and that the resulting job losses in industrialized countries do not imply any great gains in employment in the countries where companies relocate and expand. The migration of jobs is not at all a straightforward one-for-one proposition, with one job gained in the new country for every job lost in an industrialized country.

Paul Samuelson, lecturing in Italy in 1992, observed: "As billions of people who live in East Asia and Latin America qualify for good, modern jobs, the half-billion Europeans and North Americans who used to tower over the rest of the world will find their upward progress in living standards encountering tough resistance." The impression conveyed here of a quid-pro-quo is misleading. The operative word is "qualify": Many are called but few are chosen.

The Whole World Is Losing Jobs

The global economy is a great leveller – but it levels downwards. As jobs are draining away from the industrialized world — over two million jobs in the last five years — Western levels of employment are not being exported to the new host countries, along with the jobs. *Fortune* writes that "when work does move to less developed lands, it's by no means automatic that the shift will bring Western levels of employment and prosperity to new host countries." In other words, there is *no* positive counterpart in the Third World, or in the former Communist countries, to compensate on a global level for the job losses in industrialized countries through relocation of production. The main reason is that "new technology and the continuing drive for higher productivity push companies to build in undeveloped countries plants and offices that require only a fraction of the manpower that used to be needed in factories back home." A consultant quoted by *Fortune* notes: "Some of the most Japanese-looking American plants are going up in Brazil." New factories abroad, even in low-wage countries, tend to be far more labor-efficient than their counterparts in the company's home country.

Secondly, new factories built abroad by American, European or Japanese companies tend to subcontract (or "outsource") far more than their predecessors did in their home countries 10 or 15 years ago and, although sub-contracted jobs are jobs, they are cheap, unprotected jobs that contribute to the world-wide deterioration of wages and conditions. The modern company is no longer structured like the classical pyramid, with management at the top, middle management and administration below and production workers at the bottom; rather, we are dealing with a flexible cluster of activities organized in a moveable pattern around a small core. That core is itself a small pyramid, although great care is often taken to disguise the underlying authoritarian relationships. It consists of headquarters management and staff and perhaps a highly specialized and skilled core labor force; all labor intensive operations are subcontracted, domestically or internationally. The corporation thus stands at the center of an interdependent network of firms of subcontractors, who in turn have their subcontractors, etc., with wages and conditions getting worse as one moves from the center to the periphery of the network.

Production and sales organizers command production facilities in different locations and countries and subcontract all or a large part of their needs. They decide what to produce, where, how, and by whom, and from where to supply which market. They sell a combination of elements, such as brand loyalty, superior organization, design and marketing, their hold over the distribution network, access to a protected market, and quality control.

Thus, the Italian clothing firm, Benetton, owns only a small part of its production and sales facilities. The shoe-producer Nike "thinks of itself not as a manufacturer but as a research, development and marketing corporation." In fact, a number of large companies now sell their name only, and leave actual manufacturing to others. Such firms include General Motors, General Electric, Kodak, Caterpillar, Bull, Olivetti and Siemens, for significant parts of their production. This, incidentally, also illustrates the absurdity of campaigns seeking to save domestic jobs by urging consumers to "buy American" or "buy European," since only a part, often a small part, of the product originates from domestic production.

Subcontracting applies to any kind of work, not just to manufacturing. We have already seen the case of companies subcontracting their accounting and other operations to low-wage countries. *Fortune* quotes the case of "typing mills" in the Philippines that will type text and numbers in a computer for 50 cents per 10,000 characters, and even they are competing with outfits in China that will do the same work for 20 cents. It therefore becomes clear that the new transnational economic order does not bring those benefits to the so-called developing countries, which are most commonly mentioned by its apologists, most notably Milton Friedman, the World Bank and the International Monetary Fund (IMF), whose "structural adjustment programs" have been the building blocks of the New World Order.

"Structural adjustment" is the name given to a set of so-called free-market policies imposed on countries by the World Bank and the IMF as a condition for receiving financial assistance. They typically include: currency devaluation, trade liberalization, cuts in social spending, privatization of public enterprises, holding down wages, business deregulation, restrictions on credit and higher interest rates. Structural adjustment programs are designed to attract foreign investments by eliminating trade and investment regulations, boost foreign-exchange earnings by promoting exports, and reduce government deficits through cuts in spending. These measures are supposed to put countries on a path to sustainable growth.

While they may well serve the purpose of attracting foreign investment, we have seen that such investment cannot serve the stated purpose, which is the gradual and general raising of living standards through progressive and sustainable development of undeveloped economies. Massive transnational investment may bring prosperity and full employment to small city states like Singapore or Hong Kong, but even in these cases legitimate questions arise on environmental, social and cultural grounds. It certainly does no such thing for the large countries in Asia, Africa and Latin America which are predominantly agricultural, and where progressive and sustainable development requires a solution to the land question and a serious attack on rural poverty before anything else. What relocations of production and services and investments by transnational corporations do is to create high-tech islands in a sea of poverty, and free trade zones which are in fact free-fire zones for transnational capital, as far as social conditions and labor rights are concerned.

The Race to the Bottom

There is a geographical version of the trickle-down theory according to which "the way that poor countries have a chance to pull themselves up by their bootstraps is precisely by exploiting competitive advantages like cheap labor that look unfair to their rich competitors." It does not work like that in the real world: in the first place, because, as we have seen above, what is being transferred from rich to poor countries is production, not jobs or incomes. In the second place, while the trickle-down effect may have a chance in societies where democratic mechanisms, such as strong and active trade unions, ensure a redistribution of wealth, in low-wage countries the power elites see to it that labor costs stay low and they split the loot with the foreign investors. The people of these countries never even get to reach their bootstraps: only the power elite gets more powerful and richer. This is where repression plays an economic role. Gangster states like Haiti and Burma may be extreme examples but the principle functions just as well in "democraturas" like Mexico, Egypt, Malaysia or Thailand, where more or less free trade unions are allowed to exist as long as they stay weak and where the outer trappings of democracy serve to conceal the iron fist.

In the race downhill to the lowest common international denominator, in which countries underbid each other and workers are forced to underbid each other, the usual argument is that a given economic sector must remain "competitive" to survive. But open-ended "competitiveness" is a no-win proposition: there is no finish line in the race to the bottom. As Jesse Jackson has said, you cannot compete with slave labor. "Competitiveness" does not in any way solve the employment problem, either from the point of view of quality or of quantity, nor is it intended to. On the contrary, globally the underbidding based on "competitiveness" leads to stagnation. As Jeremy Brecher wrote in "Global Village or Global Pillage?" (*The Nation*, 12/6/93): "As each work force, community or country seeks to become more competitive by reducing its wages and its social and environmental overheads, the result is a general downward spiral in incomes and social and material infrastructures. Lower wages and reduced public spending means less buying power, leading to stagnation, recession and unemployment. This dynamic is aggravated by the accumulation of debt; national economies in poor countries and even in the United States become geared to debt repayment at the expense of consumption, investment and development. The downward fall is reflected in the slowing of global GNP growth from almost 5% per year in the period 1948-1973 to only half that in the period 1974-1989 and to a mere crawl since then."

To understand the political and social implications of "competitiveness" and of the massive relocation of production to low labor cost countries — both undeveloped or former Communist — it is important not to lose sight of the economic role of repression.

The Economic Role of Repression

In a celebrated and infamous ad in a trade paper of the U.S. Garment industry, the wages of a garment worker in El Salvador were advertised as follows: "Rosa Martinez produces apparel for U.S. markets on her sewing machine in El Salvador. *You* can hire her for 57 cents an hour." In later versions of the same advertisement, Rosa's wage had dropped to 33 cents an hour. There is a reason for this wage level: the country has had a civil war for decades, with over 40,000 deaths. As in Guatemala, it was a war of the ruling class, backed by U.S. interests, against their own people, where the labor movement was destroyed several times over, through physical extermination, terror and intimidation, together with the parties likely to defend the people's interest against those of the elite. It was a war for the purpose of depriving the people of the means of defending themselves.

The newly developing industrial parks in Indonesia, 12 miles across the Strait of Malacca from Singapore, employ workers from Java and Sumatra at a third the cost of comparable labor in Singapore. They live under a military dictatorship that has had to murder over half a million people in 1965, by the lowest count, two million by the highest, to seize power and to crush the labor movement.

China, the largest and cheapest labor market opening up to transnational capital in the world today, is the product of a terrorist police state which has exterminated an estimated 150 million of its own citizens by starvation and repression. Vietnam, another totalitarian police state with state-run trade unions, is the latest candidate for Asian "tiger."

Russia has a working class that is only now emerging from seven decades in which the state killed 40 million people, again, at a low count, to wipe out every vestige of a civil society with its autonomous institutions. And the other former Communist countries of Eastern and Central Europe, with 40 years of Communist rule behind them, are economically, socially and psychologically destroyed societies, where the social fabric has all but disintegrated and even such basic notions as the public interest, or the common good, have been discredited by their association with official rhetoric under the Stalinist regimes. These are societies that have been engulfed by the ideologies of free enterprise, sometimes espoused by the very same people who would maintain the political structures of the old police states, more often by adventurers and opportunists, fusing into a new capitalist ruling class, just as ruthless but far more corrupt than that of the beginnings of the industrial age, united in their hatred of workers and of any form of an independent labor movement, in their distrust of democracy and in their subservience to transnational capital.

Brazil, another favorite country for transnational investment, is a society overwhelmed by its own poverty because of decades of military dictatorship, where the army and the police made sure that unions remained docile and opponents were either jailed or murdered.

Economic blackmail continues: when electronic workers in Malaysia tried to organize a national union two years ago, Texas Instruments and others threatened to pull out of the country if the government allowed it and unions are now accused of "acting against the national interest," an accusation that is not to be taken lightly in a country with an authoritarian and egotistic Prime Minister armed with an arsenal of repressive internal security legislation. Enterprise-level unions are the only legal form of organization in Chile, Guatemala and Thailand. In Colombia, formally a parliamentary democracy, the national center, CUT, reported last year that nearly 800 trade union leaders and activists had been murdered since the foundation of the organization in 1987.

"Trade unionists in the Americas have continued to be subjected to a far-reaching twin offensive against their most basic rights," the International Confederation of Free Trade Unions (ICFTU) observed in its 1993 "Annual Survey of Violations of Trade Union Rights." "The first element of the attack is the tragically familiar use of violent extra-legal repression which has persisted, and even intensified, in countries which have undergone the political transition from military dictatorship to formal democracy. ... The second element of the attack on trade union rights is constituted by the wave of restrictive legislation which has been introduced across the continent." It does not take specialized knowledge in economics, elaborate theories of Asian exceptionalism or speculation on the economic effect of world religions to understand why capitalism in its most rapacious and destructive forms is sweeping the planet, virtually unopposed: what we are dealing with here are the effects of decades of repression, armed violence and fear.

Before the globalization of the world economy, when national and regional economies were still protected by trade barriers, when political borders still meant something in economic terms and when international communications were slower and more costly, a slaughter of tens of thousands in El Salvador or of hundreds of thousands in Indonesia may have been regarded as a horrendous crime by some, perhaps even by many, in the far-away industrial democracies, but it did not affect their societies. Today, 30 years later, with the world economy as one, and Indonesian workers working as if side by side with European or American workers, the stench of death lingering from a massacre there 30 years ago, means unemployment, sweatshops and poverty in Europe and the U.S. today.

Rosa Martinez earning 33 cents per hour in El Salvador, perhaps less at the time of writing, because those who fought for higher wages were killed, over and over again, is working next to American garment workers. Even 10 years ago American academics like S. Sassen-Koobin in an essay in *Women, Men and the International Division of Labor* (State University of New York, 1983) noted: "There is growing awareness in the industry that wages in New York City are increasingly competitive with those in the garment industry in southeast Asia ... the availability of immigrant labor in New York City makes location of factories here increasingly profitable." Here the hand of the dead indeed reaches out to seize the living.

The American and international labor leaders who were boasting in 1964 of having contributed to the overthrow of the Goulart government in Brazil by getting their tame Brazilian unions to cooperate with the military in the putsch — another famous victory in the war against "Communism" — knew at the time that they were participating in a criminal act. What they did not realize is that they were also contributing to undermining the job security of their constituency, the American workers, 30 years later.

None of the people who now live in poor countries chose to be poor: they were forced into poverty by repression. Their only chance of breaking this vicious circle of poverty and terror is by securing democratic institutions which open up the space for unions to breathe and struggle and to get some power for workers and for ordinary people. In this fight, their best, and often their only, ally has been organized labor in the industrialized countries. But of course in these countries, its traditional heartland, the labor movement is also under attack. This is what the cry for deregulation, for flexibility in the labor market, is all about. A director of Courtaulds PLC, the British chemical company, says that industry needs "major cuts in costs and living standards ... the realization that we must work harder for less money is not there yet." In order to achieve this, the power of unions in North America and Western Europe must be broken.

Global Union Busting

In response to impending union mergers in the public sector in Britain, Rupert Murdoch's *Times*, as early as March 1992, railed against "great combinations of labor" and spelled out the conservative definition of the "successful unions of tomorrow": "They will be essentially staff associations, based in the individual workplace. They will be unideological except in understanding that their members' prosperity is linked to that of their employers. They will uphold individual contracts and workers' legal rights. ... Worker organizations have a role in updating management." That is where the New Right wants labor to be: in divided and powerless enterprise-based "staff associations" permitted only to handle individual grievances and to promote the employer's prosperity.

It is difficult to imagine that such a program can be imposed across the board in the industrial democracies without abolishing democracy. But democracy can no longer be taken for granted, even in its traditional bastions. What is new in the attack on trade unionism in the industrialized countries is that it is also a break with the policies of social consensus, sometimes also called neo-corporatism, that characterized the social relations of the leading industrial democracies in the post-war period. Capitalist business in the industrialized countries is now breaking free of the moral constraints imposed on it by the defeat of fascism at the end of World War II. The passage of time and the right-wing control of most media in Europe, North America and Japan is gradually freeing business from the opprobrium of having financed and supported fascism in Europe and extremist nationalism in Japan. It is also blurring the memory that trade unionists and socialists led the democratic resistance and paid the highest price to secure the future of global democracy while the leading elite of the business world, with very few exceptions, were enthusiastic supporters of the fascist war machine, collaborated in the extermination of the Jews and other ethnic and political victims of fascism and made a fortune out of the blood of millions. Whatever else Nazism in Germany, fascism in Italy and in other European countries, military dictatorship in Japan, might have been, they were the most ambitious and temporarily successful union-busting exercise in modern history. The current attack on the trade union movement is an attempted counter-revolution against the democratic revolution carried out by the Resistance movement in Europe, against the New Deal in the United States, with all its cultural, philosophical and political dimensions and against post-war democratization in Japan.

The counter-revolutionary character of the rise of the New Right accounts for some of its most bizarre aspects: the undertone of revenge, the mix of arrogance and scurrility, of provocation and nervousness. This was apparent in the tone of the last Republican administration in the U.S. and in the pronouncements of leading Thatcherites, but also in the former Communist countries where reactionary and fascist groups have made a strong come-back. Prime Minister Vaclav Klaus of the Czech Republic says that one of his country's big problems is the political "infiltration" from Western European trade unions and social-democrats; Istvan Czurka, the leader of the right-wing split from the MDF, the Hungarian government party, says that crime and cultural decline in Hungary have "genetic origins" and that the country is a victim of a world-wide Jewish-liberal conspiracy. In Romania, former prominent Stalinist propagandists and Securitate agents are now leading extremist nationalist parties and publishing fascist newspapers. Milosevic in Serbia and Tudjman in Croatia are holding on to power through the same poisonous mix of Stalinism and fascism and it was on this same platform, of course, that Zhirinovsky, the KGB's candidate in the last Russian elections, successfully conducted his campaign.

The threat to democracy is now universal, and touches all regions and politico-economic zones. That is one of the reasons why the issue of democratic rights has such fundamental importance. The ability of workers everywhere to organize world wide, North and South, East and West, to establish effective international links and to support each other, depends on it. That mutual support is one basic building block of what we mean by global solidarity. That has to be our answer to transnational capital operating in a global labor market.

It is in the common fight for human and democratic rights, that the labor movement in all parts of the world, in the traditional industrialized countries of the "North," the underdeveloped countries of the "South" and the former Communist countries, has the strongest imaginable common interest. Those who are trying to tell Asian workers, for example, that the struggle for human rights is a protectionist ploy of Western trade unions to save Western jobs are cynical liars. As Asian workers, and others, well know, one cannot trade dignity for prosperity and anyone who tries will lose both.

ICFTU general secretary Enzo Friso has pointed out that if it were true that the exercise of democratic rights was a hindrance to economic development the most repressive countries should also be the richest, whereas the opposite is true: "The folly and corruption that has disfigured the whole history of development is the direct consequence of the way that unrepresentative rulers have ignored or repressed their citizens."

At stake are not just labor rights. But their affirmation is an integral part of, and a precondition, for a development consistent with the interests of society in general from an ecological, social or cultural point of view.

The Human Rights Imperative

In a remarkable 1992 report entitled "Indivisible Human Rights – The Relationship of Political and Civil Rights to Survival, Subsistence and Poverty," the New York-based Human Rights Watch demonstrates that "subsistence, indeed survival, often depends on the existence of political and civil rights, especially those related to democratic accountability." Contrary to the claims of certain governments, particularly in Asia, that social and economic rights (basic needs such as food, clothing, shelter) must first be met before the luxury of political freedoms can be granted, the report demonstrates the link between democratic rights on the one hand, and freedom from famine, environmental destruction and enforced poverty on the other. These democratic rights include freedom of expression, association and assembly, free and competitive elections, and freedom of movement and residence. The key issue is democratic accountability, that is, the ability of the people to discuss and review the policies of the executive authority and establish checks on that authority if its policies are not deemed by the people to be in the public interest.

The rulers of countries which deny their people's basic democratic rights are in fact hindering, not promoting, their development. They are selling their people's labor and their countries' resources for the short-term gain of a small and often corrupt ruling class and, if justice were served, they would be tried for high treason.

Let us now look for a moment at the consequences for the so-called industrial democracies of denying democratic rights in Third World and former Communist countries. The industrial democracies are few. They are, broadly speaking, the industrialized countries of the OECD: Western Europe, North America, Japan, Australia and New Zealand. In the post-war world, they represented the prosperous, democratic and open societies, which formed the power structure underpinning the world order that had emerged after the defeat of fascism in Europe and Asia. While they tended to keep their democracy to themselves (after all, it was the U.S., the U.K. and France which most aggressively fought popular and progressive movements, propped up conservative rulers and protected transnational investments all over the Third World) their societies nevertheless allowed the political space for democratic forces to develop which, at different times, had a significant impact at the international and world level. These include the labor movement, the environmental movement, and the women's movement, among others. They are rooted in democratic opinion and protected by democratic institutions. They are, organizationally, financially and politically, the principal support of an emerging world wide civil society and the principal, if not the only, allies of all peoples fighting for their liberation and their own democratic rights.

Democracy and prosperity in the industrial societies were the principal gains of the victory over fascism. Both are now under threat in a stagnant global economy with a global labor market where the living standards of a vast majority of the world's population are held at the lowest possible level by the dictatorship of the gun, the torture chamber and the killing fields.

Democracy Undefended

As we look at the world wide threat to democracy, we must keep uppermost in our minds the unreliability of leading democratic governments, so far as the defense of democracy is concerned. Recent history demonstrates clearly that the governments of the United States, whether Republican or Democrat, of the European Union and Japan are not interested in democracy. They are interested in stability. Citizens concerned with the future of democracy can make no worse mistake than to expect relief from democratic governments.

The abject betrayal of democratic and pluralist Bosnia-Herzegovina is the result of a deliberate decision by Western governments not to oppose Serbian and Croatian fascism. Western policy toward Eastern and Central Europe has been to support the World Bank's and the IMF's "structural adjustment" policies which have undermined the economic and social foundations of democracy while delivering the former Communist countries defenseless to transnational capital. Nor is the strange listlessness of the German state, and of other European governments, in dealing with the criminal activities of well-organized fascist gangs, an encouragement to democrats at home and abroad.

Japan, the regional superpower, has signaled to the Thai military, a source of corruption in all of Southeast Asia, and to the Burmese military, which runs one of the most viciously repressive regimes existing today, that they have nothing to fear. Its reprimands to the SLORC of Burma have all the punch of Thatcher, in her day, protesting violations of human rights in South Africa. The Australian Labor government, craving acceptance in Asia, is courting the Indonesian dictatorship and making it known that the defense of human rights is no longer one of its priorities.

The inaction of democratic governments in the defense of democracy world-wide has led to a new world crisis: the sudden and enormous growth of the world refugee population. In November 1993, the UN High Commissioner for Refugees reported that in 1992 world refugee numbers increased by 10,000 a day. Overall refugee numbers have risen from 2.5 million in 1970 to nearly 44 million today. More than 19 million have been forced abroad and a further 24 million have been driven from their homes and are "internally displaced" refugees, the victims of "ethnic cleansing" and other forms of persecution. Never before have there been so many people in search of protection and asylum. According to the report, the main causes are "violent conflict and the chaotic breakdown of civil order." It says further that "making sure that human rights are respected where people live, so that they do not have to flee to find protection, is a matter of the greatest urgency." You might think that this common sense conclusion would be a priority concern of democratic governments. You would be wrong. The priority concern of democratic governments is to strengthen police measures to keep the growing refugee population out of their countries.

The European Union has generated a new body, which was supposed to be secret and which is not accountable to elected officials at any level. It is called the K4 Committee and it is composed of national security officials with broad powers to coordinate the fight against international crime such as drug trafficking and money laundering, but also against illegal immigration and asylum. At the head of its list of concerns is reportedly illegal immigration: "the process of erecting still higher barriers against refugees from Bosnia and elsewhere are already well advanced." Plans to co-ordinate policies on the forcible expulsions of unwanted immigrants and a new high-tech fingerprint system for asylum-seekers are also under way." We now have to ask ourselves how long democratic institutions, even in the small part of the world where they are today taken for granted, can survive given massive permanent unemployment and steadily worsening living and working conditions, along with the pressure of immigration. Millions of refugees are knocking at the doors of the prosperous democracies because their countries are engulfed in war and terror, and are being kept out by the military and the police.

Even some employers are getting worried. An increasing number of top managers of European companies are concerned about social breakdown caused by the business decisions of corporations. A manager for Allied Signal Europe NV was recently quoted as asking: "Can society sustain 20% unemployment? Where will it lead? Who's looking at this?" Schmidheiny, one of Switzerland's corporate leaders, has become internationally active in protecting the environment. Long before anyone else, Antoine Riboud, CEO of the French food transnational BSN, advocated a social consensus based on the recognition of trade unions, and he has stated publicly that the unions he wants to deal with should be strong and independent. We may yet find allies even among some companies, those few with a more thoughtful and responsible management than the rest.

Democracy cannot survive if transnational capital succeeds in imposing its economic solutions at the world level, and succeeds in imposing the social standards of, say, China, Indonesia, Russia, Brazil or El Salvador on the workers of Western Europe and North America. The way democracy in Europe or in America can be undermined, weakened and ultimately destroyed can take many forms, but we can be sure of one consequence: unchecked world domination by transnational capital means the end of many things, in particular the end of the labor movement for a long time, perhaps for a century, as a significant force for progressive change in the world — even as a potential for building such a force.

The Irrelevance of Nation States

What are the options available to us? The traditional remedy, seeking to achieve political power in the national context and pass protective legislation, has become largely outdated and ineffective, although it should, of course, be used for as long as possible for what it is worth.

The globalization of the world economy is rapidly restricting the space where decisions on economic and social policy taken at national level make any difference. Nation states and national legislation are becoming increasingly irrelevant because domestic economies are conditioned more and more by external forces over which national economic, political and social actors have no control.

This point was made with extraordinary clarity by Richard Gardner, appointed U.S. ambassador to Spain in November 1993, who said that having consulted the 33 American firms doing business in that country, he had to let the Spanish public know that American investors were losing interest in Spain because of high labor costs, the "rigidities of the labor market" and deficient infrastructures. This statement comes at a time when the Spanish government is preparing for a showdown with the unions over precisely these issues: control over job security and conditions of employment.

The growing irrelevance of nation states helps to explain why governments in different countries, coming from opposite ends of the political spectrum and elected on entirely different programs, end up following more or less similar policies. Walter Wriston, former chairman of Citicorp, described how "200,000 monitors in trading rooms all over the world" now conduct "a kind of global plebiscite on the monetary and fiscal policies of the governments issuing currency. ... There is no way for a nation to opt out." Wriston recalls the election of "ardent socialist" Francois Mitterrand as French president in 1981. "The market took one look at his policies and within six months the capital flight forced him to reverse course."

Trading blocs and geographical zones of economic cooperation will no doubt multiply and become stronger, but they merely relegate the same problem to a regional level. At best, it may become easier to secure social clauses in trade agreements to enforce minimum social standards as a condition of access to a trading bloc, although the failure to secure such clauses in the recently-concluded re-negotiation of the GATT agreement offers little encouragement for this expectation.

What, then, is there to do? It is not too difficult to devise sensible Keynesian alternatives to the catastrophic course presently followed by the leading governments, the Bretton Woods institutions and the other decision- and policy-makers of the "international community." Beyond these, there is the gigantic task of reinventing a society organized around the priority of meeting human needs at a time when a significant and increasing part of humanity is denied a material reward for productive and creative work and where the notion of work, therefore, has to be separated from the notion of income, and the notion of income from the notion of wages or salaries. The immediate difficulty we are facing, however, is that we are not in an argument about who has the better ideas. We are in an argument about power. The question is therefore one of organization. Organizing is what the labor movement used to be best at doing, but not in its present state of disorientation and confusion. In order to organize effectively, the labor movement must learn to think globally.

Global Organizing

Organizing has to start from new premises. Trade unions in the industrial democracies are on the defensive; in some countries their numbers have been decimated, their margin for negotiations has narrowed to very little. In many countries employers have gone from the acceptance of social consensus to a policy of confrontation. In the former Communist countries, both successor organizations of old unions and the alternative organizations arising from the political opposition are disarmed by hostile, authoritarian governments, demoralized members and massive unemployment. In the Third World, unions are unable to stem the pauperization of their countries and generally do not have the support of sympathetic governments as in the past. In such desperate straits, many organizations turn inward, in the mistaken belief that concentrating on domestic issues will help solve the immediate problems of their members. In the new world situation, the opposite is true: There can no longer be any effective trade union policy, even at the national level, that is not global in concept and international in organization. Not surprisingly, the small, weak and beleaguered unions in Third World countries have understood this best, since economic dependency, and therefore interdependency, has been a fact of life in their society throughout their experience. It is in the traditionally strongest union movements that provincialism and complacency are most entrenched, even at this late stage. The experience of repeated defeats is not necessarily the mother of invention.

A global approach has to involve the membership to a far greater extent than has been customary. A transnational corporation needs to be seen as a whole for those who work in it and bargain with it. Within the European Union, draft legislation instituting regional works councils is a step in this direction, but it also carries the danger of fostering the notion that a European organization is an end in itself, and of strengthening nationalist propaganda casting the workers of other regions as competitors and enemies. A trade union approach must deal with the company as a world wide structure, and must have the objective of organizing the company wherever it operates. New forms of company organization require new forms of union organization, crossing traditional jurisdictional lines and forming coalitions of unions adapted to the specific nature of the company and of the problems it poses. International collective bargaining, including coalition bargaining of international, national and local trade union structures where appropriate, must become a priority of unions dealing with TNCs.

Restructuring at the national level is a crying need in many countries to pool scarce resources and develop specialist services, non-existent at the present time, capable of comprehending company and government policies, to develop counter-strategies and to turn them into organizing drives. How can the AFL-CIO afford some 90 unions when the overall organizational density has sunk to below 16%? How can the French trade union movement afford five national centers with an organizational density below 12%? New Zealand, with a population of 3 million, had over 300 unions when the conservative government took power. They learned the hard way. Important union mergers have taken place, and are still under way, in Australia, Britain and Japan. Let them hurry. There is nothing wrong with mergers, and largeness in itself is no threat to democracy. There are numerous bureaucratic and ossified small unions: smallness is no guarantee of democracy, but in general a guarantee of impotence.

In a global perspective, union strength must not be undermined by sectarian considerations. Union strength must be preserved where it exists and the value of a union movement must be judged on the basis of its ability to defend its members' interests regardless of past politics. It is wrong, for example, to acquiesce in the seizure by the state of union assets in the former Communist countries on the grounds that they are goods stolen from the workers when the state controlled the unions. If these assets can play a role today in strengthening the union side against the now really existing reactionary capitalist states, by all means let them remain in union hands.

The successor organizations of the former Communist unions should be supported wherever they have reformed enough to form a line of resistance against the "structural adjustment programs" which prepare the ground for neo-Stalinism and fascism. It is foolish to seek to isolate representative trade union organizations with a proven ability to defend their members, on the grounds that they are, wholly or partly, tainted by a Communist past.

Union education programs need to focus on the implications of the New World Order to enable the membership to comprehend what has been happening to them and what is likely to happen next, and to prepare them for the effort of world-wide organizing. How many unions have education programs and, of those that do, how many deal with the New World Order, which is the reality their members face every day? As a rule, there is no discussion of international issues at the membership level.

Many more resources need to be put into international union activities if the movement is to become effective globally. At present, a small number of unions, even national trade union centers, in industrialized countries have international departments and, where they exist, they are understaffed, typically with two or three people. In many countries, international relations is something the president or another official does on the side, in addition to many other duties. Budgets for international activities are, for the most, part ridiculously low, and clearly show that, in the minds of most union executives, international activities are an unimportant sideshow.

More important, the nature of international activities is misunderstood and misinterpreted. Back in the economic and social halcyon days of the 1950s and 1960s many unions, especially in the industrially developed countries, had sufficient industrial and financial strength to largely take care of their own interests and had no need for international support. For many, international activity was recreational and diplomatic, at best charitable and declarative. Verbal denunciations of colonialist and (sometimes) imperialist injustice, together with financial contributions, which might appear generous but in fact often amounted to less than donations to domestic charities, seemed to cover the ground as far as international activities were concerned. With this came a patronizing attitude to international trade union organizations and a certain amount of complacency in looking at society and the world.

Very few unions relate international programs to the problems of their members at the point of production and when they do, it is more a fire fighting exercise, typically in response to a threatened plant closure, rather than a systematic, long-term and pro-active program of educating the membership to the world wide connections of company policies to government policies.

The memory of past abuses lingers on — unions allowing their so-called international programs to be used as fronts for the intelligence operations of governments or as pretexts for junkets by top officials who rarely reported back what they were doing abroad. In the best of cases, honest officials of goodwill regarded an international program as a kind of charity, and would help weak unions abroad in the same spirit as contributing to the Red Cross. But those who look on international trade union action as charity, miss the fundamental point of trade unionism: solidarity, in contrast with charity, is a reciprocal relationship. Charity is top-down, solidarity is based on the acceptance of mutual responsibility. Shrinking budgets of both governments and unions, and to a lesser extent rising membership awareness, have put a stop to most of the political hi-jinx and manipulations. What remains, is that most union leaderships, as well as union members, have a very superficial, if any, understanding of the world they live in.

Organizing must be done in its political context with political means, centered on the defense of human rights, the core issue around which not only workers but all other victims of the New World Order can be organized and coalitions built that have political depth and staying power. This requires the defense of human rights as a categorical imperative. To be credible, there can be no selective defense of human rights, even if consistency inconveniences some trade union centers with a tradition of submitting to authoritarian governments or deferring to the principle of "non-intervention in the internal affairs of countries."

The International Labor Movement

Doesn't this mean re-inventing the international socialist movement? If the Socialist International (SI) were the kind of organization its name implies, unions would not have to take charge of the political dimension of labor action quite to the same extent that is being suggested here. The Socialist International, however, is nothing of the sort. It is a forum for leaders of mostly European socialist parties to meet and exchange views which are in general friendly to labor when their parties are in opposition and hostile to labor when their parties are in government. It is the small parties that need, and demand, an international organization capable of action; their demands are unheeded.

The large parties prefer an organization that cannot interfere with their own priorities. They make sure that it stays weak at the center, and that its policies never reach beyond the minimum common denominator they can agree on. Since their main concerns are national, that common denominator remains low. As a result, the Socialist International is utterly unable to produce an independent interpretation of the present world, much less to deal with it. Just as the defense of democracy cannot be left to democratic governments, the political dimension of labor action cannot be left to the SI.

A global approach to labor organizing and labor action implies a profound reorganization of the existing international labor movement, composed in essence of the ICFTU, which is the federation of territorial organizations such as national centers, and the International Trade Secretariats (ITSs), which are 15 or so federations of unions covering specific industries or economic sectors.

The ICFTU is at a delicate stage of its development and faces a political paradox. On the one hand, it is at the apex of its history. Its competitors are much diminished: the Communist World Federation of Trade Unions (WFTU) has lost most of the government support it relied on, as well as most of its affiliates, and its infrastructure and political network is in disarray. The Christian World Confederation of Labor (WCL) is little more than a Catholic Action propaganda group, dependent on only one strong and representative organization, the Belgian Confederation of Christian Trade Unions. A number of former WFTU affiliates and independents, which used to maintain equidistance, have now joined the ICFTU, which numbers an all time high of some 150 affiliates, in over 100 countries with a membership of approximately 110 million.

For practical purposes, the ICFTU today is the representative labor international, the only one that matters. Yet, on the other hand, it is a directionless giant. Those who regarded its primary function as fighting the Cold War are now disoriented. The obvious alternative does not occur to them: that now is the time to pick up where the serious labor internationals of the past left off. An international organization of labor formed for the purpose of conducting labor's struggle for its own and society's emancipation is beyond the imagining of those who are largely ignorant of past experience, contemptuous of history and theory, and afraid of struggle.

The ICFTU Executive Board is composed of officials of national trade union centers who are preoccupied with national issues and think in national terms. They have a vested interest in believing that there are national solutions for their members' problems and are caught in structural constraints which obstruct a global vision. This is one of the reasons why a number of national trade union centers which, through their access to public development funds, have supported international trade union activity in the past, are now starting to give direct aid to unions in former Communist or in developing countries by-passing international trade union organizations. Such bilateral assistance creates chaos, increases the danger of corruption and weakens international trade unionism at the time it most needs strengthening, but it plays well for the home audience.

ICFTU activities, which should be the cutting edge of international labor action (defense of human rights, organizational and political support to unions in former Communist countries and in the Third World, action on TNCs in cooperation with the ITSs) are underfunded and undervalued. The institution lives far too much in a bureaucratic and abstract world where form takes precedence over substance and preoccupations with turf, jurisdiction and status overshadow the original purpose of the exercise.

The ITSs have different problems. Edo Fimmen, the secretary of the International Federation of Trade Unions (the "Amsterdam International") for a brief period after the First World War, then general secretary of the International Transport Workers' Federation for most of the 1920s and 1930s, understood and tried to solve most problems 70 years ago that we are still trying to solve today. He regarded the ITSs as the most appropriate form of trade union organization to conduct international labor struggles. In a prophetic book, *Labor's Alternative — The United States of Europe or Europe Limited*, he predicted that "just as the development of capitalism has always determined the organizational form of its opponents, has given rise first of all to local and subsequently to national trade unions, so capitalism will become, if not the originator, at least the furtherer of the international organization of the industrial workers."

Fimmen was under no illusions on the capacity of the ITSs of his time to rise to their historical task: "We are still far short of this point," he wrote. "Several years are likely to elapse before the ITSs (which are still in the very earliest stage of their activity, and most of which are as yet devoid of substantial importance) will have won, practically as well as theoretically, the leadership in industrial struggles."

Seventy years later, after a second world war and the subsequent Cold War set the labor movement back for decades, many ITSs are still "devoid of substantial importance" in terms of their capability of successfully conducting international labor struggles. His conclusion, however, remains inescapable: "Still, however weak and imperfect in respect of organization the ITSs may be, however little international, nonetheless the development of capitalism will compel them to take up the task that is incumbent on them unless the proletariat is to lapse internationally into a condition of more hopeless dependence and enslavement than that of the working class in its national subdivisions today."

At this stage, the ITSs need to strengthen their capability for effective intervention at any time, anywhere in the world when trade union rights are threatened, but they must also be capable of sustained action over the long term. In short they must acquire the means of exercising power in defense of the public interest in such a way that they cannot be ignored by governments or transnational corporations, however large and powerful. This cannot be achieved without a concentration of available resources, and that in turn means a series of mergers to create a smaller number of larger and more effective organizations. These are slow processes because they have to be democratic, involving collective decisions by loosely federated organizations where differing political cultures, organizational and financial structures and personalities have to be meshed. But they are inevitable if the ITSs are to carry out their historical terms of reference. It is not difficult to see that in terms of the resources needed for effective organization, servicing and action, an effective defense of workers' interests requires not the present 15 ITSs but seven at the most, each with the critical mass enabling it to organize in depth and to successfully sustain long-term and costly struggles. The closest possible linkage is needed between the ITSs and the ICFTU, because alliances will constantly be needed between ITSs, national centers and regional organizations to tackle specific issues.

Today more than ever it is necessary to reform the ICFTU as a joint organization of ITSs and national centers, with a dual (territorial and industrial) structure, to facilitate joint action between a number of partners in changing coalitions, to adapt to specific problems in a rapidly shifting international environment, and to introduce an international dimension in the strategic thinking of the world labor movement beyond international labor statesmanship and diplomacy.

There is an obvious objection which is rooted in post-war international labor history. When the WFTU was formed as a united world-wide international federation including the state-controlled labor organizations of the USSR and its new satellites, as well as the social-democratic unions of Europe and the American CIO, a struggle for control immediately developed between the Soviet bloc and its Communist-led allies on the one hand and the social-democratic unions on the other, which eventually led to a split and to the formation of the ICFTU, with the WFTU remaining under Communist control. One of the contentious issues was the status of the ITSs, which the Communists wanted to incorporate into the structure of the WFTU as departments, whereas the social-democratic trade unionists, who were in control of the ITSs, insisted on their independence.

The following years amply demonstrated the superiority of the ITSs over their Communist counterparts, the Trade Union Internationals (TUIs) that the WFTU had set up within its structure after the split. The independence of the ITSs — including from the ICFTU — gave them a high degree of flexibility and mobility, together with a higher degree of professionalism and militancy than any other international labor organization. The question therefore arises whether these advantages would not now be lost if the ITSs became part of the ICFTU structure.

This is unlikely because the ITSs of today and tomorrow are very different organizations from those of the post-war period or from the ones of Fimmen's time. Today's ITSs, and even more so tomorrow's, if the anticipated merger process materializes, will be substantially more influential than many national centers. In a common international structure, they would not find it difficult to play their own role as equals. It is these equal relationships that would ensure the health and stability of the organization.

Rebuilding the Movement

What other building blocs of solidarity are available? The vast edifice of the pre-1930s social-democratic labor movement in Europe lies in ruins, and these ruins are impressive still as witness to past greatness, much like the lost cities of vanished civilizations.

But there is evidence of life in these ruins and many mansions are still inhabited. The labor movement in all its vastness still has immense resources at its disposal. Their effective use is a question of understanding the priorities.

In this respect, relations with the social-democratic and labor parties are best left to the trade union movement in the different countries. The current state of relations varies considerably from country to country, ranging from the traditional relations of close cooperation to open hostility. At issue is the ability of the parties purporting to represent labor's interests to develop a credible alternative to the neo-conservative New Right rather than merely succumbing to it ideologically and politically. At the international level, the trade union movement would no doubt welcome an opportunity of cooperating with the Socialist International in a mutually supportive relationship. In practical terms, those who have tried have not succeeded, for the reasons described earlier.

But the organizations of the labor movement also include a vast array of social and cultural organizations: women's and youth organizations, educational associations and schools, hiking and touring clubs, sports clubs, travel agencies, consumers cooperatives, banks and housing cooperatives. The sense of belonging together to a single movement, of representing an alternative society and a counter-culture, is now much weaker than even after the last war, but there is enough of it left to pick up some of the pieces.

Two instances come to mind: the workers' aid organizations and the workers' educational associations. Both have their own international federations. Workers' aid organizations were originally founded for the purpose of taking care of the victims of the class war: in the 1920s and 1930s literally so. In the 1950s and 1960s when conventional wisdom in the labor movement had it that the class war was over, that most of labor's goals had been attained and that further progress required as seamless as possible an integration in the existing social order, workers' aid organizations became de-politicized, as well, and like everyone else concerned with welfare, on relieving the victims of natural disasters: floods, earthquakes, famine. From the 1970s and the rise of the politics of guilt, many started giving priority to development projects: bore holes for water in the desert, planting seedlings on sand-dunes.

Today, when labor is fighting with its back to the wall, questions have to be asked regarding priorities: do the contributions of workers' aid organizations to disaster relief bring a positive benefit to the labor movement as a whole, even though they are a drop in the bucket compared to government or private charity contributions? If the objective was to earn brownie points with the bourgeoisie, has anyone ever thanked us? Have our contributions resulted in a measurable increase in influence? For that matter, what have the contributions of American unions to the various community chests, hospitals and other charitable causes done to strengthen the labor movement in the United States? And how much of a difference would the same amounts of money have made had they been spent in paying the salaries of organizers, improving the quality of labor publications, paying strike relief? Why doesn't labor help labor? No one else will.

The same goes for workers' education. In the complacent 1950s it was alright to assume that general adult education could be a legitimate goal for a workers' education association. Today, the educational needs of the labor movement as a movement are immense. The whole political culture of the labor movement has to be passed on to millions of people who have been cut off from it for several generations. What is now being done in trade union study circles, summer schools, party schools and foundations merely scratches the surface. At the international level, the International Federation of Workers' Education Associations is the only organization of the labor movement that combines trade unions at various levels of activity, party institutions, think tanks and workers' education associations. It is uniquely well placed to become the laboratory where the labor movement develops its new ideological instruments, provided that this is perceived as its principal priority.

We can no longer afford the luxury of labor movement institutions relieving symptoms rather than treating the causes of social diseases. Treating symptoms is the proper province of the state and, of course, there we have one of the major battle lines in our war with the New Right. Humanitarian donors abound when it comes to relieving the victims of social disasters but only labor is capable of dealing with the root causes of social disasters and preventing their recurrence. Global solidarity — both geographical and qualitative — is the concept that meets the present needs of the movement.

Finally, the international labor movement must take the lead in building new international coalitions with civic and social action groups, which have grown both in numbers and in strength since the 1970s. Over ten years ago, in an article in *The New International Review* (Vol. 3, No.1, 1980), this writer suggested that coalition building had to be an essential element in an international labor strategy: "the building of broad popular coalitions, with the trade union movement at their center, but bringing together many civic groups, issue-oriented movements and other popular groups that perceive, each in its own way, the social threat that corporate power represents and whose areas of concern overlap, in different degrees, with that of the labor movement." Today, lower communications and travel costs have allowed the development of more cross-border action and information. More than ever, the basis exists for the emergence of a global civil society in which the labor movement can and should play a leading role.

# Labour Strategies: Options and Perspectives [2002]

*Excerpt on the talking points presented in the form of an invitation letter to IFWEA's roundtable discussion in Oslo. September 19-20, 2002. IFWEA is the International Federation of Workers Education Associations.*

**We are members and citizens of the social-democratic and socialist labour movement in its broadest sense that includes political parties, trade unions, workers' education organizations, solidarity and welfare organizations, cultural and leisure organizations, women and youth organizations, and others. We are members and citizens of this movement each in our own countries and also internationally, through the international organizations where we are active.**

This movement is facing an existential crisis: it is a crisis of identity, of direction and of purpose. If our original goal was to create, through our joint efforts, a society based on justice, freedom and security worldwide, we are no closer to it than we ever were.

We are losing the struggle for society.

A drastic shift in power relations in favour of transnational capital has taken place: transnational capital is reordering the world economy in its own interests, with the support of the conservative government of the leading world power and of the leading European governments, through the Bretton Woods institutions, the World Trade Organization and the EU institutions.

The immediate consequences have been growing social inequalities, social disruption, the undermining of social protection, the spread of poverty world-wide, and new and growing threats to the environment, potentially life-threatening for humanity.

Technological developments, including biotechnology, are largely under corporate control. They are not only rapidly changing people's lives, but are also raising political and ethical issues which the labour movement has, with some exceptions, failed to address.

The ideological barrage from conservative think tanks, academic institutions and media has successfully promoted the belief that human welfare can best be achieved by individual solutions, thus undermining social cohesion and values like solidarity, compassion and cooperation.

Migration, caused by global inequalities, wars and repressive regimes, has become a major political and social issue in many countries, leading to the emergence of far-right movements; The labour movement has in general failed to adequately address this issue.

Trade union membership is declining, with some notable exceptions, in most industrialized countries, in many underdeveloping countries and in all transition countries: repression accounts for much of this decline, although economic and social developments, and the movement's own internal weaknesses, are also a factor.

The collapse of bureaucratic collectivism and of its totalitarian institutions in the former Soviet Union and its block has not led to a social-democratic revival, as many of us had hoped, but to the expansion of capitalism in its most brutal forms and to the discredit of the concept of socialism -- a posthumous victory of Stalinism.

Relations between the trade union movement and social-democratic parties, especially when in government, have become problematic in many countries, and also at international level: trade unions and their traditional political allies often and increasingly diverge in their analysis of the problem and in the solutions they advocate.

Organized resistance to the hegemony of transnational capital has come mostly from the new social movements, which have developed in most cases independently of the labour movement and in some instances in opposition to it.

For us, as members and citizens of the labour movement, these are challenges which engage our responsibility. There is no one else who is responsible for our movement and for its future except ourselves, and the time to act is now.

Our movement still has huge resources at its disposal, if we are able to join the forces available. The labour movement can become a formidable and ultimately successful force for social change. We do not need to lose the struggle for society and we have a fundamental responsibility to make sure that we don't. But we have to ask ourselves serious questions. They range from the general to the specific. Here are some of them, in no particular order:

(1) Many millions of people are struggling for a better life every day, if for no other reason, because they have no alternative. Are we prepared to lead and organize these struggles? If so, by what right and with what credentials? Are we prepared to reaffirm a socialist perspective in these struggles and to challenge the dominant conservative ideology (otherwise known as neo-liberalism, neo-conservatism or the "Washington consensus")? If we are not, do we believe that the struggle for a better society can be successfully conducted within the limits of the "Washington consensus"?

(2) Does the international trade union movement (essentially the ICFTU and the Global Union Federations) have a strategy for social change? If so, what is it?

(3) The labour movement, through its national and international organizations, is spending tens of millions of dollars every year in development aid (mostly public funds). What proportion of this money has demonstrably and measurably contributed to strengthening the labour movement nationally and internationally, and to changing the international balance of forces in favour of labour?

(4) Some social-democratic and labour parties have severed the historical privileged links with the trade union movement, and have declared that, as far as they were concerned, trade unions were just another pressure group among others. How do we deal with this, as socialists, trade unionists, workers educators? The trade union movement is political in everything it does and needs a political dimension. If its historical allies are withdrawing from their old relationship, what conclusions should the trade union movement draw from this? What conclusions for socialists?

(5) Industry-based, enterprise-based trade unionism is shrinking everywhere, largely because of changes in the structure of companies (from producers to coordinators of production carried out on their behalf by others). Are there other forms of trade union organization which can successfully organize the new (and old) unorganized, particularly in the informal economy? What does "social

movement trade unionism" mean and what makes it different?

(6) Trade union rights are challenged everywhere. In some countries, trade unions are targets of outright repression (Colombia is the worst example, but there are many others). In most industrial democracies certain rights which are basic human rights (such as the right to strike, especially when it comes to solidarity strikes) are severely curtailed. This is not a problem for the trade union movement only: it is a problem for the whole of the labour movement because it strikes at the root of our collective power. Some of us have campaigned for trade union rights for some time. What can we do to broaden and strengthen such campaigns? What can we do to change the mind of certain labour governments which endorse restrictions of trade union rights decreed by conservative governments that preceded them?

(7) How does the labour movement relate to the new social movements (f.ex. ATTAC, Greens, women's movements)? Are they our allies? If so, under what conditions? Are we prepared and capable of forming coalitions with such movements (i.e. certain NGOs) to create a broad-based popular mass movement for social change (back to question(1))?

(8) The Socialist International is no longer an organization in any recognizable sense but a forum for (mostly European) socialist politicians. By its own choice, it has no relations with the international trade union movement. Many in the trade union movement, also disillusioned by their own social-democratic or labour parties, have given up on the SI as a lost cause. As socialists, we cannot take this lightly. Are those of us who are active in SI member parties prepared to pursue this issue? Is it possible, or even desirable, to seek a new relationship with the SI based on a constructive and practical alliance in pursuit of common goals? If so, what goals? More broadly, what can be expected of the SI today and what can it deliver?

Despite the collapse of the Soviet block and of Stalinism as an ideology, authoritarian regimes remain in place in some of the successor States of the USSR. China has developed a system that can best be described as market Stalinism. Stalinist regimes remain in place in Vietnam and in Cuba and North Korea remains locked into its own bizarre version of totalitarianism. Just as in the past significant parts of the democratic labour movement blurred ideological differences in the name of the "realpolitik" of their governments, so today "constructive engagement" policies are gaining ground, most notably with respect to China and the Chinese State labour organizations, with equally disastrous political results. For many reasons, the political identity of democratic socialism, and its incompatibility with any form of totalitarian ideology anywhere, needs to be reaffirmed.

We do not believe, of course, that a two-day seminar can do justice to such important and complex issues. We do believe, however, that such a discussion needs to be started. So far as we are aware, it is not taking place anywhere, and we believe that these issues can only be ignored at our collective peril.

As the IFWEA already includes in its membership workers education associations, trade unions and Global Union Federations, social-democratic party institutions, labour service organizations, think tanks and labour colleges, we think we are well placed to host a discussion on broad labour movement issues. We are prepared to make this seminar the first of several. However, we are looking at this as the beginning of an open-ended political process, and we would welcome other organizations joining us in moving it along.

1. http://www.globallabour.info/en/atom.xml
2. http://www.globallabour.info/en/index.xml
3. http://www.globallabour.info/en/
4. http://www.globallabour.info/en/2011/12/post_6.html
5. http://www.globallabour.info/en/2012/01/post_7.html
6. http://www.globallabour.info/en/
7. http://www.globallabour.info/en/2011/12/post_6.html
8. http://www.globallabour.info/en/
9. http://www.globallabour.info/en/2012/01/post_7.html
       [   http://www.globallabour.info/en/2011/12/labour_strategies_options_and.html

# The WEA & the Future of International Workers' Education: Rebuilding the Movement [2003]

*The following is a speech delivered to the "WEA & the International Workers' Education Movement Conference" held at Congress House, London, May 22, 2003.*

Brothers and Sisters,
Friends and Comrades,

**It is a great pleasure and honour to convey to you, on behalf of the International Federation of Workers' Education Associations, our warmest greetings and best wishes on the occasion of the Centenary of the Workers' Education Association of England and Scotland.**

Your organization has a long history, much longer than that of our International Federation, of which it was one of the founders, but your history is also part of ours, together with that of many other organisations that have joined forces to build the International Federation.

On occasions such as this, history is remembered and honoured. But what is history? It is the sum-total of the struggles, controversies, sacrifices and the hard work involving thousands of people who shaped our movement, who created its identity and its values.

This is why history, contrary to common belief, is not about the past. Because it creates identity and values, it is about the future.

Organisations need roots to grow, and they cannot understand what they are and where they are going unless they understand where they have been and where they came from, because only then the ultimate purpose becomes clear.

What does history tell us? It tells us that our movement originated in not one but in a diversity of social and political traditions, including trade unionists, ministers of religion, academics, activists of the women's movement and of the co-operative movement, liberals and socialists, later on activists from the liberation movements. What brought them together in a common endeavour was their commitment to social justice, to a vision of society based on justice and freedom.

What they meant was not only economic justice, but also justice in the relations between men and women, and justice in the relations between individuals, that is to say individual rights, human rights, democratic rights, the exercise of democratic power under the rule of law, freedom of expression, freedom for individuals to assert their dignity and to develop their full potential as a human beings, through co-operative and mutually supportive relationships among equals.

The institutions of the labour movement, such as trade unions, and the mechanisms of social protection and social welfare the labour movement sought to establish by political means, ultimately exist to protect the ability of the individual to develop his or her potential, to protect the time and space each individual needs to grow, and in this context workers' education is part of a liberating and empowering process.

All of this defines our concept of democracy, which, for us, has never been an abstract goal but above all a method, since we all know how closely ends and means are intertwined, and how each end determines its own means. This is why our movement has always believed that workers' education has to be participatory and driven by the workers themselves because, as Marx put it when he wrote the Rules of the First International, "the emancipation of the working classes must be conquered by the working classes themselves" -- and no one else will do it for us.

These are our values and this is our identity. They have not been easy to defend at the best of times and we have always been in a struggle, although at times it appeared that this struggle was muted, and we could even entertain the illusion that we were advancing through the natural progress of society.

Today, my friends, the situation is very different. These are not the best of times. Our values and our goals are under challenge. We are facing an onslaught on our movement, world wide, of a kind that we have not experienced since the 1930s.

In the last twenty years or so, the globalisation of the world economy has meant an enormous increase in the power of transnational corporations at the expense of the nation State, that is, the geographical space in which the labour movement has been accustomed to function and where democratic control, such as it is, is exercised. The geographical space in which the transnational corporations operate is the whole world: they are global, we are not. What we have so far is international networks of national organizations, each of which think and react in national terms. That is not good enough.

A huge shift in power relationships has taken place. The mobility of capital has given transnational corporations unprecedented economic power. They also exercise political power through the international institutions, which they control through their government proxies: the World Trade Organisation, the World Bank, the International Monetary Fund. Most importantly, they are in control of the world's hegemonic superpower: the United States. There has not been an American administration in recent history that has been so directly and so blatantly connected to corporate interests as the present Bush administration.

This is an administration that pursues its goals with the utmost ruthlessness, the ruthlessness that we know well from the industrial practices of its sponsors. The Iraq war is a good illustration: none of the reasons for which it was ostensibly declared hold water, the real reason, negligently and barely concealed, is to entrench a right-wing Republican administration in the United States for a generation, and the domination of that administration over the world, for a generation.

In 1952, two American science fiction authors wrote a book called the Space Merchants, also known in its serialised form as Gravy Planet. It pictures a dystopia where corporations are literally ruling the world -- it is the syndicalist dream turned upside down, where it becomes a nightmare. Fifty years later, that fictional dystopia looks dangerously close to our reality.

We are facing this onslaught at every level: in the industrial democracies, social welfare and social protection are being dismantled, democratic rights and union rights are being eroded; the rest of the world is caught in a poverty trap, often maintained by repression, from which there seems no escape. Through a cynical distortion of language, individualism becomes a rationale for the loss of individual rights, democracy becomes a justification for repression, the freedom of some translates into the servitude of the majority.

If this was the whole picture, it would be a bleak picture indeed. But this is not the whole picture. We are also witnessing an unprecedented movement of popular resistance.

Last February, over ten million people where demonstrating in the whole world against the war in Iraq. This has never happened before in history. And it did not come out of nowhere. It would be inconceivable without the worldwide demonstrations against the World Trade Organisation, which preceded it. It would be inconceivable without the meetings of the World Social Forum of Porto Alegre, now in its third year. This is the Global Justice Movement, growing with each of its actions as it emerges from the depth of popular revolt with the battle cry: "another world is possible".

That is what we believe: another world is possible. That is the world we have been fighting for for the last hundred years, the world we carry in our hearts and in our minds.

How do we bring it about, this other world? We need to build alliances. We want to be part of the Global Justice Movement -- many of the members of our International Federation already are -- but we also want to make sure that our values and our identity, our specific goals and methods, prevail. We do not want just another world, we want a better world and to achieve this we need, first of all, to build a coalition with those who share our values.

The way forward is clear when we look back at our history. The emergent workers' education movement was carried by the two strongest institutions of the labour movement of the time: the trade unions and the co-operatives, and it is not an accident if its representatives share a platform before you today.

Let us work together to rebuild the labour movement in its broad, historical sense. Let us work together purposefully, including wherever possible the many other organisations that grew out of the historical labour movement, for example those providing welfare and solidarity, those organising women and youth, those working for a sustainable environment and, yes, also the labour parties, at least where they are not fighting us.

The division of labour between the different branches of the labour movement, which emerged over the years no longer meets the needs of our time. It is now time to bring together what has grown apart through neglect, complacency and the territorial instincts of self-perpetuating bureaucracies. We must pool our resources and we cannot go on working as if we were each of us alone in our world. We are now facing a global threat to our future and if we do not work together we may lose our future.

If we succeed in rebuilding our movement, we can become a formidable force in the Global Justice Movement, giving it a hard core and a sense of direction and then, yes, we have a chance of making a better world possible.

I thank you for your attention.

1. http://www.globallabour.info/en/atom.xml
2. http://www.globallabour.info/en/index.xml
3. http://www.globallabour.info/en/
4. http://www.globallabour.info/en/2010/10/civil_society_a_contested_terr_1.html
5. http://www.globallabour.info/en/2010/10/political_education_and_global_1.html
6. http://www.globallabour.info/en/
7. http://www.globallabour.info/en/2010/10/civil_society_a_contested_terr_1.html
8. http://www.globallabour.info/en/
9. http://www.globallabour.info/en/2010/10/political_education_and_global_1.html
10. http://www.globallabour.info/en/2010/10/rebuilding_the_movement_dan_ga.html

# The International Labour Movement: History and Ideologies [2003]

*Center Praxis Conference: "The Anti-Totalitarian Left: Between Past and Future", Moscow, June 21-22, 2003*

Dear Friends and Comrades,

**In the first place, I would like to congratulate you for having organized this meeting and, more importantly, for all the work you have done in the last four or five years which has led up to this meeting. The creation of the Victor Serge Library, which has now become a foundation, the establishment of the Praxis Center, the publication of "Memoirs of a Revolutionist" in Russian, are remarkable achievements under very difficult material and political circumstances.**

Your choice of Victor Serge as a reference is in itself a challenge. Victor Serge remains in history as a representative of the Left as it always should have been: a person of integrity, incorruptible and fearless, always clear about ultimate objectives, with a sure political instinct, with a vast experience of the revolutionary movement of his time and with the gift of communicating all this in clear and simple language. These are the qualities we most need in our labour movement today, so the first challenge, if we take Victor Serge as a reference, is to ourselves.

The second challenge is, of course, to our opponents and, yes, not to put too fine a point on it, our enemies. We have many, and they are the same Victor Serge had to face in his time. They are inside the movement, the bureaucracies that stifle us, including residual Stalinism, but not only, and outside, the other and older class enemy, more powerful than ever today.

Victor Serge is part of our history and history, contrary to common belief, is not about the past, it is about the future. History is the sum-total of the struggles, controversies, sacrifices and the hard work involving thousands of people who shaped our movement, who created its identity and its values. Because it creates identity and values, history is about the future. Organizations and movements need roots to grow. They cannot understand what they are and where they are going unless they understand their own past and their own origins, because only then the ultimate purpose becomes clear. This is why the theme of this meeting is very appropriate: we are indeed between the past and the future, which are linked – the present is a mere instant.

I have been asked to speak on the international workers' movement and the Left. You might say that this is one and the same thing, and in a general historical sense they are, of course, closely intertwined. We also need to look, however, at some attempts that have been made to separate labour in its organized form (the trade union movement) from the Left, and to understand their significance. The latest, and the most important one, has been taking place for the last ten years in the post-Stalinist societies, where the concept of the Left has been hi-jacked and compromised by Stalinism.

Broadly speaking, there are four periods in the history of the international labour movement: first, from its origins to World War I; second, the inter-war years; third, the period from the end of World War II to the collapse of Stalinism as a political system; and finally, the present period of globalizing capitalism.

The first period is that of the ascendancy of the labour movement, of the First and Second Internationals. That is where the foundations of the movement were laid. The defeat of the Paris Commune and the split between Anarchists and Marxists put an end to the First International but, a few years later, the Second International, appeared to pick up where the First left off. The socialist and trade union movements were closely linked and went from strength to strength. Socialist mass parties arose in Central and Western Europe, as well as strong anarcho-syndicalist unions in Southern Europe. The May Day campaign gave the movement international cohesion.

This phase of the movement comes to an abrupt end on August 1, 1914. Much has been written about the political collapse of movement before the tidal wave of nationalism on that day and I have no new explanation, much less a one-size-fits-all analysis. The usual explanation, combining subjective and sociological factors ("the treason of the reformist leadership"), does not explain everything. It does not explain, for example, why the revolutionary syndicalist leadership of the French CGT collapsed in the same way as the leadership of the orthodox Marxist social-democratic mass parties. Nor does it explain how it came about that great leaders and thinkers suddenly turned into cowards and collaborationists, why those who resisted can be counted on the fingers of two hands.

It is clear that the movement was just not strong enough, not ideologically, not politically, not culturally, and not organizationally. Resolutions against war, solemnly and unanimously adopted at socialist congresses, like the Basle congress of 1912, turned out to be irrelevant. We need to think more about why this was the case. Obviously, the strength of nationalism, and the ability of the ruling classes to manipulate it to their advantage, had been seriously underestimated. This also happened later, under other circumstances, and it is still happening today.

On our side, it was not so much a matter of overestimating our forces. Lenin and Trotsky, trying to get some sleep in Smolny, said to each other: if the Germans don't come through, we are finished. They realized that even if they won the war in Russia, the revolution would not survive unless it spread to Western Europe. We all know this didn't happen. What did happen, was substituting voluntarism to real strength, and the weakness of the revolutionary option opened the way to Stalinism.

The following period, roughly from the Russian Revolution to the outbreak of the Second World War, was dominated by the bitter and increasingly irreconcilable split between the social-democratic and the Communist movements. Early attempts to re-establish the unity of the Left came to nothing. The suppression of the non-Bolshevik Left in Russia, followed by the suppression of organized tendencies within the Bolshevik party, the invasion and occupation of social-democratic Georgia, the Stalinization of the Communist Parties after 1926 and finally the extermination of any form of opposition in the 1930s made reconciliation impossible. Anti-fascist and popular front "unity" policies promoted by the Communist parties proved to be tactical manoeuvres to be turned off or on according the requirements of the foreign policy of the USSR. Stalin's intervention in the Spanish Civil War demonstrated that the only unity the Communist parties would accept was where they were in total control.

The defeat in Spain and the suppression of the CNT for the next four decades also ended revolutionary syndicalism as a significant force in the international labour movement.

It is at this point that the big questions concerning the nature and the identity of the Left begin to be asked, and they all hinge around the nature of Stalinism as a social and political system. As early as 1929, Karl Kautsky challenged the socialist nature of the USSR by pointing out that the State was controlled by a ruling clique, which collectively owned the means of production through its ownership of the State. Writing of nationalization in that context, Kautsky observed that social-democrats and Communists only shared the word, not the content. Regarding final objectives, they had nothing in common.

In that, he understood the situation better than Trotsky who maintained to the end of is life that the USSR was, because of the State ownership of the means of production, some sort of socialist entity: a "degenerated workers' State".

In the 1940s, a number of Marxist theoreticians picked up where Kautsky left off. Most came from the Trotskyist tradition: Max Shachtman and Joe Carter in the US, CLR James, Tony Cliff in Britain, Cornelius Castoriadis in France; Milovan Djilas came of course out of Yugoslav Stalinism. The common denominator of all these analyses was this: the USSR (and States established on the same model) represented a new class society, based on the collective ownership of the means of production by a new ruling class through its control of the State; this ruling class maintained itself in power by military and police repression, exercising total control over all aspects of social life. In this system, the working class is doubly oppressed: as citizens through the police State, and as workers through State-controlled institutions of labour administration, called "trade unions" – here, too, one could say, we share the word, not the content.

These discussions took place in the midst of a historical catastrophe of huge proportions. Fascism had wiped out the labour movement in most of Europe: first in Italy and Portugal, then in Germany and Austria, then in Spain then, as the German armies occupied nearly all of the continent, everywhere except in Britain and a few remaining neutral or unoccupied countries. The Jewish Labour Bund was destroyed together with the population that supported it. Stalinism had contributed to the destruction of the independent Left in Europe, and had of course exterminated hundreds of thousands of socialists, anarchists and Communists in Russia itself, later in the occupied countries of Eastern and Central Europe.

Victor Serge describes this period very well, in his memoirs and in his novels: "The Case of Comrade Tulayev", "Midnight in the Century" and "The Long Dusk".

No one has so far established a reliable statistic of the losses of the Left in the three decades following the Russian Revolution, but we can safely say that about two political generations of activists and leaders disappeared in that period, more than that in Portugal and Spain where fascism lasted longer, more than that in Eastern Europe with 40 years of Stalinism, or in the territory of the former USSR, with 70 years of Stalinism.

This leads us to the fourth phase, the post-war period. The social-democratic labour movement emerged from the war superficially victorious, actually greatly weakened by its losses, and far more dependent on the State than it had been before the war. This was partly due to its war-time alliance with the Allied powers, partly to its objective weakness under conditions of economic reconstruction, partly because most of the leading post-war governments in the principal industrial countries were either social-democratic or at any rate socially-oriented and prepared to support the legislative agenda of the labour movement.

The Communist labour movement also emerged very strongly at first, as a dominant force in France and Italy, but also strong elsewhere in Europe, building on its prestige in the resistance movement (which it had joined only after 1941, when Nazi Germany attacked the USSR) and by the prestige of the USSR as the principal land-based power in Europe that had defeated Nazi Germany.

In Eastern Europe, where the trade union movement had never been strong in the first place (with the exception of Czechoslovakia), the surviving social-democratic, independent Left and dissident Communist cadres quickly disappeared in the jails and labour camps of the KGB. Trade unions were forcibly dissolved and replaced by State organizations for labour administration.

At this point, the Cold War became the new global political reality. Each of the two superpowers were deploying tremendous financial and political resources to control the labour movement in support of their bloc. The labour movement became polarized and the position of all those who were seeking to maintain an independent trade union movement based on an independent class interest became very difficult.

I think that this is where we temporarily lost the battle for the identity of the Left. The insights of those who had analysed the USSR in Marxist terms as a new class society, and who had recognized that Stalinism, anti-capitalist though it may have been, was certainly not socialist in any recognizable sense of the word, were the insights of a minority. It had some influence in the labour movement, perhaps more than is generally realized, but it could not dominate the political debate.

The political debate was dominated by conservatism and Stalinism. The Stalinist propaganda machine beat the same drum for four decades: the USSR and the bloc under its control were the "socialist countries" – actually "really existing socialism" (as opposed to the unreal and non existing variety some of us were trying to maintain as a serious political option). The Internationale, although it had ceased to be the national anthem of the USSR in the 1940s, was sung at Stalinist meetings, where red flags were also flying, and Stalinist "trade unions" were seeking a role on the international scene based on a terminological deception.

This view of the Communist movement as an acceptable variety of socialism rather than a fundamental break with the original purpose of the movement gained widespread popular acceptance after the war. This happened in several ways: (1) cultivating the myth of the October Revolution, and of the USSR as the incarnation of the values of this revolution; (2) hiding and obliterating the realities of working class life in the USSR and the occupied countries; dismissing factual reports as "enemy propaganda"; (3) corrupting Western opinion makers (writers, artists, journalists, politicians, trade unionists, etc.), including a number from the non-Communist Left, in many ways ranging from subtle to primitive; (4) intimidating opposition from the Left and within the Left.

A further difficulty for socialists trying to deal with this situation was the fact that many, probably most, of the members of Communist mass parties, typically in France and Italy, had joined in the sincere belief that they were joining a socialist movement, for much the same reasons as others, or even the same people under different circumstances, would have joined a social-democratic or independent socialist party. Most rank-and-file Communists in fact believed that they were joining a more radical and consistent socialist movement than social-democracy could offer.

It took several severe shocks to jolt such members into seeing through the tissue of deceptions and lies which had blinded them. With the experiences of the pre-war generation (the Moscow Trials, the Hitler-Stalin pact) largely obliterated by World War II, it would take experiences such as the Hungarian Revolution of 1956, or the repression of the Czechoslovak reform movement in 1968, to make normal Communist Party members understand the nature of their movement and leave.

The misappropriation of the terminology and the symbols of socialism was actively supported by the conservative propaganda from the Right, which had every interest in identifying socialism with Stalinism in order to discredit the socialist idea with the Stalinist reality.

Meanwhile, the democratic Left in the labour movement had itself largely abandoned the ideological battle by the 1970s and 1980s. In the first place, the social-democratic parties had been diluting their identity over the years, playing down their socialist origins and purposes in favour of "social market capitalism". Partly as a result of the same process, the Socialist International had become mainly an informal club of European social-democratic leaders rather than an ideological reference point and an organizing tool. Towards the USSR and its bloc the policy was to strengthen co-existence and, as government policy with various variants of "Ostpolitik" increasingly dictated party policy, this meant accommodation rather than confrontation.

In the trade union movement, the most confrontational elements, such as the AFL-CIO, were campaigning on a basic human rights platform, not a broader ideological platform. So far as ideology was concerned, the AFL-CIO had bought into an American version of the "social market economy" and was not explicitly seeking to defend any form of alternative Left.

The European social-democratic unions had also stopped asserting their political and ideological identity. Several factors explain this: first, the dilution of social-democratic ideology at the political level, as already mentioned; second, the desire to accommodate the Catholic unions, in a perspective of eventual unity at European and international level; thirdly, the same confusion as in politics between the policy of States (where the objective was peaceful coexistence) and the international policy of the trade union movement, which is to defend a class interest. Consequently, by the 1980s, very few social-democratic unions were campaigning against Stalinism, and certainly not on the basis of representing a better Left, or a genuine Left. At international level, the IUF was one of the few organizations which tried to maintain this line.

Finally, the stability of the Stalinist system was greatly overrated. The general assumption was that co-existence was to be a long term relationship, with eventual convergence over decades. No one expected the system to collapse when it did, nor as suddenly. Even those who believed that it had to collapse eventually, did not expect this to happen in the time scale it did, so events caught the labour movement unprepared at every level: ideologically, politically, organizationally.

For all these reasons, the democratic trade union movement was unable to offer a political alternative to workers in the former USSR and in Central and Eastern Europe when the Berlin Wall came down and the USSR collapsed. At the very time its historical enemy had left the scene in disgrace, social-democracy was unable to provide an alternative. Mainly because of its ideological and political weakness in the West, the economic and social order that emerged in the East after Stalinism was not any form of social-democracy but bandit capitalism with a primitive ideology of social Darwinism.

The response of the emerging trade union movement in the successor States of the USSR and in Eastern Europe was understandably confused. In both East and West the collapse of Stalinism was widely perceived as a defeat of socialism and the ideology of large parts of the new trade union movement in the East became conservative syndicalism or anti-socialism in various forms, or else residual Stalinism in some of the old structures. The continuity with the pre-war and pre-Stalinist labour movement is broken and there are no visible attempts to recover legitimacy and inspiration from this earlier period. The main exception is the Czech Republic, where historical social-democracy has re-established itself as the dominant party of the Left and the trade union movement largely identifies with it.

As we are entering the 21st century, the situation has changed again. The main feature of the present period is the emergence of the new social movements, single issue movements and protest movements against globalizing capitalism dominated by transnational corporations. They are capable of forming powerful coalitions: the World Social Forum is one of their platforms. Some originate in authoritarian traditions, most are anti-authoritarian as well as anti-capitalist.

These movements are filling a void left by the labour movement as it retreated from its broader social concerns and responsibilities and they now represent a new challenge to the international labour movement: is it going to join the coalition of those calling for an "alternative globalization", basically on an anti-capitalist platform, or is it going to remain suspended in what is essentially a lobbying activity with the international financial institutions, the EU and other inter-governmental institutions?

The period we have entered is full of paradoxes. The international labour movement (essentially the ICFTU, the GUFs and the ETUC) has never been as united in its history as it is today; at the same time, it has never been as directionless and devoid of wider social perspectives. It has never been as representative in the institutions as it is today, yet about 90% of the world's workers are not organized. Globalizing transnational capitalism is triumphant and bestrides the world scene with imperial arrogance; at the same time, it has called forth the most powerful anti-capitalist movement since historical socialism left the scene as an organized international movement. Stalinism is dead, but a Stalinist party, which has embraced capitalism, controls about one third of the population of the globe.

The labour movement, at national and especially at international level, will be unable to resolve these contradictions, each of which is a challenge, unless it reinvents its political dimension, a new Labour Left.

The general question of the World Order is put to us in very urgent and pressing terms. We are facing an onslaught on our movement, world wide, of a kind that we have not experienced since the 1930s. We are facing this onslaught at every level: in the industrial democracies, social welfare and social protection are being dismantled, democratic rights and union rights are being eroded; the rest of the world is caught in a poverty trap, often maintained by repression, from which there seems no escape. This obviously calls for a global political response. The Global Justice Movement, which emerged from Porto Alegre, declares: "another world is possible". We agree. We believe another world, and a better world, is possible. How do we bring it about? Let us not be under any illusions: we are facing very powerful and very ruthless interests. Challenging them means war, and we better realize we are in a war. We cannot win this war unless we create the broadest possible popular alliances, and this means politics: a political platform of a Labour Left.

The vast majority of the world working class today is not organized. Why is this? Partly because the working class has changed, partly because over a large part of the world trade unionism is repressed. One of the major changes in the world working class is the growing informalization of work and the growth of the informal economy, which is outside of the scope of traditional union organizing. Organizing in the informal economy again requires political skills and the creation of alliances, in this instance principally with women's organizations. Such political skills, much less a political vision, are not currently in evidence.

Fighting repression of trade unions is a human rights issue, and this too calls for political alliances, at the very least with the human rights movements. Alliances are based on reciprocity, and this means that the trade union movement must be prepared to defend a broad range of human rights issues, most of which should be normal trade union concerns anyway.

China is a huge issue all by itself, at the same time a human rights and a political issue. One would imagine that formulating and implementing a policy for the international labour movement on the largest most repressive State in the world would be a relatively simple matter. In fact, it is on this issue that the difficulty of reaching a political consensus has been most glaring and it is probably on the China issue that the political decomposition of social-democracy in the labour movement has taken its most shocking forms.

Depressingly, the lessons of dealing with the so-called "trade unions" of the former USSR have not been assimilated. There is no evidence whatsoever that "constructive engagement" on the part of Western trade unionists, over decades, contributed in any way to the transformation of the former State labour organisations of the Soviet bloc into genuine trade union organisations. That process was driven by workers' revolts of the same kind than that which is currently building up in China. Yet, the same arguments are now advanced to justify "constructive engagement" with the Chinese State-controlled labour organizations which, in some surprising instances, amounts to servile collaboration. Ultimately, the issue will be decided by the Chinese workers. Given the situation, our ambitions are modest: to be as supportive as we can of the democratic labour opposition, and to minimize the damage caused by the collaborationists, where we can.

The process of developing a new Labour Left in the international trade union movement is complicated and difficult. It amounts to the reinvention of social-democracy, in part against the social-democratic parties themselves, or at least parts of them. It will have to integrate the experiences and the insights of the independent Left, essentially derived from Trotskyism and revolutionary syndicalism. It will have to take on board the sensitivities and concerns of the new social movements, of what has become the Global Justice Movement, where labour should be an actor, not a spectator.

Actually, all of this is already happening: I am not describing a program for the future, but a process already under way, complicated and difficult as it may be.

Let us go back to history. There cannot be an a-historical Left. We need historians more than ever. As I said in the beginning, history is about identity and values. The reference points of a new Labour Left are the experiences of the old Labour Left, its aspirations and ambitions, its victories and its defeats, and its amazing resilience, after all, against all odds. We are counting on labour historians, not to develop a new ideology, that is the task of this and future generations, but to tell us how all of these things came about. We need to understand our past to shape our future.

I thank you for your attention.

# Political Education and Globalization [2004]

*IFWEA Seminar: Global Network: Political Education & Globalization, Eastbourne, October 9, 2004.*

**The labour movement is today in a crisis that has complex and interacting reasons, both objective and subjective. This crisis manifests itself in different ways at different levels, both in national and international organizations. The aspect I want to address today is the crisis of identity and orientation, and what it means to us in terms of workers' education.**

This crisis of orientation, arising from a lack of clear objectives and of a long-term vision, is now widely perceived, even in organizations that have a culture of denial and complacency.

In the key document for its forthcoming congress, "Globalizing Solidarity", the ICFTU is unusually self-critical. For example, the document states that -- a number of affiliates have expressed the view that the ICFTU needs, in some way, to be "trade unionized", to be converted into the type of international trade union centre that workers in the globalised economy are said to need. This type of thinking has not generally been accompanied by very clear proposals about how such a conversion could be undertaken, nor about its specific content. Nevertheless, it does reflect a concern that our international is not properly linked to trade union action at national level, and provides a diplomatic service when what is needed is services for organizing, for bargaining and to deliver effective solidarity."

Elsewhere, there is a full page listing often-heard criticisms of the ICFTU, among which: "that the ICFTU has not been able to adapt to historic change. Born in a specific context of geo-political confrontation, and as a participant in a struggle now ended it has lost its initial rationale and been unable to fashion a new one which it is capable of implementing."

The document stops short of a discussion of the long-term historical vision of the ICFTU and of the international labour movement in general, perhaps because no one has yet clearly challenged the underlying ideology of the ICFTU. Such a challenge is not easy to mount precisely because the ideology is underlying and assumed rather than explicit, but what sticks out is the tacit acceptance of the existing social and economic system as a given, which of course needs to be improved upon but not fundamentally challenged and replaced by a better one.

Nevertheless, this critical examination of many of the assumptions on which the ICFTU has operated is without precedent. Although no comparable self-examination exists, to my knowledge, in other international trade union organizations, such as the ETUC or the GUFs, critical discussion does exist among their member organizations.

Among the GUFs, so far as I am aware, only the IUF is prepared to engage internally in a serious discussion of current labour movement issues, but in a number of national centers discussions on the future of the labour movement are in progress, often in ways limited by national circumstances but reflecting a general unease with past and present practices and future prospects.

For those of us who have been critical over the years of the practices and the policies of the trade union movement, in particular the international movement, the usual thrust of our criticism has had a limited objective: that of strengthening the trade union movement as it is, in the hope that its internal dynamics and the necessity to respond to increasingly aggressive attacks from employers and anti-union governments would produce positive changes within it, almost by an automatic process.

In that sense, the criticism of the ICFTU of its critics is to the point (no clear proposals on exactly how to go about transforming the labour movement). Typically, our themes have been:

- the democratization of the movement, more involvement of the membership and better membership control of the structures;
- as an objective in its own right, but also as part of the democratization process, the feminization of the movement: better access to the structures for the women within it, taking on board the women's agenda;
- organizing as a priority (this also often in connection with the women's issues, f. ex. in the informal economy);
- "internationalizing the movement", i.e. how to support the GUFs and how to supplement their action through international networking (f.ex. international study circles);
- fighting for basic workers' rights and union rights.

Some of us have raised the banner of "social movement unionism", meaning in general a politically aware and capable form of trade unionism, linking up with other social movements in a broad front of resistance to neo-liberalism, to the roll-back of social welfare and the achievements of the post-war trade union movement (mostly in Europe and North America), in alliance with other social movements and pro-labour NGOs.

Very few, if any, have raised the question: to what end? Why do we want a stronger, more effective, more militant, more political trade union movement?

One obvious answer is: to prevent the workers getting more beaten down by their exploiters by means we are all too familiar with, ranging from dismissal and blacklisting to murder.

That's the obvious objective: to strengthen the movement to enable workers to protect themselves against the worst forms of abuse they are exposed to. Of course, it needs to be done.

But is it enough? If we were winning this fight it might be, but we are losing.

Even the most militant of us have been waging defensive battles. And, across the board, we have been losing ground, despite some local victories. These should not be underestimated, because they show what solidarity can do, even against very powerful enemies, but, in and by themselves, they do not change the general picture. The reason is that global transnational capitalism can run circles around us notwithstanding local and limited victories, and will continue to do so until we can mount a serious challenge to the system itself.

Are we ready to challenge the system? and do we have an alternative?

I was struck by a conclusion of the Global Network African Regional Seminar (Cape Town, September 8), which noted:

"We don't speak of socialism but of social transformation or social change. Is this because of an acceptance of capitalism or is it because of the need to re-theorise our struggles and experiences and cater for the differences and new forms that have emerged and are emerging?"

It is true that we have been avoiding the "s" word and I think it is indeed because we need to "re-theorise our struggles and experiences."

We cannot challenge the system successfully until we have an alternative. Historically, this alternative has been socialism. But socialism is also undergoing a crisis, and that is a crisis of the meaning of socialism.

Take the case of Eastern Europe, and what used to be the USSR. These were self-described "socialist countries". In fact, the Stalinist regime that was imposed on these countries was the very opposite of socialism by any historical definition, including -- and especially -- that of Karl Marx. But today, it is very difficult to promote socialism as an ideology for the labour movement in any of the former so-called "socialist countries" because it is identified with one of the worst repressive regimes in history, and the memory of the movement that preceded it, and that was destroyed by it, with its identity and values, is erased.

Take the case of Latin America. Socialism, closely linked to anti-US imperialism, is very popular. But that includes acceptance and support of Cuba as a "socialist country", even though it is nothing more than the Caribbean form of Stalinism, which most Latin American trade unionists would never dream of imposing on their own countries.

Take the case of West-European social-democracy, the historical ally of most of the European trade union movement. Socialism, as an objective, has disappeared from the program of practically all social-democratic parties, and where social-democratic parties are in government, they are, for the most part, driving through neo-liberal programs undistinguishable, but for details, from their conservative opponents.

In most of Western Europe, the trade union movement has had to oppose the policies of neo-liberal social-democracy.

Take the case of North America, where a surprising number of the leading cadres of the trade union movement are socialists, but the prevailing ideology of the movement is conservative syndicalism, even in Canada, where a social-democratic party exists, but is not supported by a majority of the unions.

How do we deal with this? Clearly, we need to re-define socialism so it again becomes recognizable as the politics which are naturally ours, those of the historical labour movement, East and West, North and South – globally.

But how, with such divergent experiences and situations, do we reconstruct an international movement with a shared identity and shared values -- not the lowest common denominator, that's what we've got today, and it isn't working. Beyond the lowest common denominator, we need an alternative explanation of the world, alternative goals for society and a program on how to get there.

Recovering the meaning of socialism in a form that is profoundly democratic and at the same time firmly anchored in the labour movement, actually its original form, is not as enormously difficult an undertaking as it may seem, although it does take some work. Much of the work is semantic. It means getting rid of the dross of vulgar Marxism, eliminating automatic language with its lazy shortcuts, which prevent thought rather than expressing it, and deconstructing neo-liberal terminology, which has perverted concepts such as "freedom", that are central to our own world view, as well as many others, that have become the common coin of current political discourse. We need to recover our language and learn to express ideas which are simple in themselves, in simple and clear language.

To recover the meaning of socialism we need to go back to the roots. Our point of departure has to be that we intend to change the world, and since the present world order is perceived as unacceptable by a majority of the world's population, we have support. So we have to go through the issues, and develop solutions.

The minimum goals should be those that are essential to human welfare: food, shelter, clothing, but also justice, equality, freedom, access to culture and education, the rule of law. On that basis, on the basis of human needs, we can challenge the present system (capitalism in its present form, however we care to define it.)

Then come the issues which are central to the power relationships: industrial democracy, workers' control of production. There is vast material of historical experience that needs to be rediscovered and related to the present realities.

When we talk about power relationships, the main point, again going back to the roots, is to remember that socialism in our meaning of the term is a democratic movement that has to be built -- or re-built – from below. Whatever system, under whatever name, including "socialism", that is imposed from above, is something else, and something we need to fight in every way we can.

This is why the industrial democracy issues are so important: because, in the context of industrial relations, they place the power issue where it belongs, with the membership.

Finally, there is the global political issue. The power of global transnational capital is expressed in political terms: through a variety of formal and informal international institutions and through the leading governments, mainly the US government and the EU. It is clear that the labour movement is in no position at this time to challenge this power at that level, even if it wanted to, which is by no means clear. Contrary to what some like to believe, it is not even in a position to negotiate at this level with any prospect of success.

To challenge the system at that level, we will need to build far more strength, far more determination and far more clarity, from below. It will take years. How soon we can do it, depends on our own hard work and on many factors that are beyond our control. Developments which we cannot foresee can push us forward or set us back. All we can do for now, is to provide a sense of direction and to make sure that whatever we do, wherever we can, goes in the same direction.

We are not alone. In different parts of the world unions are also grappling with these same problems, and in the margins of the labour movement, socialist scholars, economists, sociologists, historians, various think-tanks, are working on the problem under discussion here, or on parts of it.

One important contribution the IFWEA could be, for starters, to make an inventory of this activity and seek to connect the various strands of socialist thought and activity as part of the process of rebuilding the movement.

Meanwhile, for us, as educators, the most important question remains: how do we connect these issues with the membership?

We need to formulate the discussion in terms that makes sense to the membership in terms of their everyday experience, without underestimating their capacity to understand the broader issues. The question is, in other words: how do we deliver socialist education to the membership?

This can only be an incremental long-term process, precisely because it cannot be done without the active involvement of the membership itself.

I don't see a committee meeting for a few months and emerging with a full-blown socialist theory and action program for our time, then putting it before the membership as an accomplished fact and expecting it to salute. We have been there before, and we know this doesn't work.

This would be a re-play of the authoritarian method and it can only lead, in the best of cases, to a schizophrenic situation where socialism is perceived as a long term abstract goal without relevance to everyday realities and disconnected from practical movement activity. In the worst case, it will lead to the rejection of the whole idea.

This was the weak point of classical social-democracy, later reproduced by the communist movement and its derivations. We don't want to reproduce these mistakes, we want to learn from our mistakes.

Political education, like any other aspect of workers' and trade union education, has to be done through and with the membership, through a broad discussion, step by step. Only through such a process can the movement recover an ideological and political base that is long lasting and solidly grounded.

Where do we start? Here are some starting points:

(1) deconstruct economic neo-liberalism (or neo-conservatism in political terms), its causes and its consequences. Deconstruct the vocabulary and the ideology, the concept of

the "free market". Perhaps we need seminars on semantics.

(2) start preparing study materials for a discussion on the concept of socialism, what it is and what it is not. To borrow from G.D.H. Cole, "what Marx really meant".

3) take the minimum goals -- what is needed for human welfare – and spell out the implications. Every discussion on minimum goals, taken to the limit, leads to an attack on neo-liberalism.

4) start a discussion on industrial democracy and workers' control.

Between these two points (3 and 4), we will be getting to an outline of a program of radical democracy that is the first step to challenge neo-liberalism.

(5) write and teach labour history: history is about identity and values, and therefore about the future. There is no future without a past.

There are no doubt other approaches that I cannot think of now, that could also be considered.

Some co-ordination of such an effort is needed. The IFWEA could have a committee on political education -- not, as I said before, to re-invent socialism, but to gather information on the work already in progress in workers' education institutions, in unions, in academic circles, in social movement NGOs, to take on board the variety of political experiences that exist and to work out a program of studies that could be broadly applicable in all parts of the world, so that comparable outcomes are achieved at all stages of a global discussion and so that a political consensus can eventually emerge.

We can, and should, involve others in this work: concerned trade unionists, scholars, historians, social activists, the women's movement, foundations, think tanks. Is the IFWEA too small a boat to carry this load? At this time, perhaps, but we don't have to do everything at once. Someone has to make a start, someone has to take the first step on this journey. And, to paraphrase Rabbi Hillel (the Elder): if not here, where? if not now, when? if not us, who?

1. http://www.globallabour.info/en/atom.xml

2. http://www.globallabour.info/en/index.xml
3. http://www.globallabour.info/en/
4. http://www.globallabour.info/en/2010/10/rebuilding_the_movement_dan_ga.html
5. http://www.globallabour.info/en/2010/10/workers_education_and_workers.html
6. http://www.globallabour.info/en/
7. http://www.globallabour.info/en/2010/10/rebuilding_the_movement_dan_ga.html
8. http://www.globallabour.info/en/
9. http://www.globallabour.info/en/2010/10/workers_education_and_workers.html
10. http://www.globallabour.info/en/2010/10/political_education_and_global_1.html

# Not With a Bang But With a Whimper [2004]

*In 2004, discussions were taking place between the ICFTU and the WCL on a merger, or rather the creation of new International, by the end of 2006. This eventually resulted in the formation of the International Trade Union Confederation (ITUC).*

**I read Noblecourt's article about the international trade union movement (Michel Noblecourt, Le big bang du syndicalisme international, Le Monde, July 26, 2004) and I had a good laugh over it. Yes, I thought this was a pretty funny article, if you have that kind of sense of humour.**

Since no one is paying attention today to either ICFTU or WCL, the idea is that a new International cobbled together by the ICFTU and the WCL, and sweeping up other international and national structures on the way, would represent a power no one could ignore.

This is a strange assumption. Power is not generated by adding together superstructures which are in themselves powerless. Numbers mean nothing if there is no political thought and no political will. Organizations are what converts numbers into action and strength. When such organizations are dysfunctional, nothing happens. Most of the 151 million members of the ICFTU and the largely fictional 26 million members of the WCL don't even know these organizations exist. In a political vacuum, 151 times zero equals zero, 26 times zero equals zero, zero plus zero equals zero.

A renewal of the trade union movement has to come from the membership. It implies the mobilization and participation of the membership, power is generated by the struggles such mobilization and participation make possible and new structures that express new power are the result of such struggles. To mobilize the membership, you need a vision and an objective.

Did the ICFTU initiate or conduct any significant struggles in recent decades? No. Did the WCL? No. Did the ETUC? No (the tragedy at Renault Vilvoorde and the gesticulations at EU summits are best forgotten). Have any of these organizations ever seriously inconvenienced the power structures that dominate our society? No.

What we are dealing with here is not a membership-driven response to the war on labour and the Left, which could indeed herald a renewal of the movement, it is a totally different process. This is a top-down, bureaucratic operation, all about structure and procedure, nothing about vision and objectives, social realities or social struggles.

Not only is the membership not being mobilized, it is not supposed to know. Amazingly, the whole operation is supposed to be secret: Noblecourt reports that the ICFTU and WCL leadership have been meeting "dans le plus grand secret" for the last few months, and have "discreetly" discussed their business in side meetings at the International Labour Conference. This is truly ridiculous. We are supposed to be a democratic movement. Why all this secrecy? Who is supposed to be kept in the dark? Is this a conspiracy? Those opposed to the idea already know anyway, so what is the point? If the ultimate objective is supposed to be the renewal of the trade union movement, should there not be the most open, most widespread, most intensive and most public discussion, on all the web sites?

Noblecourt tells us that the chief artisan of the operation is Emilio Gabaglio, former general secretary of the ETUC. That does tell us something. Gabaglio is an authoritarian centralizer, and Noblecourt also tells us that the new International is likely to look like a "world-wide ETUC" - presumably, without the European Commission to pay for it. That is hardly a "big bang" of the trade union movement. This is building an air-raid shelter for panic-stricken bureaucrats.

Interestingly, but not surprisingly, the idea of folding the Global Union Federations into the new structure has come up yet again in the context of the "big bang" discussions (as rumour has it, through leaks from all those secret talks). We all remember, of course, where this idea first originated: from the greatest authoritarian centralizers of all times, the WFTU. Fortunately it failed then and it will fail now. Not that very many GUFs today are in the forefront of significant struggles (that is a separate story), but such stirrings of life in the international trade union movement as are left, that's where they are. Subordinating them to a centralized structure that is unable to make things happen but can only prevent things from happening would mean killing the last remaining structures of the international trade union movement with a potential for delivering to the membership. If you want to know, look at the European Trade Union Federations.

Noblecourt finally reports that most of the elements of the grand blueprint remain to be spelled out (in secret discussions, one presumes). There is a lot about process and structure, but he also mentions common demands, and the perspective of arriving at "social change" through trade union action. He finally asks if the new International will "openly claim to be reformist". This is really naïve. The issue has long ago ceased to be "reform or revolution", it is now "reform or submission". A seriously reformist trade union International would be quite a left-wing challenge.

One would never guess that all this discussion takes place in the context of the most important mobilization of social movements that is unfolding since the end of the last world war. Are we in a bureaucratic bubble, impervious to what is going on around us? Our membership certainly isn't, because it can't afford to be.

The social movements say: "another world is possible". That's what we used to say, and we even had some pretty good ideas what this other world might look like. Unless and until we go back to basics, and recover our original vision, with a perspective of fundamental social change, there will be no "big bang" and no renewal of the international labour movement.

The starting point must be to challenge the legitimacy of the system. We need to establish standards based on our own values, and clearly say that the only legitimate purpose of any form of social organization, whether local or world wide, or of any enterprise, or of any inter-governmental or economic structure, or of an economic system, is to serve human welfare: the satisfaction of basic needs, and these do not only include food, shelter and clothing but also justice, equality, freedom, access to culture and education, the rule of law. There is no other source of legitimacy.

These values and basic principles together constitute a program of radical democracy diametrically opposed to the currently hegemonic neo-liberalism, and these should become the elements of a basic program which the labour movement will defend at all levels with all appropriate means.

This brings us to the power question. What our leaders need to ask themselves in their secret conclaves is: do we have real enemies or don't we? if we do, who are they? are we engaged in a worldwide power struggle or not? is losing an option? what do we have to do to prevail?

A Trade Union International worthy of its name would reallocate its resources away from sterile "dialogues" with the institutions of transnational corporate power that are killing us; it would massively invest in organizing in transition countries, where the FDIs are going, to rebuild the movement there; it would keep trade union rights in China on top of its agenda; it would give full political and financial support to those GUFs that are taking on transnational corporations; it would build alliances with workers' movements in the informal economy and other social movements instead of keeping them at arms' length; it would declare war on governments which are attacking social welfare and workers' rights, regardless of their political colour; it would do so publicly and unashamedly, by publicizing the issues as widely as possible, so as to keep the membership informed and involved and to build political support. Had the ICFTU been doing this for the last few years it would not have to worry about merging with anyone today.

A Trade Union International worthy of its name would proudly proclaim: we represent the world's working class, we represent most of the world's population, and we are fighting to change the social and economic order to make the world a fit place for human beings to live in. Is this too radical? What is the alternative?

There is, of course, always an alternative. In this case, it is the further decline of the movement. It means accepting the downward spiral of lower levels of ambition, lower capacities of delivering, lower levels of support from the membership, more mergers for the sole purpose of cutting costs, further loss of fighting capacity, strength and authority. No reshuffling of useless structures will solve these problems. Instead of greater unity, there will be further fragmentation. Some organizations will collapse, others will fight on, others will survive as empty shells, for grandstanding at the WEF, if they are still invited.

This is the way the movement, as we know it, will end, not with a bang, but with a whimper. We will then have to wait a decade or two until a new movement emerges. If we get another chance.

# Organizing in the Global Informal Economy [2004]

*Bogaziçi University Social Policy Forum: Changing Role of Unions in the Contemporary World of Labour, Istanbul, November 26-27, 2004*

The Informal Economy

**Workers in the informal economy are all workers in unregulated and unprotected work – a majority by far of all workers in the world. (1) This includes all work in informal enterprises as well as informal jobs (jobs that pay no benefits or provide no social protection). such as own-account workers (for example home-based workers or street vendors) and some wage workers, for example casual workers without fixed employers, most domestic workers and even factory workers in unregulated and unprotected work, typically in the free trade zones. Because they lack protection, rights and representation, they remain trapped in poverty.**

The debt crisis of the underdeveloping countries, the dismantling of the public sector, the deregulation of the labour market under the structural adjustment programs of the IMF and the World Bank, and the succession of economic and financial crises since 1997, has pushed millions of people in Africa, Asia and Latin America out of formal employment and into the informal economy. They are not in the informal economy by choice, but as a means of survival.

In addition, the structure of the modern transnational corporation has been changing. From a producer it is becoming the coordinator of production carried out on its behalf by others. By eliminating the jobs of permanent full-time workers, by outsourcing and subcontracting all but its core activities, and by relying wherever it can on unstable forms of labour (casual, part-time, temporary, seasonal, on call), management deregulates the labour market and shifts responsibility for income, benefits, and conditions onto the individual worker.

The outer circle of this system is the submerged world of micro-enterprises and industrial outworkers, in the industrialized countries mainly immigrant workers, often without residence and working permits, with deteriorating conditions as one moves from the centre to the periphery of the production process. Most of the so-called own-account workers under contract to a transnational corporation are in fact disguised employees who have lost their rights as employees.

Globalisation has tended to informalise work everywhere: the protection of workers in the formal economy is threatened under the impact of global deregulation, even while the workers in the informal economy remain integrated into global production and marketing chains. What is particular to the informal economy is the absence of rights and social protection of the workers involved in it. In every other respect, the formal and informal economies form an integral whole and, whilst it is easy to identify the core elements of each, the borders between them are blurred and shifting.

For the most part, informal workers are women. A majority of workers expelled by the global economic crisis from regulated, steady work are women. As the ICFTU has reported (2), women are the principal victims of the casualisation of labour and the pauperisation created by the crisis, and have therefore massively entered the informal economy, where they had already been disproportionately represented, even before the effects of globalisation had made themselves felt.

The growth of the informal economy cannot be reversed in the short or medium term anywhere in the world. Formalizing the informal economy on a world scale is an illusion. In the current global economic and political context, no State or regional grouping of States has the ability or the political will to set in motion the macroeconomic changes that would create universal full employment under regulated conditions. On the contrary, for the foreseeable future we can expect more deregulation and a further growth of the informal economy. The issue is therefore not "formalizing" the "informal" but protecting the unprotected. That, of course, is also a way of "formalizing", but it implies a different approach: organizing from below rather than regulating from above.

Workers' Rights

Workers' rights are under attack, to one degree or another, in all countries, by means we are all too familiar with, ranging from blackmail with threats of relocation, to dismissal and blacklisting, to murder. In most countries, however, workers' rights are at least formally recognized and some protection exists against the worst forms of abuse they are exposed to. This is not the case in the informal economy, where workers, until recently, were not even recognized as workers and most of the time face the employer as individuals. Fear is pervasive: fear of losing one's job, however bad, fear of losing security, however fragile. The lack of legal protection of workers' rights in the informal economy is therefore an overriding issue.

At the International Labour Conference in 2002, the ILO for the first time addressed this issue. The "informal sector" was an agenda item and, after intense discussions between representatives of workers, employers and governments, conclusions were adopted where basic workers' rights, access to work and social security and organisation and representation are all identified as being elements of decent work which should be enjoyed by workers in the informal economy. These are the most significant points made in the conclusions (3):

> 1. The ILO Declaration on Fundamental Principles and Rights at Work and its Follow-up and the core labour standards are as applicable in the informal as in the formal economy.

2. Workers are not defined by their employment relationship but by the work they do and their dependent position in the production process. Therefore own-account workers are workers (not micro-entrepreneurs) and are entitled to the same rights as other workers.

3. National legislation must guarantee and defend the freedom of all workers, irrespective of where and how they work, to form and join organisations of their own choosing without fear of reprisal or intimidation.

4. The ILO should "identify the obstacles to application of the most relevant labour standards for workers in the informal economy and assist the tripartite constituents in developing laws, policies and institutions that would implement these standards".

5. The ILO should also identify the legal and practical obstacles to formation of organisations of workers in the informal economy and assist them to organise.

In 1996, the International Labour Conference had already adopted the Home Work Convention (Convention 177), which aims to promote "equality of treatment between home workers and other wage earners, taking into account the special characteristics of home work and, where appropriate, conditions applicable to the same or similar type of work carried out in an enterprise" (meaning sweatshops). In its operative part, the convention says that "equality of treatment shall be promoted, in particular, in relation to: (a) the home workers' right to establish or join organizations of their own choosing and participate in the activities of such organizations; (b) protection against discrimination in employment and occupation; (c) protection in the field of occupational safety and health; (d) remuneration; (e) statutory social security protection; (f) access to training; (g) minimum age for admission to employment or work, and (h) maternity protection."

This convention was secured by a thin majority of government and workers' votes against fierce opposition from the employers' group who, when the convention was adopted, declared that they would prevent its ratification wherever they could. So far, they have been largely successful: only four countries have ratified (Albania, Finland, Ireland and the Netherlands).

Organizing

Ultimately, of course, any real guarantee for implementation and enforcement of labour standards in the informal economy depends on the organisation of informal workers into trade unions. Only by organization into unions can informal workers hope to get their rights recognised. As for the unions, they need to organise in the informal economy to survive. With approximately 90 percent of the world labour force unorganised, and union density declining as the informal economy keeps growing, organising the workers in the informal economy everywhere has now become a crucial issue for the labour movement. Without a serious and sustained effort on this issue, it is impossible today to even think of organizing a majority of workers on a global scale - and unless we succeed in this we cannot change the existing global power relationships to our advantage.

What are the obstacles to organising in the informal economy? Some are structural: the dispersal of the labour force into individual workplaces makes traditional union organizing difficult and calls for new approaches. Some are ideological, such as backward trade union thinking, wedded to the myths and customs of rust-belt trade unionism based on traditional male manual work. Yet, even though informal workers in many instances do not have previous trade union experience or a trade union culture, they have nevertheless organized themselves into unions, as workers do, even without formal trade union backing.

The problem is not so much in the South, where traditional unions, for example in Africa and Latin America, have been often successful in organising informal workers. At the same time, informal workers have also created their own organisations. In India, where 97 percent of the labour force is in the informal economy, the Self Employed Women's Association, which represents informal women workers, now has a membership of over 700,000. In countries like Brazil, Korea or South Africa where trade unionism is a militant social movement, there are also significant advances in organising in the informal economy.

It is in Europe, North America and Japan that unions have so far largely failed to develop successful organising strategies in the informal economy. In an advanced industrial country like Britain, 64 percent of the workplaces are unorganised (4) and, although many of these in theory represent formal employment, they employ in practice a casualised, contracted out and insecure workforce whose wages and working conditions are typical of those existing in informality.

In addition, a vast number of workers, such as home workers, do not relate to any particular workplace or, like domestic workers or workers in sweatshops, are scattered among thousands of micro-employers. With a few notable exceptions, such as Northern Europe, the picture is the same throughout the industrialised world and, much worse, in the countries of the former Soviet bloc.

Some unions, for example in Britain (T&GWU, GMB), Germany (IG Metall), France, Italy, Spain and the US (SEIU), have made serious efforts to organize informal workers, with some success, but so far this is only scratching the surface.

If one assumes, as we do, that the problem of organising workers in the informal economy is a major priority to be addressed and resolved by the trade union movement, it is clear that the trade union movement has to develop new approaches: it has to take on board the women's agenda (defend women's issues, take more women into its leadership, hire more women organizers, adjust its procedures and practices to become more women friendly); it has to organize on a community basis as well as the traditional work-place based organizing, and learn to work with associations; it has to develop political programs that reflect the needs of society at large and of the informal workers within it. The trade union movement has to see itself as part of a broad coalition, which is the Global Justice and Solidarity Movement, where it can find the allies it needs and where it can contribute its sense of purpose and its organizational strength.

Here too, obstacles must be overcome, in particular a deep-seated mistrust in sections of the trade union movement of working with NGOs, justified in some cases, and entirely misplaced in others.

Equally, advocacy and service NGOs involved with informal workers have in some cases been reluctant to engage with the trade union movement, partly because of bad experiences, but most often because of perceptions based on mistaken assumptions and political prejudices.

Coalition Building

There has been some progress recently. A coalition of women's NGOs, informal workers' organisations, international and national unions and workers' education organisations has come together in the last four years to drive the organizing agenda forward. This coalition was also instrumental in securing the conclusions of the 2002 International Labour Conference.

Its main elements are:

(1) National unions, mostly in Africa, which originated in the formal economy and, as their members lost their jobs through deregulation and privatisation, followed them into the informal economy. One example is the General Agricultural Workers' Union (GAWU) of Ghana, which expanded its area of work to non-waged workers and subsistence farmers after structural adjustment programs in the 1970s caused its membership to drop from 130,000 to 30,000. Another

example is the Uganda Public Employees Union (UPEU). In the 1990s its membership dropped from 108,000 to a mere 700 as a result of the privatisation of government services. The union then drastically changed its outlook and scope: it revised the concept of "public employee" from the traditional narrow meaning of civil servants to a much broader concept of anyone engaged in serving the public, such as, for example, street vendors. As a result of these changes and a new organising drive, its membership started to grow again, reaching 17,000 by 1999.

(2) Women in Informal Employment Globalising and Organising (WIEGO): an international network of women's unions, NGOs and individuals in academic institutions and international organisations, with the aim of promoting the organisation of informal women workers into unions world wide. WIEGO is a research back up and a policy think tank for informal workers' organisations, with a secretariat at Harvard University. It also organises foundation funding for many organising initiatives.

(3) The Committee for Asian Women (CAW), a network of women's NGOs and unions based in Bangkok, with 28 members in 13 Asian countries. Since 2001 work in the informal economy is its main priority.

(4) Global union federations such as the IUF and the ITGLWF have been supportive of informal women workers' organizations because of direct experience in their area of work: home workers, nearly all women, account for a significant part of world production in tobacco products (bidi workers in India) and of garments, other textile products and footwear. The International Transport Workers' Federation (ITF), the Public Service International (PSI), UNI and, most recently, the ICFTU, have also showed support and interest.

(5) The International Federation of Workers' Education Associations (IFWEA), at its congress in 2000, decided that supporting union organisation of workers in the informal economy, through workers' education, was one of its priorities. One of its main affiliates, the WEA England and

Scotland, working with the Zambia Congress of Trade Unions, established a WEA which, in turn, through a series of seminars, was instrumental in the establishment in October 2002 of the Alliance of Zambian Informal Economy Associations (AZIEA), with over one million members. AZIEA members are mostly street and market vendors (many of them former miners in the Copper Belt who were laid off as the mines shut down, but who do have trade union experience) and some transport workers (mini-bus drivers and their helpers).

(6) The International Restructuring Education Network Europe (IRENE), based in the Netherlands, has organized several meetings on workers in the informal economy in Europe, in co-operation with trade union organisations (FNV, ETUC) and other allies (WIEGO, IFWEA).

(7) HomeNet and StreetNet, are international networks of, respectively, home workers and street and market vendors. HomeNet is dormant at this time, but StreetNet transformed itself into an international federation at a founding congress held in Seoul in March 2004, which was attended by 58 delegates from 15 organisations. It elected an executive with a president from Korea, a vice-president from India, a treasurer from South Africa and a secretary from Zambia. The co-ordinator (a staff position) is from South Africa. The International Council has five members from Africa, two members from Latin America and one member from Asia.

(8) The Self Employed Women's Association (SEWA) of India, based in Ahmedabad, Gujarat, now with over 700,000 members, is one of largest unions of informal workers in the world. It has been instrumental in building this coalition: it is affiliated to the IUF and the ITGLWF (as well as to ICEM, which, however, has not so far been active in organising informal workers), it has been the main active element in WIEGO (its founder, Ela Bhatt, is Chair of the WIEGO Steering Committee), it is an affiliate of the IFWEA through the SEWA Academy and it is a member organisation of CAW.

In December 2003, SEWA hosted an International Conference

on Organising in the Informal Economy in Ahmedabad. The conference was co-sponsored by HomeNet Thailand, the Nigeria Labour Congress, SEWA, StreetNet International and the Ghana TUC, and was attended by sixty participants (16 from Africa, 28 from Asia, 5 from North and Latin America, 2 from Europe and 9 from international organisations). The conference elected an International Co-ordination Committee (ICC) whose task is to ensure that the decisions of the conference are followed up. The ICC met last June in Geneva, at the International Labour Conference.

(9) The Global Labour Institute (GLI), based in Geneva, has been at the center of much of the co-ordinating and networking activity between the principal actors of this coalition.

Coalitions such as these, without strong formal structures but with a capacity of working effectively together as a network, can become a powerful force for positive change and for driving the organizing agenda in the informal economy.

Notes:

(1) Women and Men in the Informal Economy: A Statistical Picture, Employment Sector, ILO, Geneva, 2002

(2) From Asia to Russia to Brazil – The Cost of the Crisis, International Confederation of Free Trade Unions (ICFTU), Brussels, May 1999

(3) Conclusions concerning decent work and the informal economy, in: Effect to be given to resolutions adopted by the International Labour Conference at its 90th Session (2002); (b) Resolution concerning decent work and the informal economy, document GB.285/7/2 (available on the ILO web site: www.ilo.org).
(4) Polly Toynbee: The workers who need trade unions most can't join them, in: The Guardian, December 27, 2002.

Further reading: ICFTU Trade Union World Briefing, March 2004: The Informal Economy: Women on the Front Line (available on the ICFTU web site).

Web sites with relevant material:

www.wiego.org
www.streetnet.org.za
www.ifwea.org
www.icftu.org
www.global-labour.org

# Organizing: Means and Ends [2006]

*Global Unions, Global Justice Conference*
*Cornell Global Labor Institute, New York, February 9, 2006*

Friends, Brothers and Sisters, Comrades:

**Before I get started, let me congratulate the Cornell University School of Industrial and Labor Relations for convening this conference and the Cornell Global Labor Institute for this pre-conference meeting. After most of a lifetime in the international labor movement, I can say that this is the most serious and broad-based effort I have ever seen to develop an agenda for its renewal. The proposed Task Force should ensure that this effort will be permanent and sustained, and therefore will have an impact over time. Thank you and congratulations!**

The fact that such a conference can take place at all, and that it has met with such an enthusiastic response, is probably indicative of the depth of the crisis we are in.

There is no question today that the labor movement is in a crisis. We are all experiencing it. What we are facing is:

serious loss of membership in most countries of the world, especially in the unions' industrial heartland in Western Europe and North America;

an inability to organize the huge and growing mass of unorganized workers, not least in the informal economy;

the lack of political and industrial power to resist and defeat repression, either in the form of a systematic campaign of murders, as in Colombia, or of State policy, as in China and many other authoritarian States, or of anti-labor legislation backed by a hostile government, as in the United States or in Australia; lack of capacity to resist the dismantling of social protection, of social services and of public property, an agenda carried out by conservative and social-democratic governments alike (as in most of Europe, North America, Australia and Japan, and, under pressure from the IMF, in Africa, Asia and Latin America).

This crisis is generally attributed to the economic, social and, ultimately, political effects of globalization, unfolding in the 1980s and 1990s: the dramatic world wide shift in social power relations in favor of transnational capital, to the detriment of labor and to the detriment of the national State in its role of administrator of a social compromise between labor and capital.

Why has this happened? The usual explanation is the new and unprecedented mobility of capital, at the same time as labor remains confined within the boundaries of the national State. At the same time, massive and permanent unemployment, also in industrialized countries, has caused the unions to lose control of the labor market even where they were traditionally strong and has substantially weakened their bargaining power. These are true insights, but they are partial truths and partial insights. The crisis of the trade union movement today is in fact the outcome of a larger crisis of the broader labor movement, which began much earlier, much before the onset of globalization. The trade union movement would not be in its present predicament, fighting defensive battles in isolation, if it had not lost, by stages and over time, its anchorage in society at large.

History advances in long cycles. To understand what has happened, we need to do a flash back, about seventy years ago or more. Fascism in Europe, whatever else it may have been, was a gigantic union busting exercise. Its consequences, and the consequences of WWII, are too often forgotten. A whole generation of labor activists, the best people, disappeared in concentration camps, in the war, or did not come back from exile.

At the end of the war, the labor movement re-emerged, superficially strong, because it was part of the Allied cause, and had won the war, whereas capital was on the defensive, having largely collaborated with fascism in the Axis countries and in occupied Europe.

In reality, the labor movement had been greatly weakened, with a decimated leadership and its capacity to act as an independent social force severely undermined. All democratic governments in post-war Europe were initially supportive of the labor agenda and consequently the trade unions, in their weakened condition, developed an over-reliance on the State. No longer was there any aspiration to represent an alternative society. Amidst the newfound peace and prosperity, the labor movement had disarmed ideologically and politically.

In the USSR and in the countries of Eastern and Central Europe under its domination, it was a different story. All traces of an independent labor movement were erased. Nearly all the cadres and activists of the socialist, syndicalist, or dissident communist movements who had survived the war perished in the labor camps and prisons of the system. A new class of bureaucrats took total control of society: in that system, so-called trade unions were in fact State agencies of labor administration.

With Eastern Europe frozen in Stalinist paralysis for fifty years, there remained the movement in Western Europe. That was a movement led by survivors, not the kind of labor movement that would be capable of meeting the challenges of an entirely new world situation.

Decades of complacency had diluted and trivialized its ideological and political heritage. Its priorities had been distorted by the Cold War. Still powerful trade union organizations were led, far too often, by blinkered and politically ignorant leaderships, geared to administering gains of earlier struggles rather than to organizing and engaging in new struggles, generally unquestioning in their acceptance of the ideology of social partnership and bereft of political imagination. The rank-and-file was educated to bureaucratic routine and to passivity.

What I am describing here of course not only applies to Europe but, for different reasons, to North America and to other parts of the world as well. I could elaborate, but I won't do it here for reasons of time and you can fill in the blanks anyway.

While the labor movement was asleep, the world changed dramatically. I already referred to the impact of new communications and transport technologies, leading to an unprecedented mobility of capital, while labor remained prisoner, mentally and institutionally, of the nation-State. The working class was also changing. Traditional bastions of the trade union movement in the mass-production industries and in the public sector were falling, while the largely unorganized service sector was expanding.

The informal economy, once thought to be a remnant of archaic forms of production destined to disappear, has, on the contrary, grown everywhere, even in the industrialized countries. If we are talking about services and about the informal economy, we are talking about women workers. Women represent a huge, and largely invisible, part of the new working class.

In the 1980s and 1990s, workers from China, India and the former Soviet bloc entered the global labor pool. That's an estimated 1.47 billion new workers joining the global system of production and consumption, effectively doubling the size of the world's now globally connected work force.

These workers are, for practical purposes, unorganized. In China, what passes for trade unions, are in fact State agencies of labor administration and do not represent their captive membership. In India, over 90 percent of the labor force is in the informal sector, where organization is still weak, and the existing trade unions, divided into eight national centers, represent a fraction of the remaining few percent. In the former Soviet bloc, the collapse of the system in the 1990s exposed the hollowness of the so-called State trade unions and left behind a weak, divided and disoriented labor movement.

Here we have the real reason for the global shift of power relations in favor of transnational capital: organized labor no longer represents a statistically significant proportion of the global labor force. With a global labor force of approximately 2.93 billion, and organized labor representing globally 170 million at the most, we get a global union density of just below 6 percent.

How do we deal with this? Obviously by organizing the unorganized. Easier said than done. This is not happening and, on the contrary, we are losing ground, so we have to ask ourselves why it is not happening and what the premises of successful global organizing might be. We have to ask ourselves: what are we organizing for? And what is the vision we hold out to people we are asking to join the labor movement?

I want to submit to you the idea that the real crisis of the labor movement is a crisis of identity and perspective, and that this is the crisis we need to resolve in order to become capable of organizing the world's working class.

In order to do that, we have to return to our roots. The labor movement, in resisting the brutal exploitation of early capitalism, was inspired by the fundamental values of justice and freedom, based on the recognition of the equal value of all human beings.

In many countries it broadened its struggle to encompass larger social goals. The first international labor organization held that the emancipation of the working class was to be, at the same time, the emancipation of all society, which would become an "association in which the free development of each is the condition for the free development of all."

Today, a serious challenge to the domination of global transnational capital cannot be mounted unless the labor movement recovers a common identity based on an alternative vision of society: the vision of freedom, justice and equality that inspired it at its origins and made it the greatest mass movement in history.

We do have an international trade union movement, such as it is. It has no vision, and it does not inspire anyone. Its principal organization, the ICFTU, has been mired for decades in lobbying activities in international institutions controlled by transnational capital. Despite the obvious failure of such activities to make any significant impact on the ground, there is no sign of a change in perspective. What we have here is an ideology of global "social partnership".

We are among those who hold that the ideology of "social partnership", which became dominant in the labor movement in the three decades following WW2, has now become the main obstacle to the necessary renewal of the movement.

Large parts of the trade union movement are still unable to come to terms with the loss of their presumed "social partners", even while transnational capital has obviously abandoned any "partnership" perspective and is using its vastly increased power to unilaterally impose its interests on society.

There is now a real danger that the majority of the trade union movement will seek solutions to its crisis by restructuring exercises that will provide the appearance of power without its substance.

This has become an international issue through the decision of the last ICFTU congress to create a new International through a merger with the WCL (plus some former WFTU affiliates and independents).

This is not a bad idea in itself, and it might even have positive effects if it develops a dynamic of its own under the law of unintended consequences (there are signs that something like this may be happening in Latin America) but the absence of any political and ideological perspective in a major policy decision by what is, after all, the leadership of world's working class, is striking.

We hear that the significance of this merger lies in that "the ideological divisions of the past" are being overcome, but we are not told what the ideology of the "new International" is supposed to be. Nor is it clear what stopped the ICFTU in the past from doing by itself what it will supposedly be able to do within a "new International" where its affiliates will represent about ninety percent of the membership.

There appears to be an assumption that such a merger, by itself, will automatically restore the power and authority that the labor movement has lost, as if the mere addition of weaknesses could produce new strength. This is magical thinking, without any basis in reality or in reason.

There is no attempt to analyze the changing nature of capitalism, which has led to a dramatic shift in power relations to the detriment of labor, nor to analyze the changing nature of the working class, which is a prerequisite of successful organizing.

But we may be wrong if we assume that the apparatus currently in charge of the international labor movement is seeking to rebuild the strength of the movement to make it fit for a successful power struggle with transnational capital.

It is disturbing to hear that the level of ambition of the "new International" is no more than to exercise more influence in the World Bank and in the International Monetary Fund. This means that they are continuing to chase the illusion of a "global social partnership" under conditions where "social partnership" is a thing of the past even in the countries where the labor movement has been strongest.

The signing on of most of the international trade union movement to the UN Global Compact is another manifestation of this policy of seeking co-optation at international level. Maintaining an appearance of bargaining without bargaining power is a theater of make believe, not a strategy of struggle.

At international level, by renouncing a unifying ideology and of a vision of an alternative society, of a global Co-operative Commonwealth based on freedom and social justice, the labor movement has narrowed its options to purely defensive ones. It has failed to connect with the new social movements that are able to mobilize millions. By restricting its agenda to what it assumes to be its core business, it has isolated itself from society and is in danger of turning itself into a narrow "interest group", as its enemies would have it.

A movement content to represent politically no more than the lowest common denominator of its members, substituting process to politics and seeking solutions to its crisis by restructuring exercises that provide the appearance of power without its substance, cannot lead or inspire society.

Yet, it must lead and inspire society.

The time has come to remember that the labor movement is not an end in itself. It has a responsibility not only to its members but to all of society, precisely because it is not a "special interest group" and because the interests of its members are not separate from those of society at large.

The stakes are extraordinarily high. The current system of global transnational capitalism, as it stands, is environmentally unsustainable. It condemns most of the world's population to poverty and virtual slavery. It divides humanity into a small minority living in gated estates of prosperity surrounded by an ocean of misery and revolt. It spends billions on means of repression. It is leading humanity to death.

Must the labor movement save humanity? Yes, of course. Who else? If not us, who? If not here, where? If not now, when? No other force in society has the potential to achieve this goal, which is the only goal that matters today.

How do we go about saving humanity? In the first place, by saving ourselves.

The first step is to recognize that the present world order is not an eternal given and to declare clearly that we are opposing it. Contrary to what some thought, we have not reached the end of history. The ideological premises of the present world order are a fraud. The free market is a fiction, there is no correlation at all between so-called free market capitalism and democracy. Capitalism is enormously adaptable, but only under threat.

Alternatives of course remain possible, socialism in the way it was historically conceived remains such an alternative. A benevolent and sustainable capitalism is an illusion, but even for those of us who would be willing to give it a try it must be clear that in order to effect positive changes we again have to become a threat.

How do we become a threat?

In the first place, this requires a break of the international labor movement with their bureaucratic complicities in the international financial institutions and other intergovernmental organizations. A policy of breaking away would send a strong signal to the transnational establishment and would in addition free resources that would become available to support more productive investments.

All policies, activities and priorities of the labor movement should be reconsidered in a different perspective, a perspective of system change: the ends and means of organizing, the allocation of resources, the conditions under which trade union development programs are carried out, the way the movement positions itself in society, its alliances and its political commitments.

This, I expect, will be the agenda of our Task Force. Here I cannot do more than mention some specific aspects.

Within the realm of the traditional trade union activity, the Global Union Federations have, in some cases, made significant progress in bargaining at international level with transnational corporations. They are, for the most part, underfunded and overstretched. Building an international fund to support these activities would be a first step to help reverse the existing power relations.

A second step would be building alliances with those who share our concerns. They represent an enormous constituency. Last year it was estimated that a billion people in the world existed on less than a dollar a day. Of these, 550 million were working. Most of these have been beyond the reach of the trade union movement. They have no stake in this society.

We need to address all workers, whatever the form of their work or areas where they work, and we cannot reach them, we cannot mobilize and organize them, unless they can see and sense a commitment on our part to a common cause based on mutual solidarity - unless we give them hope.

Most of the working poor are in the informal economy, that is, in unprotected and unregulated jobs, both self-employed and working for wages. There is a growing international movement of workers in the informal economy and since women are over-represented in that sector this is largely a women's movement. These are our natural allies and, indeed, one of their largest and most dynamic organizations, the Self Employed Women's Association of India, has joined several Global Union Federations. For no good reason, the ICFTU has been keeping this movement at arms' length, although there are now signs that this may be changing.

Women organizing are a source of tremendous energy: they are resourceful, militant and unafraid. In a number of countries they are joining unions at a faster rate than men, yet the labor movement has been slow to recognize their contribution and to include them at all levels of responsibility. They are now spearheading organization in the informal sector. Our answer to the feminization of poverty must be the feminization of the labor movement.

The working poor also include hundreds of millions of rural workers: small peasants, landless peasants, day laborers and casual workers. They are also getting organized, they also want to change the world and they are also our natural allies. I was looking forward to share this platform today with José Bové, one of their outstanding leaders. The US immigration authorities decided otherwise, and I am deeply indignant that Bové was refused access to this country and to this conference. They will not stop us. Tierra y Libertad! Land and Freedom! This great watchword of the revolutionary unions in Mexico in the beginning of the last century, and in Spain in the 1930s, should be our common program.

We need to build alliances with those who are seeking to protect our natural environment. This will not be easy, because it means that trade unions, which are committed to defend their members' jobs, will have to reconsider the methods of production and, indeed, the product itself, that guarantee these jobs.

I know you can't smoke in this city and at one time I represented tobacco workers. They were a small group to begin with, and their jobs were destroyed by the companies through mechanization, far more than by anti-smoking campaigns. But what about auto workers? Can the world afford an auto industry based on present assumptions? And will the social and environmental impact of Wal-Mart become any less destructive once it recognizes a union? Who needs huge hypermarkets?

These are difficult questions but we must deal with them because we have no other option: what is ultimately at stake here is the survival of human life on this planet. That is an issue the labor movement cannot walk away from. We must deal with these issues and find solutions in the interest of society, which also includes our members.

We need to strengthen alliances with the academic world, draw on its research capacity and its capacity to organize exchanges of ideas and policy discussions. This conference is actually an illustration of such an alliance and an important step in strengthening these links.

But the labor movement also needs to invest far more in educational activities and in supporting those organizations that are engaged in workers' education in a labor movement perspective, such as the IFWEA. The movement needs this ideological and political back up. I know I am also preaching here for my own parish, but how else are we going to counter the vast array of reactionary think tanks generously funded by reactionary billionaires, in public opinion and within our own membership?

Finally, we need to take democracy seriously, both internationally and within our own movement. We must be consistent with our own principles: we define a union as an organization of workers democratically controlled by its own members, who decide on its policies and activities. I am fully aware that within our movement this definition is sometimes honored more in breach than in observance, but there is a world of difference with organizations that are structurally and by definition controlled by employers, or by the State where the State is the employer.

In situations like China, or like Cuba, or like any other authoritarian State that represses any independent expression of civil society, the organizations that purport to represent workers cannot be our allies. They are obstacles to the alliances we need to build with the workers of these countries. Organizing internationally in this context can only mean, for the time being, reaching out to and defending those incredibly courageous individuals who are facing jail, psychiatric internment or labor camps to defend the kind of unionism we believe in.

In addition, democracy has to be in the first place our own commitment in our own organizations, also at international level. Democracy is not only a goal, it is a permanent process, which cannot be separated from the goal. We do not believe that union strength can be built, or re-built, at any level, without the involvement of an aware, informed, motivated and militant membership. It certainly cannot be done under conditions where most of the members are not even aware of the existence of the organizations that purport to speak in their name.

To re-connect the membership to a perspective of international struggle requires a realistic assessment of the situation, the political will to change it, a vision of an alternative, the democratic reform of the movement and a global program of action. Education, organizing and struggle must go hand-in-hand.

We will continue to support those working for the reform of the labor movement through struggle, reconstructing its identity as a movement for democratic social transformation, with a common vision of an alternative, and better, society.

I thank you for your attention.

# International Framework Agreements: A Reassessment [2006]

*The following paper was presented at the workshop of the International Institute of Labour Studies (IILS) on "Cross-Border Social Dialogue and Agreements: an Emerging Global Industrial Framework?", ILO, Geneva, December 15 and 16, 2006. Together with the other papers presented at the workshop, it was published as an ILO/IILS publication in 2008: "Cross Border Social Dialogue and Agreements: An emerging global industrial relations framework?", ed. Konstantinos Papadakis, 288 p.*

Introduction

**Soon it will be twenty years since the first agreement between an international trade union organization and a transnational corporation (TNC) was signed. Sixty such agreements or International Framework Agreements (IFAs), have been signed since and it may be assumed that more will be signed in the coming years. A considerable body of academic and trade union literature has developed to discuss their significance. It seems appropriate at this point to review this discussion in the light of what was originally intended, of what has developed since, and of future prospects.**

This chapter depicts a number of historical events, which constitute key benchmarks in the emergence of trans-national labour/management relations and agreements. We first explain the original intention of the trans-national negotiations undertaken between the International Trade Secretariats (ITSs) and TNCs in the 1960s (section 1), as well as lessons drawn from this original experience (section 2). We then focus on the history of first IFA (Danone, 1988) and the reasons which might have motivated the TNC in reaching this agreement (section 3). We then highlight the differences between IFAs and corporate codes of conduct (section 4) and the relation between IFAs and European Works Councils (section 5). We conclude by discussing the issue of whether IFAs can still be considered to constitute elements of an emerging global labour relations architecture, within a political and economic context increasingly hostile to trade union rights.

The Original Intention

It is not difficult to trace back the origins of the International Framework Agreements (IFAs). They originate in the response, in the 1960s, of three International Trade Secretariats (ITSs, now renamed Global Union Federations or GUFs) to the growing influence of transnational corporations on industrial relations, also and especially at national level.

The three ITSs were the International Federation of Chemical and General Workers' Unions (ICF), the forerunner of the present International Federation of Chemical, Energy, Mine and General Workers' Unions (ICEM), the International Metalworkers' Federation (IMF) and the International Union of Food and Allied Workers' Associations (IUF), the forerunner of the present International Union of Food, Agricultural, Hotel, Restaurant, Catering, Tobacco and Allied Workers' Associations.

The International Transport Workers' Federation (ITF) was of course the first ITS to conclude international agreements with employers' federations in the maritime industry and is thus the pioneer of international collective bargaining. Most recently, in 2000, the ITF concluded a sectoral agreement with the International Maritime Employers' Committee (IMEC). This, however, is a special case that should be examined separately (see, Lillie in this volume who examines a key episode in the history of the cross-border social dialogue in the maritime shipping industry, i.e., the adoption of a consolidated ILO Maritime Labour Convention following global trade union campaign against flag of convenience shipping and negotiations between the ITF and ship-owners). The three industrial ITSs were inspired by the American example of co-ordinated bargaining or coalition bargaining, which had been developed by unions in the Congress of Industrial Organizations (CIO), particularly the United Auto Workers' Union under the leadership of its president Walter Reuther. After the merger of the American Federation of Labor (AFL) and the Congress of Industrial Organizations (CIO) in 1955, the Industrial Union Department of the AFL-CIO continued this strategy.

The basic idea was simple: to prevent the existing fragmentation of the movement to become a factor of division and weakness when bargaining with a multi-plant corporation:

"In the United States, trade union jurisdictional lines in certain industries are extremely blurred [...] This results in several unions having bargaining rights for different plants of the company. Each is therefore confronted by the total combined strength of the company although it may be bargaining with a local plant official [...] To offset this very great disadvantage in power at the bargaining table, the Industrial Union Department of the AFL-CIO (IUD) has developed a co-ordinated bargaining program. Under this plan all unions with collective bargaining rights within a plant of a given company work out their demands and bargaining strategy jointly. Thus a company would have a single set of demands and a single strategy to contend with, backed by a number of different unions in a common front. Although still in its initial stages, this plan has already achieved some notable successes, particularly with General Electric, Westinghouse and other companies." (Levinson 1972: 103-104).

The same factors which led North American unions to adopt the coalition bargaining strategy would apply even more at international level, where by definition, in almost all cases, different national unions would hold bargaining rights in different production sites of the same company.[4] Consequently, the necessity of working out "their demands and bargaining strategy jointly" would be even more compelling in terms of the objective of building an international countervailing union force to counter the "combined strength of the company" and it would make the coalition bargaining strategy even more relevant.

However, in addition to working towards creating an international collective bargaining situation where union and management power would be more evenly balanced, in seeking to co-ordinate union activities at TNC level the ITSs also responded to the perceived need of their member unions for mutual support in conflict situations, whether within a formal bargaining framework or not.

In the event, the ICF itself successfully practiced this strategy in many instances, starting in the middle 1960s (Levinson, 1972: 112-17). The ICF action against the Saint-Gobain glass company in 1969 attracted international attention. It was simultaneously conducted in four countries including a twenty-six day strike in the United States, and it was the first major international trade union action based on the principle of coalition bargaining in the post-war period.

The IMF based its response to transnational corporations on similar principles, starting in the automobile industry. The first IMF auto workers' conference focusing on TNCs was held in Paris in 1959. Successive conferences in the 1960s progressively built up a strategy of World Auto Company Councils for the nine world corporations, accounting at the time for 80 percent of the Western world's production. The first three World Auto Councils (Ford, General Motors and Chrysler) were set up in June 1966, the fourth (Volkswagen-Mercedes Benz) was established in November 1966, and the

---

[4]  The exceptions are the labour movement in the United States and Canada, and in the United Kingdom and Ireland, where some unions hold membership and collective bargaining rights in both countries.

fifth (Fiat-Citroën) in November 1968.

Through these world councils, the IMF organised specific actions, such as the participation of an experienced negotiator from the union in the country of the parent company in local negotiations at a subsidiary location. They also organised communication of economic and collective bargaining information between unions operating in the same company and intervention by unions who had the support of the parent company in strikes at subsidiary plants.

A conference of the IMF World Auto Company Councils, held in London in March 1971, defined specific demands for each of the councils and adopted a declaration which stated in part:

"On the collective bargaining front it is imperative that the centralized control of the international corporations be countered by the closest possible co-ordination of unions in all nations representing the workers of each such corporation [...] Help must be given, in every country where it is needed, to organize the still unorganised workers of such corporations. Collective bargaining rights, including the right to strike, must be won in every country where they are now denied. National affiliates of the IMF must be provided with all the help they require to strengthen their organizations and to train their members and leaders to bargain more effectively with their employers.

"We call for meetings of representatives of each of the IMF World Auto Company Councils with the top policy-makers of these respective international corporations. Among the priority items to be discussed at such meetings are information concerning investment and production plans and job security.

"Common expiration dates should be established for collective bargaining contracts in all nations, corporation by corporation, so that the full weight of the totality of the firm's organized workers can be brought to bear upon each corporation, under conditions in which all unions involved are free of contractual restrictions."

In 1967, the IMF had established a Commission for Multinational Corporations to co-ordinate its general policy in this area. The action program was extended beyond the auto industry to the machine and electrical engineering industries, with international meetings of unions in General Electric, International Harvester, Philips and Honeywell, among others.

Also in 1967, the IMF established a European Committee of Metal Trade Unions, as a co-ordinating body of the IMF in what was then the European Economic Community. This Committee worked to establish bargaining rights with several transnational corporations, but focused particular attention on Philips, the Dutch electronics industry corporation.

The unions' short-term objective was an agreement securing parity of treatment of workers employed by Philips in different countries, as well as the protection of workers affected by technological change. A longer term goal was an international collective bargaining agreement covering working conditions (including wages and hours) and union rights and representation in the plants.

From 1967 to 1970, three meetings were held between representatives of the European Committee and Philips management officials. In the first meeting (September 1967), the discussions centred on the effect on employment and wage rates of changes in production processes resulting from technological innovation and from international production transfers. An agreement was reached to hold further discussions at a later date.

At the second meeting (June 1969) management agreed that unions would be given previous notice of important transfers of production from one country to another and of any changes in the limits set on production within individual plants. Management also agreed to consider union proposals on readjustment and vocational training measures for workers affected by technological change.

The third meeting (September 1970) dealt primarily with work organisation and future developments of the company's economic activities. Philips representatives agreed to consider the European Committee's demands for a permanent labour-management liaison committee, a comprehensive labour policy and of discussions at international level in advance of proposed layoffs and international transfer of employees. They also agreed that if production transfers were undertaken, the "redundant" workers would be guaranteed full wages and social security contributions for at least six months and that special protection would be extended to worker over fifty years old.

After this meeting the Philips management apparently decided against continuing to engage with the unions in a discussion of their labour relations at international level. A fourth meeting, planned for 1971, was to discuss the possibility of establishing a permanent joint advisory committee which would examine employment, social policy and industrial relations problems within the Philips group, but "owing to the company's increasing hesitancy" this was indefinitely postponed (Levinson, 1972: 132).

A "Philips European Forum" was formed in 1996 as a European Works Council (EWC) under Article 13 of the EU directive. Like other EWCs, its mandate is limited to "information and consultation". In February 2001, the IMF held its first Philips World Conference, with about 60 participants from 18 countries, which established a Steering Committee and a Task Force to build an effective information network. The conference also considered that the establishment of a World Works Council, "to complement the existing European Works Council (European Philips Forum – EPF)" was necessary, because "Philips gears its decision-making to the global level. The emerging trend whereby production plants are moved to low-wage countries requires a global organization of trade unions and company employee representatives." (IMF, 2001). There is no IFA covering Philips.

The International Union of Food and Allied Workers'

Associations (IUF) had taken an active interest in international co-ordination of trade union bargaining since 1958, when it undertook a comparative survey of wages and working conditions in British-American Tobacco (BAT). The issue was also on the agenda of sectoral conferences in 1961, for the meat and tobacco companies.

BAT was in fact the first company where the IUF organised solidarity action between member unions in different countries representing workers in the same TNC.

The action was in defence of the Pak Cigarette Labour Union (PCLU), which represented workers at the Pakistan subsidiary of BAT. The PCLU was formed in 1961 but was denied recognition. Instead, the union faced lockouts, arrests, dismissals and fines. In February 1963 the union went on strike during which its general secretary was jailed for four months and twelve union members were dismissed. The IUF organized financial support for the dismissed workers and called on its members at BAT to raise the issue with their local management. In December, the general secretary of the British Tobacco Workers' Union, Percy Belcher, travelled to Karachi officially representing the IUF and helped bring about negotiations between the union and the company. These negotiations resulted in the reinstatement of the dismissed workers and of the union's general secretary, as well as in the first ever collective bargaining agreement reached between any union and employer in Karachi.

In May 1964, the issue of TNCs was on the agenda of the 14th Congress of the IUF in Stockholm, which adopted the following Resolution on International Collective Bargaining:

"The Fourteenth Statutory Congress of the International Union of Food and Allied Workers' Associations, meeting in Stockholm from May 27 to 30, 1964:

CONSIDERING the dominant position of international companies in all aspects of economic and social life;

CONSIDERING the growing ability of such companies to

mobilize their full international potential in collective bargaining with single national unions;

CONSIDERING the threat arising to national trade union organizations from inadequate communication and coordination in their dealings with international companies;

DIRECTS the Executive Committee to take all appropriate measures to secure the recognition of the IUF as an international negotiating body and to perfect an appropriate procedure for conducting international negotiations in the food and allied industries under IUF sponsorship."

Following the congress, the IUF approached BAT with the proposal to establish a permanent joint negotiating body but did not meet with a positive response. However, the IUF continued to organise international coordination at TNC level, typically in the context of a conflict situation.

One such action was in support of a strike by the US Bakery and Confectionary Workers' Union in October 1969 against the National Biscuit Co. (Nabisco), involving unions from ten countries where Nabisco had subsidiaries. The strike was successfully ended two weeks after the initial call for international solidarity.

The 16th IUF Congress held in Zurich in July 1970 again noted the concentration of power taking place at international company level and stressed the need to strengthen union co-operation at that level. It called for regular meetings of unions representing workers in the major TNCs as well as for ad hoc meetings in emergencies and for exchanges of union delegations to observe each others' negotiations within the same TNC.

In May 1972, in Geneva, the IUF held its first World Conference of Nestlé Workers, which established a Nestlé Permanent Council. The tasks of the Council were to: (a) contact the management of Nestlé Alimentana SA on international questions or at the request of affiliates; (b) call future Nestlé conferences; and (c) follow up on the decisions of the Conference.

The Conference adopted a statement which formulated demands on job security and wages policy, but also on the respect of union rights and on union participation in management policy decisions.

The statement also included a political demand: it invited Nestlé to "contribute to the development of underdeveloped countries" in particular by the following measures:

1. ensure the equitable distribution of its subsidiaries' revenues, whether in the form of wages or taxes;
2. bring the prices of Nestlé products to a level where all consumers will be able to purchase them;
3. bring its influence to bear to guarantee fair prices for the primary commodities which it processes;
4. follow a policy of processing primary commodities where these originate, without thereby creating employment problems in its subsidiaries located in industrialized countries.

Finally, the participating unions agreed to "increase, through the IUF secretariat, the exchange of information and experiences concerning their relations with Nestlé, thereby laying the groundwork for more effective co-operation at the level of the company" and to "mutually support their demands and their struggles."

It was also decided that the IUF secretariat should publish a Nestlé bulletin and such a bulletin did appear on an approximately monthly basis until most IUF periodical publications were replaced by a web site in the late 1990s.

In June 1972, a delegation of the IUF Permanent Council met with Nestlé management at the company headquarters in Vevey to discuss the conclusions of the World Conference, after having agreed that these talks could not become a substitute for management/labour relations at the national level.

The management representatives assured the IUF delegation that the company considered good relations with the unions of utmost importance and in particular attached importance to the respect of trade union rights by its associated companies and subsidiaries, that Nestlé intended to make the safeguarding of jobs a priority, and it would seek an understanding with workers' representatives on the material and social impacts of lay-offs resulting from rationalisation measures.

The management representatives also said that the company would issue appropriate recommendations to companies manufacturing or distributing Nestlé products whenever such companies would not observe the parent's firm policy on these two issues.

Concerning Nestlé's role in the "underdeveloped countries", the company stated its desire to contribute to the establishment of equitable prices for primary commodities, particularly for coffee and cocoa, at a level which would permit the development and consumption in producing countries.

Both parties agreed that further meetings between representatives of the IUF Permanent Council and the Nestlé management should take place at the request of either of them.

However, relations soured in 1973 when Nestlé management refused to discuss the anti-union policies of Stouffer Foods, a recent acquisition in the US, and when it refused to intervene in a conflict at the Chiclayo plant of Perulac, its subsidiary in Peru.

The dispute in Chiclayo occurred when the workers who had struck in sympathy with a walk-out at another Nestlé plant in Lima (Maggi) returned to work on April 10 to find that non-union workers were the only ones being paid for strike days. This resulted in another strike which lasted six weeks, with the workers occupying the plant. In a solidarity action organized by the IUF, unions representing Nestlé workers in fifteen countries supported the strike. A decisive intervention by the

New Zealand Dairy Workers' Union, which threatened to close down the Nestlé powdered milk plant which supplied all Nestlé operations on the South American Pacific coast, tilted the balance.

The final settlement on May 23 met all the demands of the Perulac Workers' Union: a lump sum to be paid to the union to allow it to compensate its members for loss of earnings during the strike, a 20 percent wage increase, paid holidays up from 15 to 20 per years, dropping all charges against union members and a commitment by management to cease discrimination against them, and retroactive recognition of the legality of the strike by the Peruvian government (which had it declared illegal on May 2).

However, the IUF regional secretary for Latin America, who had visited the union during the strike was arrested on May 5 and expelled from the country on May 9. In July, he returned to Peru and was only subjected to a short police interrogation, but almost a year later, the regional secretary and the general secretary of the IUF again visited Peru, having been invited by the Perulac union to participate in the inauguration of its new premises. On March 24, 1974, they were arrested in Chiclayo by security police led by an official who held a paper with Nestlé letterhead in his hand, transferred to Lima and expelled on March 26.

After that, relations between the IUF and Nestlé became decidedly frosty for several years. A thaw set in 1989 when the then IUF president Günter Döding, also president of the German Food and Allied Workers' Union NGG, met with Helmut Maucher, Nestlé CEO whom he had known as director of Nestlé Germany, and over dinner decided that Nestlé could recognise the IUF as its international social counterpart.

This led to a resumption of annual meetings between a reconstituted IUF Nestlé Council and Nestlé management, but only at European level. These meetings were eventually formalised in 1996 as an EWC (the "Nestlé European Council for Information and Consultation – NECIC). Nestlé has, however, so far refused to sign an IFA with the IUF.

Except for two informal agreements on training and equal opportunities, such agreements as exist are only procedural (frequency of meetings, composition of the delegations, countries to be included). Even on procedure, contentious issues arose: the IUF insisted that the workers' side should only include union members (officials and lay members from the production sites), Nestlé wanted to include an "independent" union in Spain the IUF did not recognise. The IUF also wanted the meetings to cover all of geographical Europe, whereas Nestlé wanted only EU countries included. The trade union issue was eventually resolved on IUF terms but the geographical issue only partially resolved.

As a parallel activity, the IUF also convened regional Nestlé meetings: most recently, for Asia and the Pacific in Manila (1999) and Jakarta (2002), for Eastern Europe in Lviv (2003) and for Africa in Cape Town (2003). The seventh Nestlé conference for Latin America took place in Buenos Aires in 2003. The director of corporate human relations attended some of these recent regional meetings. Since 2004, the IUF has established a network of regional Nestlé co-ordinators based in Bangkok, Johannesburg, Montevideo and Moscow.

In 1998, Nestlé adopted "Corporate Business Principles" which affirm, among other things, the "respect of the right of employees to join legally recognized labour unions". However, the establishment of formal mechanisms of communication between the IUF and Nestlé did not reduce the number of conflicts. In all parts of the world, including Europe, unions have been in conflict with local Nestlé managements in recent years over a wide variety of issues, including union rights issues.

2. Conclusions from Experience

The main conclusion that can be drawn from the experience of the ICF, IMF and IUF in the 1960s and 1970s is that their work in co-ordinating international union activities at TNC level was in fact a basic trade union response to a new development affecting the structure of their employer counterparts: the concentration of capital and the shift of the place where corporate power was exercised and decisions made from the national to the international level.

This response was intended to be a strategy of trade union struggle and it was motivated by the need to make this struggle more effective under the new conditions, which affected industrial relations world wide. International co-ordination was viewed as a tool through which unions could build up a countervailing power comparable to that of the TNCs they were facing and level the proverbial playing field.

From that perspective, international framework agreements, although a logical outcome of international negotiations, were not the principal objective. The principal objective was rather to build union strength at TNC level to achieve any number of basic trade union aims, such as successfully conducting solidarity actions. This is something the ITSs would have had to do in any event, and it is still part of their basic functions, whatever institutional form it may take.

No IFAs existed in the 1960s and 1970s and those few companies (for example, BAT, Philips, Nestlé) which had agreed to meet with ITS delegations to discuss industrial relations problems affecting their entire operations quickly drew back when they realised that the ITSs involved expected some form of binding commitment and serious changes in their corporate practices. Although disappointing, this did not stop the ITSs from further building union coalitions and organizing at TNC level.

The situation may best be understood by comparing the international with the national or even local level. Trade unions exist to defend the interests of their members in a variety of ways over a wide range of issues; they do not exist exclusively for the purpose of concluding collective bargaining agreements (CBAs), although this is part of their normal activities. But when it comes to bargaining, because they must defend their members' interests against opposing interests, trade unions must always be prepared for conflict and organise for conflict, even as they negotiate. A collective bargaining agreement is, in an institutionalised form, the temporary outcome of a conflict situation, whether latent or open, soft or hard. It reflects, in an institutionalised form, the balance of power, at any given time, between the contracting parties. This is why there are strong and weak agreements.

International collective bargaining is only different insofar as there is no international legal framework, such as exists in most countries at national level, to provide a guaranteed legal status to any labour/management agreement reached at international level. Since such agreements are therefore entirely voluntary, they depend even more on the balance of power between the contracting parties at the time they are concluded. This is why there are strong and weak IFAs, and this is also the reason why there are so few of them.

3. The First International Framework Agreement

The first international framework agreement was signed by the IUF and the French transnational food company BSN, (re-named Danone in 1994), on August 23, 1988. It is entitled "Common Viewpoint IUF/BSN" and states that the parties agree to promote co-ordinated initiatives, throughout the BSN group, on four issues:

> 1. " A policy for training for skills in order to anticipate the consequences of the introduction of new technologies or industrial restructuring. To achieve this objective, the social partners will seek to integrate this aspect into present and future plans for training;
>
> 2. A policy aiming to achieve the same level and the same quality of information, both in the economic and the social fields, in all locations of BSN subsidiaries. To achieve this objective, the social partners concerned will seek, both through national legislation as well as collective agreement, to reduce the differences observed in

terms of the information between one country and another or between one location and another;

3. A development of conditions to assure real equality between men and women at work. Developing jobs and work processes have led to distortions between the situation of men and women; the social partners will therefore evaluate, location by location, the nature of the different initiatives to be adopted to improve the situation;

4. The implementation of trade union rights as defined in ILO conventions Nos. 87, 98 and 135. The social partners concerned will identify where progress can be made in improving trade union rights and access to trade union education."

The adoption of the "Common Viewpoint" was preceded by a number of meetings, since 1984, between an IUF delegation, normally composed of the IUF general secretary, a member of the IUF staff responsible for coordinating BSN activities and representatives of the French IUF affiliates (the CFDT and Force Ouvrière food workers' unions), with Danone management, normally composed of Antoine Riboud, CEO, the director of human resources and a member of his staff.

In 1986, a first meeting between the management and delegates from IUF affiliates in Belgium, France, Germany and Italy with membership in BSN was organized by the IUF in Geneva. This meeting was the first of annual meetings which have regularly taken place since, with growing participation, to include all of geographical Europe and representation from the rest of the world. On the management side, central management (the CEO, HR director and staff), as well as all national directors in Europe, would participate. The joint meeting would last one day; the workers' group meets the day before to prepare and the day after for evaluation and to discuss the follow-up. The company bears the expenses of all meetings. The IUF appointed a coordinating union (the CFDT Food Workers' Union) for the Workers' Group and its national officer responsible for Danone would chair the joint meetings.

It was agreed that all IUF/Danone agreements would cover the entire operations of the company in all parts of the world. Neither the agreements, nor the joint meetings, nor their agenda, were therefore "European" in nature, but worldwide in scope. Unions representing Danone workers outside of Europe (Africa, Asia/Pacific, Latin America and, for some years, North America) would be represented at the joint meetings by the IUF regional secretaries for these regions. In some meetings, unions from outside Europe also participated.

Follow-up agreements to the "Common Viewpoint" were concluded in 1989 (on economic and social information for staff and their representatives, and on equality at work for men and women), in 1992 (on skills training), and in 1994 (on trade union rights). In 1997, a further agreement was signed on measures to be taken in the event of changes in business activities affecting employment or working conditions. This agreement, the first of its kind at international level, served as a basis for a specific agreement on social standards applicable to all plants affected by the industrial restructuring plan of 2001 for biscuit operations in Europe.

Following the adoption by the EU of its European Works Council directive in 1994, an agreement establishing a Danone information and consultation committee was signed in 1996. The IUF commented as follows:

"This committee, although functioning within the framework or European legislation, continues the work carried out by the IUF since 1984 on behalf of its affiliates and also continues the positive features characteristic of Danone-IUF relations since 1984:

1. trade union recognition
2. at enterprise level: workers' representatives are exclusively trade union delegates;
3. at national level: full-time national officers are included in the trade union delegation;
4. at international level: the secretariats of the IUF and

of the ECF-IUF are members of the new structure and the other regional secretaries of the IUF represent Danone workers outside Europe. Danone accepts that in a transnational company with a global spread of activities, the international trade union movement represents the global counterpart.
5. shared responsibilities: the themes for discussion are decided jointly, and the meetings are chaired by the IUF international co-ordinator Pierre Laurent.
6. Finally, the committee does not confine itself in an information and consultation role, as the EU legislation suggests, but continues the momentum of IUF-Danone relations by being a forum for negotiations on the crucial issues of concern to all Danone workers." (IUF, 1997)

The Danone agreement, including its subsidiary agreements, remains the most far-reaching IFA to this day, and has set the pattern for further IUF agreements with TNCs (Accor, Chiquita, Fonterra) and others (Tørres and Gunnes, 2003: 9).

There has been some speculation as to why Danone was the first company to agree to an IFA of this nature. The personal views of Antoine Riboud, its founder and CEO until 1996 when he was succeeded by his son Franck, were undoubtedly an important factor. Antoine Riboud, who died in 2002, was a progressive Catholic with links to the Socialist Party and viewed trade unions as legitimate counterparts at all levels. As he declared in a meeting with an IUF delegation, he wanted strong unions in his company because he could not imagine leading his company against its employees and without respecting their rights. There is no doubt that this was his sincere belief. Riboud was a man of honour.

The recent experiences of the IUF at that time, however, also played a role. It became apparent to all TNCs in the IUF's scope that it was becoming a serious counterpart, including Danone. As we have seen, the IUF had sustained a bruising conflict with Nestlé in 1973, although in the end it had been resolved on union terms. In 1980, the IUF conducted a major conflict with the Coca-Cola Company, in order to secure the survival of a union (and indeed the physical survival of its officers and activists) at a bottling subsidiary in Guatemala. An international campaign involving solidarity strikes at Coke plants in several countries, demonstrations, and negative publicity, with wide-spread support from NGOs and political groups, obliged the Coca-Cola company to buy the subsidiary plant, recognise the enterprise union and intervene such that the then government ceased is anti-union terror campaign, at least in that plant.

This, however, was not the end of the story. Four years later, the directors Coca-Cola had put in charge of the plant absconded with the cash and declared the plant bankrupt. The workers, who had become aware that this might happen, occupied the plant on February 18, 1984. The IUF again made representations to the Coca Cola Company, and the company initially refused to take responsibility, as in 1980.

The assumption by the company that the IUF would not be able to replicate its campaign of 1980 proved unfounded. In fact, the 1984 campaign was even stronger than the first one. It involved: unions which had previously stood aside (notably in the US and in Canada); a union television crew from New York who visited the occupied plant to document the occupation;[5] a professional accountant from the Interfaith Council for Corporate Responsibility in the US who discovered how the directors had cooked the books which they had left behind in their precipitated departure; more solidarity strikes; waiters in the Philippines and supermarket cashiers in Sweden refusing to serve or sell Coke, and more. The damage to the company image was enormous.

After three months, the company wanted to settle. On May 27 company representatives (the corporate HR director and regional directors) met with an IUF delegation (the general secretary, the North American regional secretary, the vice president of the principal North American affiliate and two

---

[5] The film is called "The Real Thing". It was shown at hundreds of solidarity meetings in many countries and, reportedly, is being shown in Coca-Cola management training courses to illustrate why bad management practices should be avoided.

officers of the Guatemalan union) in Costa Rica. After two days of tense negotiations the company agreed to sell the plant to a reputable buyer, guaranteed that the new owners would recognise the union and the existing CBA, agreed to employ and pay the workers occupying the plant until it reopened, and agreed that the plant would reopen with all its workers and that no-one would be laid off. On that basis, the IUF called off its boycott.

The implementation of the agreement took several more months. Coca-Cola was looking for a buyer, the workers were still occupying the plant and the IUF was standing by to resume the international solidarity action. Finally, on November 9, the company announced that they had found a buyer: a consortium led by Carlos Porras Gonzáles, a reputable economist who had run businesses in El Salvador. New negotiations then had to be conducted with the new owners, which were concluded on February 1, 1985, just over two weeks short of the anniversary of the start of the occupation, and the plant re-opened on March 1. The final settlement corresponded to the agreement reached with Coca-Cola on May 27, 1984, although the plant reopened with only 265 of the 350 workers who had been occupying it (the others were re-hired in the following months). Since then, the Guatemalan union has become the core of a national food workers' federation and the CBA has been regularly re-negotiated, although the plant now has other owners.

The IUF has had many meetings with Coca-Cola top management since to discuss problems arising in the Coca-Cola system, and also reached agreements on specific issues, but without a formal framework.

When the IUF met with the Coca-Cola management representatives on May 25-27, 1984, at a time when the company was obviously ready to make extensive concessions to put an end to the conflict, the question arose whether the IUF delegation should demand the establishment of a general IFA as part of the settlement. The IUF general secretary decided against it because, with the lives of the workers in the plant still under threat (the Guatemalan army had surrounded the plant since the beginning of the occupation and was still there), it was his opinion that the IUF should not risk delaying the settlement by introducing extraneous issues. The overriding priority had to be to protect the Guatemalan affiliate and its members. The IFA could wait.

The Nestlé conflict in 1973 and especially the conflicts with Coca-Cola in 1980 and 1984/5 had received extensive press coverage. The IUF had demonstrated its capacity of creating serious inconveniences to even large and powerful TNCs and it may be safely assumed that by 1984 at the latest the IUF had caught the attention of all leading TNCs in its field of activity.

The Danone agreement was not reached in the context of any conflict with Danone and all discussions and negotiations were conducted in a friendly atmosphere of mutual respect and trust. It would be wrong to suggest that Danone had become interested in concluding an IFA with the IUF because it feared a conflict with the IUF: no serious conflict was on the horizon and, given the Danone corporate philosophy, it was highly unlikely to arise. It can, however, be said that Danone had perceived the IUF to be a serious international counterpart and had come to the conclusion that signing an agreement with the IUF was not only a moral and political imperative but also a smart business move.

4. IFAs and Codes of Conduct

The distinction between Codes of Conduct and IFAs is sometimes ignored or blurred. For example, a list of IFAs established by the Friedrich-Ebert-Stiftung, in 2002, is called: "List of Codes of Conduct/Framework Agreements", as if they were interchangeable. A footnote says: "Some GUFs call the agreements 'Framework Agreements', not Code of Conduct, because there had been only a few principles fixed in the first agreement which often have been extended by additional agreements. For instance in the case of Danone the first agreement of 1988 has meanwhile been developed by six other agreements."

This is, of course, not true. Neither the IUF nor anyone else ever called the Danone agreement a Code of Conduct, nor did anyone ever suggest that a Code was in any sense stronger than a Framework Agreement.

A similar list, by SASK, the Finnish trade union development agency, in 2005, is also headed "Codes of Conduct/Framework Agreements", with a similar footnote.

A positive article about IFAs in the IMF journal Metal World (Nilsson, 2004) introduces the subject by referring to IFAs "or Codes of Conduct, as they were formerly called" and goes on to say that IFAs were called Codes of Conduct "before that expression was compromised." The article later correctly points out some of the fundamental differences between Codes and IFAs, but the fact is that IFAs were never called Codes and that the concept of Codes was compromised from the beginning as a management-driven public relations exercise.

The ICFTU and some GUFs have developed "model codes of conduct" as potential stepping stones to IFAs or for lack of a better alternative. But some analysts have pointed out with reason, that:

"With this voluntary initiative by management to implement social policy rules as business principles, weak unions and workers' representatives will tend to have little say in taking this further to a framework agreement that commits both management and unions. There is reason to consider this a barrier to adopting global agreements that commit both management and unions, and thus a hinder for trade union recognition." (Tørres and Gunnes, 2003: 45).

On the subject, these authors also note:

"Codes of conduct covering issues of social responsibility are becoming more frequent. However, the extent to which this is facilitating improved communications and dialogue between employees and management is more doubtful. [...] There is [...] a danger that codes are seen as something more than they really are, and used to deflect criticism and reduce the demand for negotiations or external regulation. [...] In some cases, codes have led to a worsening of the situation for those whom they purport to benefit." (Tørres and Gunnes, 2003: 443).

Most trade unionists, analysts and researchers make a clear distinction between IFAs and Codes of Conduct.

The ICFTU notes that "the content of a framework agreement is often similar to the language found in some of the codes of conduct that companies have adopted for their suppliers and which cover some, or all, of the fundamental rights at work. However, that does not mean that a framework agreement is the same thing as a code of conduct. It is not.

"There is a fundamental difference between a code of labour practice, which is a unilateral management pledge, mainly made to address public concerns, and a framework agreement, which is recognition that the company will engage the relevant international trade union organization and discuss issues of fundamental concerns to both parties." (ICFTU, 2004)

Others have been even more explicit. Riisgaard notes that code of conduct responses are frequently an example

"where businesses [...] have embraced codes of conduct as protection against public opinion and as a means to sidestep demands for unionisation. The RUGMARK certification system for example guarantees that no child workers have been used in the production of the labelled blankets, but does nothing to secure the rights of the remaining workforce [...] A 1998 ILO investigation of 215 codes found that only around 15 percent refer to freedom of association or the right to collective bargaining, and likewise a 1999 OECD investigation shows that only around 20 percent of the 182 investigated codes refer explicitly to the ILO conventions on freedom of association and the right to collective bargaining [...] As seen in the examples above, one can seriously question whether most voluntary initiatives reflect NGO or business interests rather than workers' interests. [...] As a result, it is important to differentiate between voluntary initiatives that are negotiated with labour and initiatives that are not." (Riisgaard, 2003: 2)

This author has pointed out elsewhere that in many cases, far from promoting labour rights, one of the main purposes of Codes of Conduct has actually been union avoidance:

"In 1990, 85 percent of the top 100 US corporations were found to have a code; in the UK, this figure was 42 percent, in the Netherlands 22 percent.[6] However, most codes of conduct that address social issues are limited in their coverage and do not address basic labour rights [...]

This comes as no surprise since, in some cases, companies adopted codes as part of a union-avoidance strategy by pre-emption, preferring to unilaterally offer a paternalistic package than have a recognized negotiating body to deal with. As the ICFTU has pointed out, 'many of the US-based companies that were the first to adopt codes were, in both principle and practice, opposed to trade unions'.[7] For example, the Caterpillar code states that the company seeks to 'operate the business in such a way that employees don't feel a need for representation by unions or other third parties' and the Sara Lee Knit Products code states that the company 'believes in a union-free environment except where law and cultures require (SKP) to do otherwise.' The DuPont code reads: 'employees shall be encouraged by lawful expression of management opinion to continue an existing no-union status, but where employees have chosen to be represented by a union, management shall deal with the union in good faith.'[8]

A second problem has been monitoring of compliance. Most codes do not provide for a credible independent monitoring procedure, or for strong enforcement and complaints mechanisms. Unions have argued that the existence of

---

[6] Kaptein, S. P. and Klamer, H. K. (1991). *Ethische Bedrijfscodes in Nederlandse Bedrijven, Nederlands Christelijk Werkgeversbond*, The Hague, quoted in van Liemt G. (1999), "Codes of Conduct and International Subcontracting: A "Private" Road towards Ensuring Minimum Labour Standards in Export Industries, paper presented at the conference on Multinational Enterprises and the Social Challenges of the 21st Century", Leuven, May 3-4.

[7] ICFTU (1997) *Labor and Business in the Global Market (ICFTU-ITS Recommendations and Guidelines Concerning Company and Industry Codes of Labour Practice, Their Implementation and Monitoring*, Brussels: ICFTU.

independent trade unions throughout the operations of transnational corporations are the most efficient monitoring system.[9] Many companies have gone to great length – and expense – to resort to other monitoring systems (creating their own, contracting out to commercial monitoring enterprises or to compliant NGOs) with dubious results." (Gallin, 2000)

After a detailed analysis of the differences between IFAs and Corporate Social Responsibility (CSR) initiatives, most commonly expressed in the form of Codes of Conduct, Gibb observed:

"When considering the argument that IFAs are no different than other CSR initiatives, or that IFAs are one form of CSR, it must be recognized that if the contribution of IFAs was limited to improving the public image or providing a marketing boost to companies, there would be as many IFAs signed as there are

---

[8] Caterpillar: Code of Worldwide Business Conduct; Sara Lee Knit Products: International Operating Principles; DuPont: Labour Relations Policies and Principles; quoted in ILO (1998). "Overview of global developments and Office activities concerning codes of conduct, social labeling and other private sector initiatives addressing labour issues", GB.273/WP/SDL/1 (Add. 1), November, Annex: endnotes 69 and 70).

[9] "The experience is that independent and secure trade unions are the most effective means of ending or of preventing the exploitation and abuse of workers. Codes of conduct are not as efficient as what workers can do for themselves when they are allowed to join free trade unions and to bargain collectively with their employer in the knowledge that their rights are secure and protected. The objectives of codes are best achieved when governments respect the trade union rights of workers. Self-promulgated codes that do not mention trade union rights give the impression that it is possible to protect workers' interests without respecting their right to organize into independent trade unions. This impression is reinforced where codes merely pledge the company to respect national laws and practice." (ICFTU, op cit, p2)

[...] "Independent monitoring by itself ... is not sufficient to ensure respect for minimal worker rights and occupational and environmental health and safety standards. No independent monitor can substitute for the independent organization of workers through their trade unions, which must be represented on the monitoring bodies for these to meaningfully do their job." (Ron Oswald, IUF General Secretary, in a letter to the International Herald Tribune, June 9, 1998)

CSR initiatives. This is not the case." (Gibb, 2005)

In a document for the IUF Executive Committee meeting in 2006, the IUF secretariat makes the same point:

"Whilst some may say that IFAs are little more than agreed 'codes of conduct' they are clearly significantly better. Unlike codes their very existence as signed agreements means they are explicitly built on union recognition at international level and therefore do not pose the danger of being used as an alternative to unions in the same way that many codes and CSR initiatives do (even those where unions somehow 'sign on')." (IUF, 2006)

Although the one obvious difference between Codes and IFAs is that most Codes are unilateral company statements whereas IFAs are negotiated labour/management agreements, it is not the only difference and actually not always the case: there are some negotiated Codes. There may be a deeper underlying issue, which has to do with the view unions take of the purpose of such agreements. If IFAs are primarily meant to address company behaviour, they may indeed appear to be no more than a stronger kind of Code: stronger, because the outcome of a negotiation, but not basically different in purpose. If, on the other hand, IFAs are seen and used as organizing tools, the contrast with Codes becomes much clearer. (Egels-Zandén and Hyllman, 2007)

5. IFAs and European Works Councils

As a rule, European Works Councils (EWCs) do not negotiate IFAs and are not signatories to IFAs.

Carley (2001) observes that:

"In formal terms, the prospects of EWCs developing a negotiating role are not very bright. The (EU) Directive provides for no such role for them, stating that their purpose is to improve information and consultation and laying down only an informative/consultative role for statutory EWCs based on its subsidiary requirements."

The European Trade Union Confederation (ETUC), whilst it supports the development of a European framework for transnational collective bargaining, which should complement the existing framework for European "social dialogue"[10], stresses that EWCs do not have a mandate for negotiations nor the right to sign transnational agreements:

"The power to do this must remain solely and strictly a trade union right, owing to their representativeness long recognized by the Commission, which also specified as much in a text. Transnational agreements as such must be left up to collectively responsible and thus players with a mandate to represent their members. [...] EWCs, which we stress were only given powers of information and consultation, are not appropriate bodies for negotiations given the current state of legislation." (ETUC, 2005)

Therefore, unsurprisingly: "The first and arguably the clearest conclusion is that from the available evidence, the practice of negotiating joint texts in EWCs is extremely rare. The research has found only 22 examples in nine multinationals. Given that there are probably 700 EWCs in existence, this represents only a tiny proportion of the total (little over 1 percent)." (Carley, 2001: 47)

The existence of joint texts in EWCs is even more rare than

---

[10] A note on terminology is in order. About twenty years ago, a new vocabulary was introduced in the public discourse on industrial relations, typically involving concepts like "social partners" and "social partnership", or "social dialogue". This vocabulary seems to have originated with the EU Treaty of Rome (1984), but has since, unfortunately, been adopted by the ILO and by most international trade union organisations. In fact, it is not designed to reflect reality but to hide it. "Partnership", by any definition, assumes shared interests. In recent years, it has become increasingly obvious that whatever shared interests may have existed or still exist between workers and employers, they are overridden by conflicts of opposing interests in most areas of industrial relations. Today, trade unions do not have "social partners" in any real sense: the accurate term would be: "social counterparts". As for "social dialogue", it is a particularly vague and meaningless term, obviously designed to dilute the reality of labour/management relations, perhaps to sidestep terms like "negotiation". Since vocabulary is never innocent, it is worth reflecting on what interest is served by introducing this kind of language.

Carley suggests, since he included six Danone agreements in that number, although, as we have seen, these were neither negotiated nor signed by an EWC but in an entirely different context and, indeed, even before the existence of the EU directive.

This does not stop Carley from claiming that the joint IUF/Danone committee which met annually from 1987 onward was "one of the first EWCs": "BSN/Danone thus established an EWC long before all but one or two other firms had done so – and long before the EWC directive was proposed – and this body (and IUF) was given a negotiating role almost a decade before any other EWC." (Carley, 2001: 34).

In fact, the IUF/Danone committee was not an EWC at all, since neither the IUF nor the company could possibly foreseen the future creation of a body that did not exist at that time. Furthermore, although-as Carley rightly points out- the joint IUF/Danone committee was subsequently "formalized" by an Article 13 agreement in March 1996, this joint committee has none of the typical limitations of the EWCs (in the sense that it is vested with negotiating powers, and is worldwide in scope). This is so precisely because it did not originate as an EWC and therefore does not conform to the standard EWC pattern.

One wonders which of the remaining sixteen "joint texts" have been similarly retroactively annexed to an agenda of bolstering an assumed EWC negotiating role. The ENI agreement (2002), for one, is also one signed by the GUF and not by the EWC.

From the point of view of an international labour strategy, three issues need to be addressed and solved in a way consistent with trade union interests, namely, the negotiation issue; the trade union issue; and the geographical issue (Gallin, 2003).

First, some EWC agreements (EFAs) explicitly rule out any negotiating role, others make provisions for certain types of negotiations. The important point here is that the content of what happens in an EWC depends on a mutual agreement of the social counterparts and not necessarily by what the Directive says. Unions should therefore push for what is consistent with their objectives and their interests, rather than voluntarily conforming to rules invented by others that work to their disadvantage.

Second, the trade union issue arises because the EWC directive is a much-diluted version of the original draft of 1980, which would have given trade unions statutory representation rights. In its final and present form, it does not mention trade unions at all, so that unions have had to fight to nail down the right of their officials to be part of the EWC and to ensure that the lay members themselves be union members. Where this has not succeeded, EWCs remain vulnerable to management manipulation or become outright management tools.

The main reason why the trade union presence, and specifically international trade union presence, is necessary, is because it represents the long term general interest of workers, whereas works council representatives are not necessarily committed to defending more than the specific interests of the workers of their enterprise as those interests appear to them at the time of the meeting. When each delegation comes to the meeting determined to defend its short-term interests, this can easily lead to a free-for-all where management can impose its own decisions. Whenever workers' representatives meet internationally, it is their obligation to reach a position reflecting the long-term general interest of all involved and, in order to do so, to negotiate the necessary compromises among themselves. Once this is done, they can confront management with a united position. Any other scenario is a recipe for defeat.

Drawing the lessons of the Renault-Vilvoorde conflict (other examples could also apply), Rehfeldt (1999) observes:

"The EWC alone will always have great difficulties when it tries to define common interests of the workforce in different European plants and in different economic situations. Union intervention will always be necessary in order to facilitate a compromise between different interests and different strategic approaches. Neither the ETUC, nor the European industry federations have yet been able to play this role of interest intermediation and arbitration." (Rehfeldt, 1999: 113)

Finally, the geographical issue arises because the directive formally only applies to EU countries, but leaves agreement on the actual coverage of the council to the social counterparts. Most companies seek to limit the EWCs to the EU only (the issue here is not so much Norway and Switzerland but Eastern Europe). The union interest is of course to secure the maximum coverage, ideally of every single operation of the company regardless of its location anywhere in the world. Thus most EWCs are confined to the EU, some cover all of geographical Europe and at least three are worldwide in scope.

Since the social counterparts are largely free to make their own arrangements when establishing an EWC, there is no reason why unions should obediently restrict themselves to the letter of the Directive. In the end, the structure and functions of an EWC boil down to a question of the existing balance of power, which, as we have seen, applies to any negotiating situation. Admittedly, given the present balance of social and political power in the EU member States and in the Commission, it is unlikely that much progress can be achieved at this time through a revision of the EWC directive.

Because the EWC represent, at least temporarily, a dead end, some GUFs, such as the IMF, have revived the World Councils. UNI, for its part has created a number of international union networks at TNC level, which appear to be in fact world councils in a more flexible form.

Conclusion: Back to the Future?

As we noted above, the significance and value of an IFA very much depend on the purpose it is intended to serve, which, in turn, is confirmed (or not) by its results.

The broader issue is to what extent IFAs can still be

considered to be the elements of an emerging architecture of international labour/management relations in a global political context that is increasingly hostile to trade union rights. In such a context, there is a danger that TNCs will be increasingly tempted to ignore "social partnership" arrangements, whilst the options for unions are narrowing down to their "core business": rebuilding power relations through struggle.

The situation of the labour movement is that it is confronted not only with the hostility of anti-union corporations and conservative governments here and there, but also with a worldwide political and social project, driven by transnational capital, which is fundamentally anti-democratic. It is about power in society.

This system of power is codified and given enforcement authority by the World Trade Organisation (WTO) and reinforced through the international financial institutions, which are also instruments of corporate policy. It is about a new hierarchy of rights in which corporate rights outweigh all others at the level of enforcement, in a world where other international institutions, such as the ILO, or Conventions on human rights, have little or no enforcement capacity.

In this world, the objective of any meaningful international labour strategy can only be to challenge and reverse the existing hierarchy of rights by changing the existing power relationships through organisation.

In this context, the role of IFAs has to be reassessed. In order to become a useful part of a global labour strategy, IFAs must be primarily understood and used as global organizing tools that can be evaluated by measurable outcomes. Where rights such as freedom of association and the right to collective bargaining are affirmed, IFAs should contain provisions ensuring that such rights are actually exercised.

IFAs must confront the employment-destroying nature of the system as a whole, which is not the same thing as fighting individual plant closures. In negotiating IFAs, the priority should be to put a stop to outsourcing and casualisation, which are now rampant throughout the manufacturing and services industries. Unions must claim the right to challenge management policies and decisions when these are damaging to labour interests and to the general interests of society. In other words, IFAs can and should become instruments of industrial democracy.

We know that very few companies would today be prepared to sign on to such a program. That is no reason to scale down our level of ambition and to refuse to develop adequate responses to the crisis we are facing. In conclusion, we cannot do better than quote from a speech of the IUF communications director addressing the same issues last year:

"We need to develop a political response to the corporate program, and we need to link this program to our members' day-to-day struggles in ways which can effectively challenge the enormous shift in the balance of power which is what globalisation is fundamentally about. While the challenge is enormous, we must never forget that the historic gains of the labour movement – gains which profoundly transformed the world we live in – seemed scarcely realizable when we first began to fight for them. We fought and we won. There was nothing inevitable about the corporate advances of the last two decades. We were simply out-organized at all levels, or failed to organize because we didn't appreciate the significance of what was taking place." (Rossman, 2003)

References

Carley M. (2001). Bargaining at European Level? Joint Texts Negotiated by European Works Councils, European Foundation for the Improvement of Living and Working Conditions, Dublin.

Egels-Zandén N. and Hyllman P. (2007). "Evaluating Strategies for Negotiating Workers' Rights in Transnational Corporations: The Effects of Codes of Conduct and Global Agreements on Workplace Democracy", Journal of Business Ethics, 76: 207-23.

ETUC Executive Committee (2006). Resolution on the Coordination of Collective Bargaining in 2006 , ETUC, Brussels.

Gallin D. (2000). Trade Unions and NGOs: A Necessary Partnership for Social Development, UNRISD, Geneva.

Gallin D. (2003). Strategies for the Labour Movement, Conference on Globalisation, LO Skolen, Helsingør.

Gibb E. (2005). International Framework Agreements: Increasing the Effectiveness of Core Labour Standards, Global Labour University.

International Confederation of Free Trade Unions (ICFTU) (2004). ICFTU Trade Union Guide to Globalisation (2nd ed), ICFTU, Brussels..

International Metalworkers Federation (IMF) (2001). Agreements from the Philips World Conference.

International Union of Food, Agricultural, Hotel, Restaurant, Catering, Tobacco and Allied Workers' Associations (IUF) (1997). Danone Bulletin, 1.

IUF (2006). Confronting and Negotiating with Transnational Companies – Development of International Framework Agreements, IUF EC 5-6 April.

Levinson Ch. (1972). International Trade Unionism, George Allen & Unwin, London.

Nilsson J. (2002). A Tool for Achieving Workers' Rights', Metal World,. 4.

Rehfeldt U. (1999). 'European Works Councils and International Restructuring: A Perspective for European Collective Bargaining?' Actes du GERPISA, 30, Evry: Université d'Evry-Val d'Essonne..

Riisgaard L. (2003). International Framework Agreements: A New Model for Securing Workers' Rights?, Copenhagen: Institute for International Studies.

Rossman P.(2005). Address to the Finnish Food Workers' Union Centenary Seminar, Helsinki, 3 June.

Tørres L. and Gunnes S. (2003). Global Framework Agreements: A New Tool for International Labour, FAFO.

Bibliography

Mike Gatehouse and Miguel Angel Reyes: Soft Drink, Hard Labour – Guatemalan Workers Take On Coca-Cola, Latin American Bureau, London, 1987, 38 p.

International Union Rights, Vol. 11, Nr. 3, 2004: Focus on Global Framework Agreements, International Centre for Trade Union Rights, London

Nikolaus Hammer: International Framework Agreements: Global Union Federations and Value Chains (draft paper), 19 p., November 2004

Stefan Rüb: Implementing and Monitoring an International Framework Agreement, IG Metall, Frankfurt, 42 p., 2006

IMF Model International Framework Agreement, IMF, Geneva, n.d.

Reynald Bourque: Les accords-cadres internationaux (ACI) et la négociation collective internationale à l'ère de la mondialisation, Institut International d'Etudes Sociales, OIT, Genève, 37 p., 2005

Jane Wills: Bargaining for the space to organize in the global economy: A review of the Accor-IUF trade union rights agreement, 2001. Interview: Dan Gallin

# Looking for the Quick Fix: Reviewing Andy Stern [2007]

**Andy Stern, president of the second-largest union in the United States, the Service Employees' International Union (SEIU), published a book in October last year[11] in which he presents himself and his views to the American public. Partly autobiographical, partly programmatic, the book was written "to help galvanize the forces for change".**

It is a strange book full of contradictions which raises far more questions than it answers. Stern denounces growing economic and social inequality but advocates making US corporations more competitive in the "global marketplace" by shifting the burden of health care and pension cost to workers. He sympathetically describes the plight of working class families who cannot make ends meet but wants workers to work harder to increase their employers' competitiveness. He declares that "the world needs global unions" but the book is full of flag-waving America-First sloganeering. He denounces the dependence of unions on Democratic politicians, only to quote admiringly and at length some of the most reactionary leaders of the Republican party. His book reads as though he was running for political office, but barely mentions issues of national concern like the war in Iraq, international relations, trade, immigration – or, indeed, workers' rights.

---

[11]   Andy Stern: A Country That Works – Getting America Back on Track, Free Press (Simon & Schuster), New York, 2006, 212 p. Further references to the book will be noted as "Stern 2006"

Stern wrote this book in his capacity as a union leader – indeed, according to George Will, the most significant U.S. union leader of his generation. His views on life and the world would be of little interest if he did not have the capacity to use his power as a union leader to further the cause of labor or to set it back. The core issue is therefore to understand clearly what his concept of trade unionism is all about. This becomes most clear when he discusses the relations he has established with the official unions in China, his views on labor/business partnerships and on international trade union work. This review focuses on these three issues.

**The China Opening**

A recent story in the Wall Street Journal[12] started with the paragraph: "As China imprisoned dozens of dissident labor activists after massive workers' demonstrations in 2002, an American labor leader decided it was time to embrace China's government-backed unions."

Andy Stern counts the opening up of relations with the All-China Federation of Trade Unions (ACFTU) in 2002 as one of his major achievements. He was persuaded to begin building relation with the ACFTU by Chinese American and other U.S. labor activists who argued that the Chinese trade unions are legitimate workers organizations and that the American labor movement should begin to open a dialogue and cultivate relationships with them. [13] Last May Stern visited the ACFTU for the sixth time, leading a delegation of the Change to Win (CtW) coalition of U.S. unions which disaffiliated with the AFL-CIO in July 2005. Stern has also hosted ACFTU delegations to the United States and recently the Los Angeles Federation of Labor signed a co-operation agreement with the Shanghai Trade Union Council, the local ACFTU branch, the

---

[12] U.S. Labor Leader Aided China's Wal-Mart Coup – Unlikely Alliance Helps Beijing-Backed Union Organize at Retailer, by Mei Fong and Kris Maher, *The Wall Street Journal,* June 22, 2007, page A1.

[13] See e.g. "Rethinking the China Campaign", by Kent Wong and Elaine Bernard, New Labor Forum, Queens College, NY, Fall/Winter 2000.

"first formal relationship between a U.S. central labor council and their equivalent in China", according to the LACFL press release. It "pledges co-operation, regular exchange of labor leader delegations, and joint work on research and organizing, especially in addressing multinational corporations operating in both cities."

These are important political developments not just for the U.S. labor movement but for the entire global independent trade union movement.. While he may not be the political brain behind them, Andy Stern is their leading public advocate.

The AFL-CIO of course does not recognize the ACFTU as a legitimate trade union organization. In 2002, when the South China Morning Post reported Andy Stern's visit, an AFL-CIO spokesperson issued a statement that the delegation in no way represented the AFL-CIO: "the AFL-CIO shares the view of the International Confederation of Free Trade Unions ... that the ACFTU is not an independent trade union but rather part of the Chinese government and party structure."

Stern is neither naïve nor uninformed. He describes the ACFTU as "government-controlled"[14] and "employer-oriented"[15]. He knows that "there is no question that workers' unrest is on the rise in China" and that, when protests follow, "Chinese authorities arrest the leaders, who can end up serving long prison sentences". He wonders what will happen "if China's rulers succeed in bottling a potion that mixes market capitalism and political authoritarianism"[16] He even pays tribute to the "brave man" who "stood still and faced seventeen approaching tanks in Tiananmen Square (actually Chang'an Avenue - dg), not knowing that his stance would become a worldwide symbol for the heroic fight for democracy in China."[17]

So, given what he knows about the ACFTU, why did Stern

---

[14] Stern 2006, p. 23

[15] Stern 2006, p. 28

[16] Stern 2006, pp. 27 and 28

engage with this "government controlled and employer-oriented" organization as if it were a genuine trade union body?

His description of his first visit to China gives no obvious answer. He sounds like a naïve tourist, awed by having been met at the airport by the head of the ACFTU International Department, and "whisked" into the diplomatic lounge. Then Stern and his delegation were received, to his "shock", in the Great Hall of the People: "with much ceremony we were guided into the splendor of the Great Hall formal reception room and treated with the formality of visiting diplomats. As the highest-ranking union leader in the delegation, I was guided to a lavishly carved, formal chair opposite the president of the ACFTU, Wei Jianxing."

He goes on to explain: "Mr. Wei was China's highest-ranking labor leader, assigned by the Communist Party. More important, he served as one of eight powerful members of the Politburo Standing Committee, China's highest governing body. Mr. Wei wielded enormous power over all the affairs of China, and his importance surpassed that of any union leader I had previously met."[18]

A far cry indeed from Stern's previous international labor travel, with "uneventful, private dinners with the host country's union officials"[19]. none of them, to be sure, wielding the "enormous power" that membership in the highest governing body of a one-party police state brings with it.

Already in 2001, the Hong Kong Confederation of Trade Unions (HKCTU) and China Labour Bulletin (CLB) had warned that visits arranged under the auspices of the ACFTU were "directly harmful to those in China trying to promote

---

[17] There are conflicting reports about the identity and fate of the "brave man". He may have been Wang Weilin, a 19-yer old student, He was arrested on the spot by the Public Security Bureau and, according to some reports, executed fourteen days later.

[18] Stern 2006, p. 25

[19] Stern 2006, p. 24

labor rights in China, either within the parameters of the official "union" or outside it" because "the ACFTU leadership milks the publicity opportunities that engagement offers, using it to shore up its credibility, while clamping down on independent labor activists and silencing the reformers." [20]

Here is how the ACFTU leadership milked the publicity opportunity of Stern's 2002 visit, in Stern's own words: after Wei "grandly welcomed" the delegation with a short speech and Stern spoke in reply, "Mr. Wei made a slight motion with his hand and, in what had obviously been prearranged, summoned the Chinese press corps. Several dozen reporters and photographers appeared and began taking notes, shooting pictures and video footage, and I later learned that our introductory remarks had been recorded, translated and broadcast to the press room."

Stern goes on to write, apparently oblivious to the real significance of the public relations theater in which he is the star performer: "For the Chinese, the photograph of an American labor leader's 'historic' arrival was worth a thousand words, and those pictures would soon appear in the China Daily News, in Russia's Tass, and, back home, in Business Week."[21]

In that context, Greg Tarpinian's (Executive Director of CtW) comment last May that "engagement is not acceptance, engagement is not endorsement"[22] is beside the point. The ACFTU is not looking for acceptance or endorsement, it is looking for recognition and legitimacy, and it got what it wanted.

Stern, echoed by others, does eventually offer a number of arguments why engagement with the ACFTU supposedly advances the interests of Chinese and American workers.

---

[20] Rethinking the Rethink – The Chinese Working Class, the ACFTU and Engagement, by the Hong Kong Confederation of Trade Unions and China Labour Bulletin, January 18, 2001

[21] Stern 2006, pp. 25 and 26

[22] quoted in: Global Labor Strategies, June 8, 2007

Some are remarkably shallow and ignorant of the experiences and views of many who have seriously dealt with similar issues, others deserve more serious consideration. Here are a few of them:

(1) China is Big and Everyone is Going There.

Andy Stern writes:[23] "Most Fortune 500 companies have invested madly in China. Representatives of both American political parties have visited China. From around the world, professors, students, journalists, athletes, artists, musicians, tourists – and unions – travel to China in acknowledgement of its rapid emergence as a power player in all aspects of world affairs."

Later he writes: "I was stunned by China". What follows is a wide-eyed description of urban development in Beijing and Shanghai. Stern concludes: "China is for real".

It is not news that, as General de Gaulle memorably remarked, "China is a very big country inhabited by many Chinese", nor is it news that China is a fascinating country that has excited the curiosity of foreigners over centuries and it is common knowledge that since Deng Xiaoping's reforms starting in the late 1970s, industrial and urban development has been spectacular.

Obviously thousands of people, representing a wide range of institutions and organizations, keep visiting China, each for their own reasons: companies to make money, professors and students to do research, journalists to write reports, as they would anywhere, athletes to compete, artists and musicians to perform and tourists to satisfy their curiosity. Governments obviously maintain diplomatic relations and exchange visits,

---

[23] Stern 2006, p. 24. There is another mention of the "Cold War" in Stern's book when he writes that "Lech Walensa and other brave trade unionists helped win the Cold War, destroying all obstacles to market capitalism." What Walensa and the other brave trade unionists actually thought they were doing was destroying all obstacles to democracy. The return to unfettered market capitalism was not on their agenda: it can only be regarded as collateral damage and a national tragedy. But Stern doesn't know the difference, or doesn't care.

sometimes at the highest level, for reasons of State. This is why Nixon visited China in 1972 and Deng visited the US in 1979.

For trade unionists to visit China in their capacity as trade unionists, there would have to be a trade union reason, which assumes that there are legitimate counterparts - either real unions or incipient democratic worker organizations - to visit. Let us have a closer look.

(2) Time to End the Cold War.

Stern writes that "American unions had a policy dating back to the Cold War of refusing to interact with 'government dominated' unions and would not recognize the ACFTU or speak officially to its leaders. I found that policy counterproductive."[24] As another American union leader put it: "The Cold War is over, the economy that they have in this country is essentially the same as we have in the United States"[25] (but not the political system, he forgets to add).

It is worth remembering that the Cold War was a period of worldwide conflict between two political blocs led respectively by two superpowers, the United States and the Soviet Union, roughly from 1946 to 1990. This was a conflict between States and, after the Sino-Soviet split starting in the late 1950s, it was never principally about China, which had its own international policy with shifting alliances, including with the United States as in the case of Cambodia when both supported the murderous Khmer Rouge regime from 1975 to 1979.

As we all know, both superpowers tried to control the international labor movement and to turn it into an auxiliary in that contest. In the case of the USSR, the control was total in its sphere of influence. In the case of the US, despite the best efforts of the CIA, the control was far from total.

---

[24] Stern 2006, p. 24

[25] Dave Arian, former president of the International Longshore and Warehouse Association, quoted in: "L.A. delegation seeks brotherhood in China," by Mitchell Landsberg, Los Angeles Times, July 4, 2007.

What was total, however, was the rejection of the Soviet system by trade unionists of all political tendencies other than Communist, not because the American government said so but because, since the rise of fascism and Stalinism in the 1920s and 1930s, no independent trade unionist would accept the idea that an organization which was part of the State machinery in a one-party police State, where workers were forcibly enrolled, could legitimately represent workers and be called a union.

This is why socialist, social-democratic, catholic, revolutionary syndicalist and conservative syndicalist unions, the AFofL, the CIO, the AFL-CIO and others refused to establish fraternal relations with the German Labor Front of the Nazis, the fascist corporations of Italy, Portugal and Spain, the All-Union Central Council of Trade Unions of the USSR and similar organizations in the countries under its control, and of course the ACFTU. All of this started long before the Cold War and had nothing to do with China except insofar as the Chinese unions are state-controlled. In fact, some international trade union organizations, such as the IUF, also refused for the same reasons to entertain relations with the so-called trade unions in Taiwan when it was a one-party dictatorship of the Kuomintang, very much in contrast to the "Cold War policies" of the time.

Communists had of course always opposed union policies isolating the Soviet labor organization and, starting in the 1970s, others also started establishing and advocating contacts. The controversies that then developed followed exactly the same pattern as is now developing over China.

In order to build a case for engaging with organizations that were obviously and admittedly part of the State machinery, the advocates of engagement had to endorse a political operation which the HKCTU and CLB have called "conceptual embezzlement", i.e. the hijacking of labor terminology to cover a reality reflecting the opposite of its original meaning, starting with the word "union"[26].

The original example of this "conceptual embezzlement" was the designation of the labor organizations of the USSR as "trade unions" and the designation as "trade unions" of all similar organizations established on that model, in all countries controlled by the USSR and in China, whereas in reality they were and, where they still exist, still are organs of the State for administering and controlling the labor force, if necessary by aiding repression.[27]

However, as long as the "conceptual embezzlement" is successful and unchallenged, the way is clear to muddy the waters by those who have a political agenda to do so, by those who choose to believe their own lies and by those who cannot tell the difference.

This brings us to the other arguments.

(3) Aiding the Reformers

The case for engagement is often made on the grounds that developing contacts with unions all over the world will help bring about positive changes even in State-controlled organizations.

---

[26] Similar instances of "conceptual embezzlement" occurred with the words "soviet", "democracy" and "socialist", but that is another story.

[27] The Public Security Bureau (PSB), which is the Chinese political police, in 1996 issued guidelines on maintaining social order which include the following guidelines for the unions:
"Trade unions must emphasise their work on politics and ideology in the work-force as well as propaganda education. Contradictions among employees and labour disputes must also be handled in an efficient manner and the union must assist the enterprise directors and party and government leaders to formulate all necessary measures to promote public security systems. The union must also co-ordinate with the PSB, organise "public order and prevention teams" to protect the internal security and order of the enterprises, as well as social order. Staff and workers should be mobilised to struggle against all forms of criminal and illegal behaviour. The union must also assist the relevant authorities to deal adequately with the education and employment of dismissed employees, workers who have committed errors and those who have completed sentences and been released."

Stern writes that "the ACFTU's willingness to transform itself to effectively counter the impact of globalization has far-reaching implications for workers everywhere." [28] and:
"I've continued my conversations with leaders of the ACFTU and have heard the frustrated voices of Chinese union officials trying to deal with foreign-owned enterprises. In 2005, I hosted the ACFTU's delegation to the United States and sensed their evolving thinking in regard to the significant challenges of a capitalist economy and the urgent need to reevaluate their role in representing Chinese workers."[29]

These comments echo the argument put forth by other American unionists and activists. For example, Kent Wong and Elaine Bernard argue that: "There is a wide range of political and philosophical perspectives among Chinese trade unionists. There is a major generational transition taking place in China, and a new emerging leadership within the government and within labor unions. Through engaging in more dialogue and exchange with Chinese workers and unions, the American labor movement could identify new leaders of China who embrace a similar perspective on global corporate domination and the need to defend human rights and labor rights."[30]

This is an argument that must be taken seriously, inasmuch as in an organization as large as the ACFTU (and, for that matter, in a society as complex as China's) there will inevitably be a "wide range of political and philosophical perspectives" and, no doubt, reflection and discussion about how to meet the challenges of capitalism and "market Stalinism". [31]

Two questions, however, need to be asked: first, in a regime that exercises total control over the permissible limits of public debate, and enforces these limits by police measures,

---

[28] Stern 2006, p. 28

[29] Stern 2006, p. 27

[30] Wong/Bernard 2000

[31] The term was coined by Boris Kagarlitsky, in: The Importance of Being Marxist, New Left Review, Nov.-Dec. 1989

how far can views that deviate from the official Party line affect policies of organizations such as the ACFTU? Second, how far can foreign visitors affect the debate?

In their reply to Wong and Bernard, the HKCTU and the CLB[32] pointed out that there was nothing new in engagement: "According to the People's Daily, the ACFTU reported that between 1994 and 1998 Chinese trade unions established 'cooperative relations' with 419 trade unions from 131 countries and regions. These included 267 trade union delegations to China and 200 ACFTU delegations sent abroad to 191 countries and regions. In addition, between 1996 and 1998, the ACFTU sent over 400 cadres on labor related study missions abroad. ACFTU Vice-Chair Zhang Dinghua made clear that such exchanges were not an attempt to build links in the international labor movement's struggle to resist the increasing international power of capital and multinational companies. On the contrary, the exchanges were an integral part of the Chinese government's foreign policy."

There have been many more delegations since this was written and many, though not all, have raised human rights and labor rights issues, with nothing to show for.

Over decades, Western European and other trade union delegations visited what they took to be their counterpart unions in the USSR and other countries in the Soviet bloc, most of them arguing that such visits promoted democratic change, which would eventually lead to co-operation on basic trade union issues, such as a common front against corporate power. Actually, as long as the system remained in place, no relations with labor organizations in the Soviet bloc ever contributed to a single joint action against a transnational corporation and when democratic change finally happened, it had nothing to do with trade union exchange visits.

Rather, these so-called "unions" collapsed like a house of cards when the States that controlled them collapsed, without the workers they were supposed to represent lifting a finger to

---

[32] HKCTU/CLB 2001

support them. The genuine unions that succeeded them, whether arising from "old" or "new" structures, have had to battle ever since against the discredit the defunct State organizations have brought to the concept of "union" and find it hard to overcome the skepticism and passivity of workers used to perceiving "unions" as tools of a repressive State bureaucracy.

Even if American trade unionists, through exchange visits (and, one assumes, aided by their own independent and trustworthy interpreters) might succeed in "identifying new leaders of China who embrace a similar perspective on global corporate domination and the need to defend human rights and labor rights" such new leaders cannot implement progressive change in the ACFTU as long as the system remains in place. For this to change, far larger forces than the trade union bureaucracy will have to start moving, and it is certainly not visiting foreign trade unionists who will influence the outcome of such political struggles.

The paradox is that Andy Stern and the other engagers are failing to see the forest for the trees. New leaders do exist and they are known, but they are ignored by Stern and the other engagers because of the political choice they have made.

A democratic trade union movement does exist in China: it is the Hong Kong Confederation of Trade Unions. An independent and democratic trade union movement also exists in Taiwan. Han Dongfang, independent labor activist and editor of the China Labour Bulletin[33], is very well known and his expertise is unchallenged. Whatever their views may be, Stern has decided that the ACFTU was the only serious show in town. He met with the HKCTU last year, but only to tell its general secretary, after a lengthy conversation, that he (Stern) was older and therefore more experienced as a trade unionist.

Nowhere in his book is there any indication that he raised

---

[33] Han Dongfang was also the spokesman of an independent union, the Workers' Autonomous Federation of Beijing, which was suppressed, together with the students, at Tiananmen in 1989

labor rights issues with his ACFTU hosts. Nor is there any indication in the statements of the CtW and the LACFL delegations that they raised such issues, or expressed any concern about the Chinese labor activists who are imprisoned because they engaged in independent labor action or tried to organize independent unions.[34], contrary to many other trade union delegations visiting China. Clearly, the "heroic fight for democracy in China" is not on their agenda.

Robin Munro, research director of China Labour Bulletin, has pointed out that, contrary to the situation ten years ago, China now in effect has a labor movement, but it is not controlled by the ACFTU apparatus: "the scale of worker unrest nowadays is so great, you can go to almost any city in the country now and there will be several major collective worker protests going on at the same time. ... So China now has a labor movement. This is an important point to just put there on the table and recognize. It is not organized. It is spontaneous, it is relatively inchoate. ... We have basically a pre-union phase of labor movement development in China today. It also has great potential, I think, for becoming a proper labor movement."

That is where the real labor movement is emerging in China, that Stern and the others have been missing because they wear blinders. They are screened from reality by the ACFTU and voluntarily submit to such screening.

How the international labor movement can most effectively assist this emerging real labor movement, in its "relatively inchoate" form, should be the issue up for debate.

(4) Organizing the Companies.

The ACFTU organizes transnational corporations. That is the main argument, which is supposed to override all objections, but it rests entirely on the assumption that Chinese trade unions in some sense represent workers' interests and on the meaning of the word "organizing".

---

[34] There are twenty-six documented cases of imprisoned labor activists in China as of June 2007. The list is not exhaustive. (IHLO, Hong Kong: **www.ihlo.org**)

Stern seems to believe that the ACFTU genuinely seeks to "reevaluate their role in representing Chinese workers" and he sees "the first sign of this reevaluation when the ACFTU resorted to traditional American tactics of 'blacklisting' foreign-owned enterprises that defied Chinese labor laws, including Wal-Mart, McDonalds's, Dell, Samsung, and Kodak".[35]

"We're just dumbfounded about how they were able to organize Wal-Mart here" said Ray Familathe, director of international affairs of the ILWU and a member of the California delegation.[36]. He well might be, if he thinks that "organizing" is what took place.

What actually happened with Wal-Mart should be perfectly clear for anyone who has read the newspapers. In 2004 an initially reluctant Wal-Mart, having been threatened with legal action by the ACFTU, accepted that "should associates request the formation of a union, Wal-Mart China would respect their wishes and honor its obligations under China's Trade Union Law"[37].

Wal-Mart was still dragging its feet until Hu Jintao, president of China, in March 2006, ordered the ACFTU to "do a better job of building (Communist) Party organizations and trade unions" in foreign companies[38]. The ACFTU then duly set up an office to target Wal-Mart in Quanzhou and the Wal-Mart "associates" duly requested the formation of a union there, which was established on July 29.

In August, Wal-Mart issued a statement saying that it would set up "trade unions" in all its outlets across China in collaboration with the ACFTU, "China's union authority"[39].

---

[35] Stern 2006, p. 27

[36] quoted in LA Times, July 4, 2007)

[37] quoted in Financial Times, November 23, 2004: Wal-Mart Gives in to China's Union Federation, by Richard McGregor

[38] China Daily, quoting AP, August 17, 2006

[39] China Daily, quoting Xinhua, August 15, 2006

and an official of the ACFTU duly "acknowledged Wal-Mart's 'active attitude' in helping set up union branches."

Joe Hatfield, president of Wal-Mart Asia, thought that a good relationship with the ACFTU was good for business development: "We think it is in line with the Chinese government's efforts to build a harmonious society."[40]

Jonathan Dong, a spokesman for Wal-Mart China, when asked why the company agreed to allow unions in China while it resists them in other countries, said: "The union in China if fundamentally different from unions in the West ... The union has made it clear that its goal is to work with employers, not promote confrontation."[41]. He said details were still under discussion, in particular whether the 2 percent of wages that the ACFTU is authorized to take as dues would apply to all employees of a store or just to union members.

In other words, what we have here is a command performance, with the ACFTU perfectly happy to front as a company union for Wal-Mart as long as it collects its dues.

Han Dongfang who does not rule out that some day a genuine labor movement may emerge within the shell of the ACFTU, had the following comments:

"The biggest number of working people in China are those who are working in factories. They include foreign investment and privatized former State-owned enterprises. From a real union organizing strategy point of view, the Chinese trade union movement should focus more on organizing these workers in the factories in order to form a solid foundation of the trade union. Even in the ACFTU's own interests, it should approach the factory workers rather than the department stores to compensate for its membership losses (after the privatization of the State-owned enterprises, the ACFTU's branch unions disappeared). But, instead of following its own need of developing membership power, the ACFTU went to

---

[40] China Daily, quoting Xinhua, August 25, 2006

[41] China Daily, quoting Reuters, August 11, 2006

Wal-Mart. Yes, the ACFTU has won international attention from this big show but it has neither increased its membership nor its real power. Sixty-two store "unions" had been set up about a year ago but none of these "unions" approached the employer to open negotiations for the workers. It was very clear that the ACFTU approach to Wal-Mart was for international publicity more than for building the Chinese labor movement."[42]

Just in case anyone might have any misapprehension about the nature of the Chinese Wal-Mart "unions", any notion of possible trade union independence was dispelled when Communist Party and Communist Youth League branches were set up in the Wal-Mart stores in parallel with the ACFTU branches.

The first two branches, at Shenyang, were established in August 2006, followed by the Shenzhen Wal-Mart in December 2006. In April this year there were already six party branches, prompting Reuters to comment: "The world's largest retailer, Wal-Mart, is now host to the world's largest communist party."

But never fear: according to Xinhua[43], the Chinese news agency, Chen Lie, head to the Organization Department of the Dongda District Committee of the CPC, was reassuring: the CPC and CYLC branches would not interfere with the business development strategy and internal management of the company. According to Chen, "the branches will encourage members to play an exemplary role in doing a good job and that will be helpful to business development."

Xinhua also quotes Zhu Hui, vice president of the Party School of the Shenyang City Committee of the CPC: "The aim of the CPC is to boost economic development, which accords with the purpose of business development of Wal-Mart and other enterprises."

---

[42] Interview in Pages de Gauche (Lausanne), May 2007

[43] Xinhua report, in China Daily, August 25, 2006. Xinhua is the official Chinese news service.

According to Liu, manager of the Shenyang outlet, Wal-Mart headquarters did not oppose the establishment of the CPC and CYLC branches[44]. Xia Jinsheng, party secretary in Wal-Marts Tianjin store, who also heads Wal-Mart's Tianjin public relations department, says that most members in Wal-Mart's party cells are midlevel or senior executives.[45]

It is quite possible that those American trade unionists who do not have a political axe to grind and who trust their own judgment and experience, will eventually see through the charade. Maria Elena Durazo, who led the Los Angeles delegation, and who believes that American unions have something to learn from Chinese workers because they "organized" Wal-Mart, after sitting through a meeting where a company executive explained the union's role, commented: "We come here and they're talking about harmony. Harmony? With someone who's just thinking about maximum profits? We just can't think that way."[46]

**Seeking Harmony in the United States**

In an interview with the Wall Street Journal[47] Stern was asked: "Do you think unions will ever be able to organize Wal-Mart in the US?" His reply: "The group SEIU's part of, Wal-Mart Watch, has not been trying to organize them but to change their business model." He goes on to say that a "traditional organizing drive" will not succeed because the odds are too strong against it. However: "I think Wal-Mart has the opportunity to create an entirely new American model of worker representation. The question is do they want partners or do they want to be held accountable in a much more public fashion?"

Stern's book has attracted a lot of attention, not so much because of the China opening, but because of his proposals for

---

[44] China Daily (Xinhua), August 25, 2006

[45] Wall Street Journal, December 18, 2006

[46] quoted in the Los Angeles Times, July 4, 2007

[47] quoted in Wal-Mart Watch, January 22, 2007

new strategic labor-business partnerships on issues of national policy, such as immigration and health care. But they also involve patterns of union organization based on labor-management partnerships.

His principles for "effective twenty-first century unions" include: "Employees and employers need organizations that solve problems, not create them." ... " Both employers and employees must begin with the presumption that all parties want a mutually beneficial relationship based on teamwork." "To maximize success, employee organizations need to be aligned with employers' market and industry structures and flexible enough to respond to ever-changing employer dynamics, and competent enough to be good partners." [48]

As one example among others, Stern mentions the national labor-management committee established by the SEIU and nursing home owners and "new state-based relationships to promote quality and employer economic stability."

These are essentially a trade-off by which the SEIU agrees to lobby for an increase in state funding for nursing homes in exchange for the companies' agreement not to hinder the union's organizing efforts.

"In California", Stern writes, "the industry and union worked with the legislature on a plan to enhance quality in nursing homes, stabilize the workforce, and provide more resources for direct patient care. The alliance secured a $660 million state legislative appropriation, which dramatically altered the fundamentals of the industry."[49]

However, this agreement with the Alliance group of nursing home operators, also involved "template" contracts, i.e. centrally pre-negotiated deals that would automatically apply to any newly organized unit and eliminate basic workers' rights, such as the right to strike, local collective bargaining rights, the right to report violations of workers' rights and

---

[48] Stern 2006, pp. 105-106

[49] Stern 2006, p. 107

patient's rights in organized nursing homes to the authorities or to the media. Moreover, the choice of which units were to be organized was left to the nursing home owners; other units were not to be approached by the union even if the workers there wanted to become members.

Unsurprisingly, this deal met with wide spread opposition, both inside and outside the SEIU. On May 31, the SEIU was forced to end the partnership after the United Healthcare Workers-West (UHW), one of its two locals that were part of the original deal in 2003, launched a campaign to re-negotiate the agreement on a different basis: union democracy, the right to aggressively advocate for workers covered by partnership agreements and full union membership rights for these workers.

In an internal document[50] analyzing the 2003 agreement from a workers' perspective, the UHW asked the question: "What kind of worker organizations are Alliance based template agreements creating, and, equally important, what are they laying the groundwork for?".

The answer: "Alliance based template agreements do not allow workers to empower themselves, nor are they conceived out of a process in which workers are truly part of 'winning' the union."

The "Lessons Learned" document goes on to say:

"Essentially the Alliance agreement gave SEIU the opportunity to organize facilities (that the Alliance employers chose) in exchange for SEIU's political power to raise reimbursement rates. ... Traditionally, for workers to organize they engage in struggle to win that right. Under the Alliance agreement this is absent. The contract that newly organized Alliance workers will have is worked out in advance with the ultimate terms of that agreement discouraging – and in some cases, preventing – workers from independently engaging in struggle to improve their working conditions. Prior to getting to the negotiating

---
[50] The California Alliance Agreement:: Lessons Learned in Moving Forward in Organizing California's Nursing Home Industry, UHW, 2007, 20 p.

table not only are the rules of engagement worked out but the nature of the 'deal' itself. Is it any wonder that we have often heard from these workers that 'the boss brought us the union'?

"Many workers who came into our union through the Alliance neutrality agreement found themselves with 'template' contracts that allowed for very little power on the shop floor with no right to strike and no clear path toward full collective bargaining rights. From UHW members' experience it is safe to state that the template arrangement created a worker organization that restricts member empowerment. Those members covered by template agreements went to the table with the expectation that bargaining would be an opportunity to not only secure economic benefits, but to change labor relations within facilities where templates restricted their right to do so. Our members have made it very clear to us: renegotiation of a new Alliance agreement must involve members – it must begin from the bottom up."

The conclusion: "If the nature of the labor agreement defined in the current Alliance templates – which restrict members' rights and ability to be empowered – is allowed to continue, what effect will this have on the fundamental nature of a union organization? What ultimately happens if we give up the right to strike as the means for workers to level the playing field with employers when needed? We would argue that it would adversely affect our mission and goal to advance and defend the interests of our members, and in fact, may come close to becoming what have historically been called 'company' unions. ..."

Does this sound familiar? Does it not recall the situation of the Chinese unions that are supposed to have "organized" Wal-Mart? Is it any wonder that Andy Stern can find nothing wrong with the ACFTU? After all, what they are doing in China is not so different from what he is trying to do in California – except that in California, his members won't let him get away with it. One can imagine Stern commiserating with the most powerful trade unionist on earth about the thankless task of keeping the rank-and-file in line to ensure harmony with the employers.

Thankfully, Stern does not have the Public Security Bureau to back him up, but he is trying to get rid of the opposition by merging it out of existence. Under a plan to merge the SEIU's California locals, the national headquarters is pushing to merge the UHW with another local, more amenable to Stern's "partnership" policies, a move the UHW has so far resisted. And, even as the California agreement was being re-negotiated under pressure from the membership, a similar agreement to the original was signed in Washington State – for ten years.

Rose Ann DeMoro, executive director of the California Nurses Association (CNA) says that Stern is "organizing corporations, not workers", and: "to him, the union is just a human resource department, or a temp agency." [51]

DeMoro's organization, with 80,000 members, is dwarfed by the SEIU's 1.9m., but it is the fastest growing union in the US, having tripled in size in 13 years, since DeMoro became its leader. If the SEIU had grown at the same rate in the same period, since Stern became its leader, it should now have 4.5m. members. The CNA, a longtime independent union, and its offshoot, the National Nurses Organizing Committee (NNOC), joined the AFL-CIO earlier this year.

In his book, Stern says that "one of the first defining moments" of his presidency of the SEIU was his settlement with Kaiser Permanente, one of the largest health care employers in California. After a history of conflict, Stern in 1996 called the company CEO David Lawrence and told him: "we need to change our relationship" (his emphasis). His conversations with Lawrence led to the "largest labor-management partnership in the history of the service sector", a "risky, colossal shift in approach."

As Stern admits, "it wasn't always easy for union members to hear that their elected leader ... was talking peaceably with the CEO of their company and promoting new relationships." However, Stern says, the members eventually accepted "a new

---
[51] quoted in: Andy Stern: Savior or Sellout? by Liza Featherstone, The Nation, July 16, 2007

approach to collective bargaining that emphasized problem solving". Joint committees were formed, an "amazing experience": "As hard as I tried, I could not distinguish the union representatives from the management representatives."[52]

This "groundbreaking relationship" produced one of the best contracts in the health care industry, Stern maintains, adding that "not every union agrees with our approach: To this day, the California Nurses Association still criticizes SEIU's arrangement with Kaiser and has chosen not to join us in the process."[53]

Clearly, the CNA remains the pea under the mattress of the SEIU princess. It also secured a contract with Kaiser Permanente, but with entirely different methods:

"When Kaiser Permanente began laying off 1,600 union nurses and demanded wage concessions, patients started to suffer. The union set up a (free call) number so people could report instances of patients dying from neglect and mistakes at Kaiser and other facilities. CNA posted those tales on its Web site, which attracted so much national attention that the health care giant not only settled with the union, it agreed to work with nurses to solve those problems as part of its labor contract. "These improvements have forged a more solid relationship", said a Kaiser spokeswoman."[54]

## Global Unions

When this writer first met him, Andy Stern did not think much of international unionism. This was at a meeting of US trade union leaders and International Trade Secretariats (renamed Global Union Federations in 2002), which the AFL-CIO had convened in Washington D.C. about twenty years ago. The idea was to introduce American unionists, especially those who had no experience of ITS activities, to the practical work

---

[52] Stern 2006, pp. 69-70

[53] Stern 2006, p.70

[54] The Rabble-rouser, by Kathleen Sharp, SFGate.com, May 6, 2007

of ITSs in confronting transnational corporations. Stern, at that time organizing director of the SEIU, visibly impatient with what he was hearing, grumbled that international trade union organizations were a waste of time and left the meeting early.

Today, Andy Stern says: "The world needs global unions"[55]. He has discovered international trade unionism in the form of "the world's largest global union federation,[56] Union Network International (UNI), with 15.5 million members", which held its last congress in Chicago in August 2005, under the banner "Imagine a Global Union".

Much of what he writes amounts to re-inventing the wheel: it is hardly news that unions have to adapt to a world without borders, or that workers in different countries who share the same employer need to co-ordinate internationally to face that employer together. These are insights and principles that have been written about and acted upon, sometimes with success, for decades. Walter Reuther introduced the concept of international coalition bargaining in the International Metalworkers Federation about fifty years ago, the first international strike in the post-war period was organized by Charles Levinson, general secretary of the International Chemical Workers' Federation, nearly forty years ago and the first international agreement in the post-war period with a transnational corporation was signed in the food industry nearly twenty years ago.

The idea of a "convergence of global movements concerned with the environment, social responsibility, human rights, child labor, gender equality and workers' rights"[57] is not new either. This kind of international coalition building has been advocated by trade unionists and social movement activists since the 1980s, mainly as a response to the disappearance of

---

[55] Stern 2006, p. 111

[56] Actually the fourth-largest, after the Education International (30m.), the International Metalworkers' Federation (25m.) and the International Chemical, Energy and Mine Workers' Federation (20m.).

[57] Stern 2006, p. 113

the socialist movement as a coherent international force in most of the industrialized world. It is now sometimes described as the emerging "global social justice movement" and it is essentially political in nature. The slogan of today's social movements, "another world is possible", is what the labor movement always stood for.

The important point here is that all concepts of international labor solidarity, of the structures established to give it a practical expression, and of the political alliances that the labor movement needs to advance its agenda, have been based on the recognition of a reality: the fundamental conflict of interest between capital and labor, national at the outset, transnational today. Of necessity, this involves power struggles at every level, and conflict.

Stern is developing a different agenda. It comes through most clearly in his interview in The McKinsey Quarterly last year[58]. The interviewer asks where the movement is going, and Stern replies: "what we're going to see happen in the next ten years, if not sooner, is a convergence of a global labor movement, a global corporate responsibility movement, and nongovernmental organizations. ... We need to build new organizations that can help people, and on the global level that will require joint efforts by unions, NGOs and corporate responsibility groups."

What if the employers are not convinced? Stern has figured out an international strike strategy that is cost-effective: "If workers are ready to go on strike in the United States, and we are ready to pay them to strike, it would be very costly. But paying workers in Indonesia or India or other places to go on strike against the same global employer isn't particularly expensive."

The interviewer, who probably cannot believe what he is hearing, insists: "So a global federation or union might decide, in effect, to outsource a strike to the lowest-cost area because

---

[58] Shaking up the labor movement: An interview with the head of the Service Employees International Union, by Lenny T. Mendonca, The McKinsey Quarterly, Number 1, 2006

the amount needed for the strike fund would be lower, and thus put pressure on one wing of a global employers' operations?"

Stern's reply: "Yes, absolutely."

This is extraordinary. In the past, when a strike was "outsourced", it was the other way around: strong unions would put pressure on transnational corporations, including through industrial action, to defend weaker unions that were unable to defend themselves because, for example, they would face extreme repression. Stern is aware of this possibility, since he mentions "outsourcing strikes to countries where strikes are legal and will not provoke government retaliation"[59] but what he is now proposing, is that unions in rich countries, specifically the United States, should in effect hire unions in low-wage countries as cannon fodder to fight their battles.

It is hard to imagine a more cynical and manipulative approach. It is also totally unrealistic. No union anywhere, except for maybe the usual, useless clients, is going to sign on to Stern's outsourced mercenary army.

In his book, Stern points out that: "With a mandate from the SEIU's 2004 convention delegates to build a global union, followed by UNI's adoption of global unionism, SEIU assigned staff to Australia, Poland, England, India, France, Switzerland, Germany, the Netherlands, South America and, soon, Africa."[60]

It is not clear why Stern believes that building a "global union" requires assigning SEIU staff to nineteen countries or more. What is the task of these emissaries, and how are they planning to go about building a "global union"? And what would that "global union" look like? Is this too sensitive and important a project to be entrusted to existing international trade union structures? Those structures of course involve mutual democratic accountability. Stern seems to have

---

[59] Stern 2006, p. 113

[60] Stern 2006, p. 112

decided on a short-cut:, create his own labor International, where he would be accountable to no one but himself.

His "global partnerships" appear to be run by staffers deliberately chosen for their lack of experience of the international labor world. One of them, expected to co-ordinate "the activities of unions that represent workers of international corporations in other countries", and who had just spent two-and-a-half weeks traveling to India, Australia and Canada, explained: "This is all brand new and everybody is figuring it out as we go. When Andy Stern asked me to do this, he said: 'I don't know what it's going to be. You are going to have to figure it out.' And that was one of the interesting parts of it. Not only do I get an interesting job, but I get to help figure out what it's about."[61]

Other staff, embedded in the SEIU's partner unions, supervise teams of organizers targeting an enterprise, working independently, without co-ordination or reference to existing union structures. Nor does there seem to be any follow-up in the event the enterprise is organized in terms of collective bargaining or lasting local organization.

This type of slash-and-burn organizing has a history: it was one of the reasons why the Industrial Workers of the World were unable to establish a lasting presence in many of the industries they organized in the early 20th century. History repeats itself, the first time as a tragedy, the second time as a farce.

What happens when his "global partnership" organizers run up against reality and understand that they are not, after all, expected to "figure out what it's all about"? Or, having figured it out, start talking back? Or realize that others have figured it out a long time ago, but differently from the way their boss sees it? And how long until the partner unions start resenting the embedded hit teams, regardless of the money Stern is able to throw around?

---

[61] quoted in Kennebee Journal, Augusta, Maine, May 4, 2005: Union ex-leader goes global, by Gary Rumal

And what about the general orientation of the entire exercise? Stern takes sideswipes at the "class struggle mentality" of unions, which he attributes to "an earlier, rough area of industrial unions"[62] and he tells the McKinsey interviewer that "confrontational models are very slow and not a relationship-building orientation to have."

The interviewer then asks how Stern thinks one can "get past the traditional confrontation between management and labor", and Stern replies that one way "is for unions to change their role to that of service provider, outsourcer of training, and benefits provider."

How does this translate into global terms? Does the SEIU plan to build "global service providers", "global outsourcers of training" or "global benefits providers" all over the world? Does Stern see it as his mission to spread the gospel of global corporatism? If that is the case, he is unlikely to retain many allies in the world trade union movement, although he will retain some. It is not impossible that Stern's neo-corporatist wisdom will surface in some form at one of the next sessions of the World Economic Forum or other international gatherings where advancing union/management co-operation is on the agenda.

Stern is not a patient man. He is always looking for the short-cut, the quick fix. Organizing a real labor movement in China takes too long? Deal with the fake. Can't convince a majority of AFL-CIO unions? Pull out, create your own federation. Organizing workers takes too long? Organize through the company.

It is a safe bet that the difficult, complex and often thankless task of building global unionism will soon outrun his patience. Building global unionism cannot be done by smoke and mirrors and by branding exercises, but only in the way genuine trade unionism is built anywhere: by education and organization from the bottom up, by organizations that are accountable to their membership.

---

[62] Stern 2006, pp. 70-71

It also requires the recognition of a reality: that the labor movement is facing powerful interests that are opposed to everything it stands for, and that it has real enemies. Their agenda is the destruction of the labor movement. It is futile to try to disarm that opposition by pretending that trade unions are something else than they are, or that they can defend interests other than those of their members and the general interest of society.

Stern often dismisses progressive policies on the grounds that they will encounter too strong an opposition, meaning that they are not acceptable to transnational capital and to the right-wing politicians at its service. The would-be realism of his partnerships with employers is ultimately based on the principle of: if you can't beat'em, join'em. But politics is not "the art of the possible", as opportunists always tell us, it is the art of making possible what is necessary.

Building global unionism takes more than just organizing: it takes organizing inspired by an alternative social and economic perspective. The roots of the labor movement, and the source of its enduring strength and resiliency, is a mission of social change, to bring about a social order based on the general interest of society. Others than Stern will move this agenda forward.

# Bureaucratism: Labour's Enemy Within [2009]

*An interview with Dan Gallin By Peter Hall-Jones\*, for the New Unionism Network (http://www.newunionism.net) 2009*

**Where does bureaucratism in the union movement come from? More to the point, how can we get rid of it?**

In an attempt to answer this question we interviewed the outspoken Dan Gallin, current Chair of the Global Labour Institute. Prior to holding this position, Gallin served 29 years as General Secretary of the International Union of Food, Agricultural, Hotel, Restaurant and Catering, Tobacco and Allied Workers' Associations (IUF). He was also President of the International Federation of Workers' Education Associations (IFWEA) from 1992-2003, and Director of the Organization and Representation Program of Women in Informal Employment Globalizing and Organizing (WIEGO) from 2000-2002. (more on DG below\*).

New Unionism: The union movement is the largest democratic force in the world today, by far. However, too many union members complain about bureaucratic behaviour at leadership level. Do you accept this is a problem, and, if so, what do you think are the root causes?

Dan Gallin: First, let's get the problem in perspective. The level of bureaucracy in unions is constantly overstated. We have much less difficulty in this area than corporations do, for instance. Of course corporations are, by their very nature, top-down power structures – what could be less democratic than your average workplace? – and I cannot imagine anything as wasteful as some management bureaucracies. Similarly, think about bureaucracy in government, or in tri-partite bodies, or in non-governmental organisations. The difference is that unions, by their very structure and purpose, are consciously committed to internal democracy, and so failures are clearly seen as such. The basic structures of unionism are democratic and the internal struggle to assert and reassert democracy is always there. Trade unions have to deliver; there is a very short time span between demand and the delivery. Think of collective bargaining, for instance. Unions are constantly being held to account by their members.

NU: Are you trying to tell us there's no real problem, then?

DG: No. I am not trying to minimize the problem. What I am saying is that bureaucracy is a pervasive feature of all institutional and organizational life. What, after all, is a bureaucracy? It is an administration, and all organizations need an administration. The problem arises when this administration develops a collective interest of its own, separate and eventually even opposed to the interests of the people it is supposed to serve.

This is serious enough in government, where the civil service constitutes a bureaucracy that can easily overreach its authority. In a democracy, the civil service is supposed to be the servant of the people. When it starts to act as its master, democracy is in danger.

In the trade union movement, the problem is even more serious because its administration, its own civil service if you wish, must represent people who have no other source of power than their organization. If this organization ceases to be responsive to their needs, they lose everything. An administration that builds its own power at the expense of the membership is betraying its trust – that is treason.

NU: If, as you say, trade unionism is inherently democratic, why is it that we hear these complaints about unions being run as dictatorships and/or oligarchies?

DG: Actually, there are not so many cases of this, in

proportion. What happens is that we have some spectacular examples of organizations which degenerate and then become notorious. They are falsely represented as typical of the movement, most often in anti-union propaganda. But there is never any guarantee against an organization, even with the best democratic traditions, being hijacked by anti-democratic cliques or personalities.

The hijacking of the Russian revolution by the Communist bureaucracy led by Stalin is a classical example. After four or five short years, a vibrant, radically democratic, revolutionary mass movement started giving way to the rule of a bureaucracy which first asserted, then consolidated power by means of terror, police and military terror against its own people, on a scale not seen before in modern times. A whole new society with a bureaucratic ruling class!

How do these things happen? In order to work, democracy needs the active support of large masses of people at all times. In a union, this means the active participation of most of the membership. Democracy is not a state of being, it is an activity, it is in fact hard work, and it is a constant work in progress. You might say the same thing about freedom.

Most people are not able to maintain a high level of commitment over time. They are not organization professionals, they need to get on with their lives, as they should, so "democracy fatigue" might set in; especially after periods of great social stress. They might not pay attention to what happens in the organization for a time, routine sets in and the professionals take over. If the leaders are not trained in the right kind of politics, if they are not persons of the highest individual integrity, and if they are not supervised and controlled, they may start treating the organization as if it were their own property.

This is why it is the responsibility of every progressive and democratic trade union leadership to maintain constitutional and practical conditions in which membership participation and control is ensured and welcomed, without making conditions of participation too onerous for ordinary members.

NU: Just by way of clarification, can you explain what you mean by "trained in the right kind of politics"?

DG: Socialist politics, of course. And by that I mean the kind of politics based on the values that were at the origins of the labour movement and that made it great: solidarity, selflessness, respect for people, a sense of honour, and the modesty that comes with the awareness of being a soldier in the service of a great cause, a contempt for self-promotion, or "le refus de parvenir" as Monatte(17) called it.

NU: Do you think the Cold War contributed to bureaucratizing the movement?

DG: It certainly did. In a situation of extreme political polarization by outside forces, it is easy to lose sight of the original purpose of the exercise.

First, let us be clear what we are talking about. The Cold War was a conflict between States, between two blocs of States, led by the two superpowers of the time: the United States and the USSR, more or less from 1949 to 1989.

However, this conflict had nothing to do with a much older conflict within the labour movement. This earlier conflict arose after the October Revolution, when the Russian Communist Party created an International of its own and declared war on all other movements of the Left unless they accepted total subordination to its dictates (1). That conflict became unbridgeable once the Communist leadership had moved to imprison and execute activists of other Left tendencies in the territory under its control, including its own opponents and dissidents. Under Stalin, this became a systematic campaign of extermination, with hit men spreading out all over the world to assassinate opponents.

It is small wonder that a majority of the Left, of all tendencies, became "anti-Communist", meaning that they organized to defend themselves as best as they could against Communist claims of hegemony and terror.

When Nazi Germany attacked the USSR in 1941, breaking the treaty it had signed two years previously, the USSR found itself part of the anti-fascist war-time alliance. Despite past history and experience, much of the Western trade-union movement, which was predominantly social-democratic, was ready for organizational unity with Soviet bloc labour organizations. The result was the World Federation of Trade Unions (WFTU), which was founded in 1945. However, it lasted only four years as an inclusive organization of the world's labour movement (though it continued, and still exists, as a Communist rump).

The unity on which the WFTU had been founded was the temporary unity of governments, not a unity of labour – none of the contentious issues between the Communists and everyone else on the Left had been resolved. When the unity of governments gave way to the rivalry between the US and the USSR for world power, the artificial top-down unity of the WFTU also broke apart.

What happened then was a race between the two blocs to secure the support – in fact, the control – of civil society organizations (labour, youth, students, women, etc.), with trade unions as prime targets.

And now comes the complicated part, which must be clearly understood. The Western governments and the non-Communist Left suddenly had the same enemy. The conflict between governments – the "Cold War" – and that earlier conflict within the labour movement, became superimposed. For some, they became indistinguishable.

This is how the war-time relationships which some socialists – and others – had formed with the political services of the US or UK governments (among others) to fight the Nazis continued seamlessly into the fight for a "free world", against the new totalitarian menace.

In reality, we were of course still dealing with two different conflicts and two distinct interests. One was fighting Stalinism to defend working class interests, the other was fighting the USSR as a rival imperialism to that of the US. These are hardly compatible positions, but the most difficult thing to comprehend in politics, especially if you have the knife at your throat, is that the enemy of your enemy is not necessarily your friend.

Despite the apparent symmetry of the situation of the trade union movement within the two blocs, the reality was quite different. In the Soviet bloc, the trade union apparatus was part of the government structures of a police state, and a fairly subordinate structure at that. Dissidence was treated as a criminal offence or as a mental disorder. So in that context, the bureaucracy issue does not even arise in connection with the Cold War -- the whole system had been thoroughly bureaucratized long before. In its first decades, that system was impossible to crack from within.

The situation in the West was much different: here a three-way battle was being fought between the advocates of an alignment on pro-American policies, the advocates and apologists for Soviet policies, and those who kept saying that neither option represented working class interests and that the labour movement should refuse to be aligned with either side.

Those of us who held the latter position believed that the lines of cleavage that mattered most in the world were not the vertical ones separating the two blocs, but the horizontal ones between the working class and the rulers of both systems, a fundamental division cutting across both blocs.

This was not an easy position to hold. The pressures to align and to conform were very strong. Having been put in charge of the AFL-CIO's International Department by George Meany (2), Jay Lovestone (3) -- the Dr. Strangelove (4) of the labour movement -- with his acolyte Irving Brown (5) and the various AFL-CIO Institutes, were running around the world buying unions with US government money, in close cooperation with the CIA , and trying to destroy any organization or individuals that did not accept their line, whether Communist or not. They were not looking for allies, they were recruiting agents.

The Soviet bloc operators were doing the same for the other side, also backed by considerable diplomatic and financial resources. The result of this competition is not difficult to guess: it spread a culture of corruption, especially in Africa where the movement was weakest and most vulnerable, but also in parts of Asia, Latin America, Europe and the United States itself, where some labour leaders were co-opted into Cold War politics, although most had no idea what the International Department was up to, and did not much care until all these operations were exposed in the mid-1960s.

In that sense the Cold War was a very powerful factor of bureaucratization in the West: it created and strengthened corrupt leaderships who no longer had to take their memberships into account, it enforced political conformity, stifled discussion, suppressed dissent and isolated all radical opposition through 'red baiting'.

NU: Some labour writers contend that the acceptance of Cold War politics, and anti-Communist purges by the leadership of the American labour movement, contributed to its paralysis during the conservative onslaught of recent years.

DG: Yes and no. It's not that simple. True enough, after the anti-Communist purges in the Congress of Industrial Organizations (CIO) and the merger with the American Federation of Labor (AFL) in 1955, the conservative elements of the AFL prevailed in the merged AFL-CIO. These people would later prove totally at a loss in the face of globalization and the conservative onslaught launched by Reagan, and continued by his successors, both Republican and Democrat.

But the problem with this reading of history is that it exonerates the American Communist Party of any responsibility in these developments. The CP and its trade union activists are cast in the role of innocent victims. This overlooks the war the CP waged against all of the Left from its earliest days: first against the IWW and the socialists, then against the Trotskyists and against every other kind of radical group it didn't control, and of course against most union leaderships, progressive or not. The CP did what it could to destroy the American Left and, like in Niemöller's poem (6), when they came to get it there was nobody left to defend it.

This said, most conservative labour leaders didn't need the Cold War in order to be ferociously anti-radical, super-patriotic and, eventually, helpless before the anti-labour campaigns of the Right. You have to remember that we're dealing here with very stupid people. They may have been street-wise and cunning, but they knew nothing about the world and couldn't think strategically. The roots of conservatism in the American union movement are very perceptively described by authors such as Daniel Fusfeld and Patricia Cayo Sexton (7). What the Cold War situation did, was to give people like Lovestone the opportunity to organize the right-wing of the American trade union bureaucracy as a base for a major international operation, and to isolate leaders of the labour Left, like Walter Reuther (8), Ralph Helstein (9) and Pat Gorman (10), as well as some good unions with a Communist history, like the ILWU and the UE.

NU: Did the Communists not at least denounce the clandestine right-wing operations the American unions were involved in?

DG: Not at all. Of course they would denounce operations like the overthrow of Arbenz in Guatemala, or of Goulart in Brazil, as examples of American imperialism in action, but there was never any exposure of the union involvement. The CIA and British government operations in the labour movement were blown open by Trotskyists and independent radicals in the mid-1960s. Then the New York Times picked up the story and it became a major scandal. But the CP had nothing to do with it at any stage. Afterwards, of course, everyone started writing about it.

NU: While all of this was happening in the US, bureaucratization must surely have been a growing problem in the European trade union movement as well?

DG: In Europe and elsewhere, for instance in Japan, the

polarized politics of the Cold War also enforced political conformity and stifled dissent, but Europe is a complicated place with many political and trade union cultures, so generalizations are not very useful. In some countries Cold War politics played a major role in the labour movement, in others hardly at all.

Far more pervasive and general were the consequences of the war. Today it is hard to imagine the extent to which the historical labour movement had been destroyed, first by the rise of fascism in the 1920s and 1930s, then by the war itself, with the occupation of most of Europe by the Nazi armies and police. In most of Europe the structures of the labour movement were wiped out, parties and unions of course, but also the entire institutional network that rooted the movement in society: welfare institutions, credit unions, co-ops, cultural and leisure time activities – everything.

Most of the leadership of the movement, right down to local level, had to go into exile, or into concentration camps, or died in the war. Many of the best people were lost. One of the important parties of the Socialist International, the Jewish Labour Bund (11), was destroyed entirely, together with the population that supported it. No one had imagined anything like this could happen, and those who had hoped that the end of WWII would usher in another period of social revolution, a re-play of 1918, had lost touch with reality.

Superficially, the unions emerged in a strong position – after all we were on the side of the victors, whereas big business had collaborated with fascism throughout Europe and had much to be forgiven for. In fact, labour was far weaker than it appeared, and far more dependent on the State than before the war. That too did not seem to be a problem at first, since most post-war governments were pro-labour in one way or another, but it did eventually lead to the loss of the political and material independence of the movement and, yes, it did promote bureaucratization.

Whereas the pre-war movement conceived of itself as a counter-culture and an alternative society, at least in principle, the post-war movement made its peace with the "social market economy" and demanded no more than a better life within the system (full employment, welfare, social protection, good wages and working conditions).

In that situation, the leadership of the movement became increasingly unwilling to maintain a whole network of flanking institutions. If you don't want to change society then you don't need to build an alternative counter-culture or an alternative economy. Think of all the money you can save. So the unions concentrated on their presumed "core business" - collective bargaining with "social partners" - the parties concentrated on elections, and the movement lost its roots in society, lost many of its think tanks and educational institutions, and lost its periphery, a sphere of influence and protection.

At the same time, you had the surge of prosperity in post-war Western Europe through the Marshall Plan. An exhausted working class, after the deprivation and the sufferings of the war, started to get its life back and became gradually more comfortable over the next thirty years. And why not? But as it played out, as a major political factor, it created a problem the movement couldn't cope with, because it also coincided with the rise of media empires, with television, financed largely by advertising. Our movement was not ready to compete at that level. This is where we lost the communications war. We lost our press and any independent expressions of working class culture, with the long-term effect of losing the culture wars in the 1990s.

Many of the issues of the vanished civil society of labour eventually got taken over by others (feminists, environmentalists, human rights activists, etc.), but that's another story.

Then, in countries like France, Italy and Greece, where the CP was dominant in the labour movement, the working class became hostage to Cold War politics and political positions, as well as labour alignments. They were frozen for about thirty or forty years. In some other countries, notably Germany, Cold War polarization also contributed to deadening the political debate and distorting trade union priorities.

Finally, European unions have become accustomed to State subsidies, in general for specific activities, such as education or participation in a host of official and quasi-official institutions and meetings. Today, in many countries, unions would be unable to function without the government subsidies they have become accustomed to.

So what do you get? A heavily bureaucratized and passive movement, initially led by survivors, then rapidly replaced by complacent and arrogant careerists who are happy to depend on the State. They administer the gains of past struggles but are unwilling to conduct any new ones, opposing any ideas they have not thought of themselves and believing that nothing must ever happen for the first time. That kind of leadership educates union members to be passive consumers of union services, not participants in struggle.

NU: You said before that, as far as Europe was concerned, generalizations were not very useful. Should we take that to include what you just said?

DG: You got me there. I think what I have tried to do is draw a common denominator, a composite picture which applies in general but not exactly in any one country. For example, in the Nordic countries, except for a short-lived split in Finland, the Cold War had hardly any impact at all. In Spain, where the labour movement emerged from a fascist regime only in the 1970s, rank-and-file democracy is a strongly-felt aspiration. All of Eastern Europe is a different situation again, and a very complicated situation, with many cross-currents. And of course there are always exceptions. There have been outstanding labour leaders like Otto Brenner (12), Wilhelm Gefeller (13) in Germany, Jack Jones (14) in Britain, André Renard (15) in Belgium. So, one has to fine-tune every national situation. But some will recognize my descriptions and, as the saying goes, if the shoe fits, wear it.

Neither do I want to idealize the pre-war labour movement in Europe. There were too many entirely avoidable and disastrous defeats. The leading labour parties of Germany and Austria had armed militias ready to fight which were awaiting orders that never came. The French Popular Front government refused to support the Spanish Republicans in the civil war, who, had they won, would have changed the course of history. Not to speak of the catastrophic Communist policies, in Germany, in Spain, all over. One needs to reflect on these defeats and learn from them. But even so, the level of ambition in those days was higher.

NU: You were general secretary of the IUF for many years, and active in the international union movement. How does the international movement cope with the problem of bureaucratism?

DG: With difficulty. You have to realize that the international movement is yet another level removed from the rank-and-file: the actual members of international trade union organizations, in a statutory sense, are national unions, not individual workers, so the international organization will reflect to a very large extent the culture and practices of its affiliated unions, particularly the large affiliates.

So, structurally, it is almost inevitably bureaucratic. The politics of the leadership, basically the secretariat and the governing bodies, makes a big difference. You can have an organization with a deeply rooted culture of militancy and a democratic culture, which will do two things: first, ensure that democratic practices are respected and encouraged in the way it operates, within its own governing bodies, and, second, encourage democratic participation within its affiliates wherever it can, for example through its educational programs, in its publications, etc.

NU: And then you have the others...

DG: Indeed. Again, it is a question of politics, of how you interpret the situation and, consequently, how you evaluate the union response required. If you believe that "social partnership" is an accurate description of labour/management relations, and that social change occurs through conversations between political leaders and experts – "social dialogue" - then you will invest your resources and energies in a lobbying operation. The privileged counterparts in these conversations will be the bureaucrats of government organizations and of employers' organizations. In meeting after meeting, you will be bargaining about words, and you will believe you have won a significant victory when you have changed a sentence in a statement. This can go on forever, and no one will ever know the difference. The workers who are members of such organizations don't even know they exist.

NU: How can workers, at rank-and-file level, learn to tell the difference between useful and useless organizations? Where does usefulness become apparent?

DG: Very simple: workers certainly can tell the difference when they become involved in a conflict. When it comes to conflict, the differences are very quickly apparent. And whether our international sell-out artists like it or not, unions are about conflict. Either the international organization pulls out all stops and the saying "one for all, all for one", (especially the second part) becomes a concrete reality, for as long as it takes, or else the international organization starts mediating instead of fighting, tries to minimize and kill the conflict, even sides with the employer just to be rid of the problem.

NU: How does this relate back to the issue of bureaucratism? Are you suggesting that bureaucracy and politics are related?

DG: They are, very much so. However, the relationship is not a mechanical one. For instance it would be simplistic and wrong to say that left-wing politics protects us against bureaucracy. If we are talking about the Communist tradition, the opposite is true, almost always, and this includes Maoism, which is actually an extreme form of Stalinism. People who come out of that school are often dangerous authoritarians. Even when they change their politics, they don't necessarily change their methods.

And of course social-democracy has its own awesome bureaucratic traditions; even anarchist and syndicalist organizations, contrary to legend, can be run in extremely authoritarian and bureaucratic ways.

No, the only form of politics which is an effective antidote to bureaucratism is the kind of socialist politics that contains a strong element of radical democracy. This goes back to Marx himself, but despite appearances, this current was never dominant in the socialist movement. It surfaces from time to time, a person like Rosa Luxemburg would be fairly typical, there were others within the political families of the Left. Eugene Debs in the United States would be another example.

NU: That's not a very broad political base. If that's all we have, is the struggle against bureaucratism lost in advance?

DG: No, because in fact we have very much more. The politics of radical democracy respond to a very deep and fundamental need felt by workers. They keep coming back to this on their own, and they very often spontaneously develop democratic forms of organizing, of conducting struggles, of running their organizations. Rosa Luxemburg understood this. This aspiration is very strong. That is the basic reason why the labour movement has such a democratic culture, despite all the pressures to the contrary from the society that surrounds it... the "old shit", as Marx called it (16).

NU: Do you see workers' desire for deeper forms of democracy extending from union HQ all the way down into the workplace?

DG: Yes, except I would put it the other way around, from the workplace - the "point of production", as the IWW used to say - to union HQ. It has to start at the point of production. As I said, this is a very fundamental need of workers, and actually very often of people in general. Think of women's movements or peasant's movements - in all progressive mass movements there is this demand for transparency and accountability in the leadership.

The point is to nurture and strengthen the politics of radical democracy, the particular strand of socialist politics which I believe is the authentic Marxism, which insists that power, where it matters, always has to remain in the hands of the workers. Today this means almost all of society, since nearly everybody is part of the working class, whether they know it or not. To get there, you have to start from the bottom, the point of production, and then build democratic institutions, like democratic unions, impose democratic procedures at every level, democratize the decision-making mechanism in public administration. We don't want to abolish bureaucracy if bureaucracy means administration, we all need administration and we want it to be honest, transparent and efficient, in our own organizations to start with, then in society at large. We want an administration built on our key values: justice and freedom. These will be the values of the society of the future - if we make it that far.

-- end --

A little more on Dan Gallin's life and work

Dan Gallin is currently chair of the Global Labour Institute (GLI), a foundation established in 1997 with a secretariat in Geneva. The GLI investigates the consequences of the globalization of the world economy for workers and trade unions, develops and proposes counterstrategies and promotes international thought and action in the labour movement. Prior to this, he worked for the IUF from August 1960 until April 1997, since 1968 as General Secretary. He was born in 1931 as a Romanian citizen, became stateless in 1949 and was granted Swiss citizenship in 1969. He studied political science and sociology in the United States and in Switzerland and since 1953 has lived in Geneva. He joined the socialist movement as a student in the United States in 1951 and has been a member of the Swiss Social-Democratic Party since 1955. He is a member of the Swiss General Workers' Union UNIA and has been a member of one of its predecessors, the Swiss Commercial, Transport and Food Workers' Union, since 1960. He served as President of IFWEA from 1992 to 2003 and was Director of the Organization and Representation Program of WIEGO from June 30, 2000 to July 31, 2002. He continues to serve on the WIEGO Steering Committee. He is currently researching union organization of women workers in the informal economy, labour movement history and issues of policy and organization in the international trade union movement.

Peter Hall-Jones is communications co-ordinator for the New Unionism Network (http://www.newunionism.net). The Network is an informal global group of union activists and labour academics who have united around four key principles: organizing, workplace democracy, internationalism and creativity. An illustrated version of this interview can be found at http://www.newunionism.net/redirects/gallin.htm

Endnotes

1. The Second Congress of the Comintern in 1920 agreed on 'Twenty One Conditions', which formalised the beginning of 'the great split': a split which was to divide the labour movement for the rest of the century. For more on what is meant by this, see http://en.wikipedia.org/wiki/Twenty-one_Conditions. Note in particular: 'In the columns of the press, at public meetings, in the trades unions, in the co-operatives – wherever the members of the Communist International can gain admittance – it is necessary to brand not only the bourgeoisie but also its helpers, the reformists of every shade, systematically and pitilessly.'

2. George Meany (1894 – 1980), president of the American Federation of Labor from 1952 to 1955, then, following its merger with the Congress of Industrial Organizations, president of the united AFL-CIO from 1955 to 1979.

3. Jay Lovestone (1906 – 1989), a founder of the American Communist Party, later leader of the Right-Wing opposition group (the pro-Bukharin faction) which dissolved in 1941. In 1943 Lovestone became international affairs director of the International Ladies Garment Workers' Union and, in 1963, director of the international affairs department of the AFL-CIO. He held that position until 1974 and as the main architect of the collaboration of the AFL-CIO with the CIA. For more on Lovestone, see: 'A Covert Life: Jay Lovestone, Communist,

Anti-Communist, and Spymaster' by Ted Morgan (New York: Random House, 1999) and 'Taking Care of Business' by Paul Buhle, Monthly Review Press, New York, 1999.

4. Dr. Strangelove: the 1964 black comedy film by Stanley Kubrick, featuring a paranoiac American general launching a nuclear attack on the Soviet Union, hoping to thwart a Communist conspiracy to "sap and impurify" the "precious bodily fluids" of the American people with fluoridated water. The US president in the film is advised by a "mad scientist" type: Dr. Strangelove.

5. Irving Brown (1911 – 1989), chief lieutenant and hatchet man for Lovestone since the 1930s, set up "anti-Communist" operations in the trade union movement, mostly in Europe, including the notorious Mediterranean Committee, organized with the help of gangsters in French, Italian and Greek ports.

6. Martin Niemöller (1892 – 1984), prominent German anti-Nazi theologian and Lutheran pastor. He is best known as the author of the following lines (and variations thereof):
"First they came for the communists, and I did not speak out—because I was not a communist;
Then they came for the socialists, and I did not speak out—because I was not a socialist;
Then they came for the trade unionists, and I did not speak out—because I was not a trade unionist;
Then they came for the Jews, and I did not speak out—because I was not a Jew;
Then they came for me—and there was no one left to speak out for me."

7. Daniel Fusfeld: The Rise and Repression of Radical Labor 1877-1918, Charles H. Kerr Publishing Company, Chicago, 1980 (ISBN 088286050X) and Patricia Cayo Sexton: The War on Labor and the Left – Understanding America's Unique Conservatism, Westview Press, Boulder/San Francisco/Oxford, 1991 (ISBN 0813310636)

8. Walter Reuther (1907 – 1970), leading organizer and after 1946 president of the United Auto Workers' union, a Socialist

Party member until 1939, president of the Congress of Industrial Organizations (CIO) in 1952, negotiated the merger with the American Federation of Labor in 1955, eventually clashed with Meany over the conservative policies of the AFL-CIO and formed a short-lived alternative center, the Alliance for Labor Action (1958-1972) with the Teamsters and a few smaller unions. On May 9, 1970, Reuther and his wife May were killed when their chartered plane crashed while on final approach to the airstrip near the union's recreational and educational facility at Black Lake, Michigan. In October 1968, a year and a half before the fatal crash, Reuther and his brother Victor were almost killed in a small private plane as it approached Dulles airport. Both incidents are amazingly similar; the altimeter in the fatal crash was believed to have malfunctioned. When Victor Reuther was interviewed many years after the fatal crash he said "I and other family members are convinced that both the fatal crash and the near fatal one in 1968 were not accidental."

9. Ralph Helstein (1908 – 1985), president of the United Packinghouse Workers of America (UPWA) from 1946 to 1968. Under his leadership, the union, a CIO affiliate, became one of the most militant and democratic unions in the US. It organized the meat packing industry in the US and Canada and played a leading role in fighting for minority and women's rights. When the UPWA merged with the Amalgamated Meat Cutters union in 1968, Helstein became vice president and special counsel. He worked with the union until 1972 and died in Chicago in 1985.

10. Patrick Emmet Gorman (1882 – 1980), a life-long socialist, International Secretary-Treasurer of the Amalgamated Meat Cutters and Butcher Workmen (AFL) from 1942 to 1976 (the Meat Cutters were an old socialist union which had a European constitution, where the secretary-treasurer, not the president, was the chief executive officer). Gorman opposed Meany on the Vietnam war and on many other political issues.

11. The General Jewish Labour Union of Lithuania, Poland and Russia, in Yiddish the Algemeyner Yidisher Arbeter Bund in Lite, Poyln un Rusland , generally called the Bund (from

German and Yiddish: Bund, meaning federation or union) or the Jewish Labour Bund, was a Jewish political party and trade union in several European countries operating predominantly between the 1890s and the 1930s with remnants of the party still active in the United States, Canada, Australia, France and the United Kingdom. The Bund opposed Zionism and fought for the recognition of Jews as an autonomous cultural community within European countries. In this and in other respects it was strongly influenced by the Austro-Marxist school of socialism, and was a left-socialist party in the Labour and Socialist International. In WWII it was active in the resistance movement against the Nazi occupation in Poland and in Lithuania, one of its leaders, Marek Edelman, was a leader of the Warsaw Ghetto uprising in 1943, and later of the Workers' Defense Committee (KOR) in 1976 and of the Solidarity movement. Edelman died in Warsaw on October 2, 2009 at the age of 90. Two leaders of the Bund, Victor Alter and Henryk Erlich, who had sought refuge in the USSR after the German invasion, were executed in December 1941 in Moscow on Stalin's orders.

12. Otto Brenner (1907 – 1972), president of the German metal workers' union IG Metall from 1956 to 1972. In 1931 Brenner left the Social-Democratic Party (SPD) which he had joined as a youth to join the Socialist Workers' Party, founded by Left Socialists and dissident Communists, too late to prevent the seizure of power by Hitler. Brenner became active in the anti-Nazi resistance, was arrested in 1933, sentenced to two years' prison and kept under police supervision until the end of the war. In 1945 Brenner re-joined the SPD and became active in the reconstruction of the trade union movement. At the head of the IG Metall he played a leading tole in the defence of democratic rights and against rearmament. In 1961, he was elected president of the International Metalworkers' Federation.

13. Wilhelm Gefeller (1906 – 1983), president of the German chemical workers' union IG Chemie from 1949 to 1969 , one of the founders of the post-war German trade union movement, active in the SPD. Strong advocate of co-determination in German industry and at international level, and of democratic

rights. President of the International Chemical and General Workers' Unions (ICF) in the late 1960s.

14. James Larkin (Jack) Jones (1913 – 2009), general secretary of the Transport & General Workers' Union (UK) from 1968 to 1978. Throughout his career he strove to increase the power and influence of shop stewards. In 1937 he joined the International Brigades in the Spanish civil war and was wounded in 1938. Jones was also Vice-President of the International Transport Workers Federation and, after his retirement, was a campaigner for pensioners' rights. His autobiography, Union Man, was published in 1986.

15. André Renard (1911 – 1962), Belgian trade unionist, active in the resistance under Nazi occupation, created an illegal united trade union movement independent of political parties and advocated its extension to the entire country at liberation, but could not overcome the split between socialist and Catholic unions. Deputy General-Secretary of the socialist trade union center FGTB, leader of the six-week general strike in 1960-1961 against the austerity policies of the conservative government. A strong advocate for the autonomy of Wallonia (the French-speaking part of Belgium).

16. "...revolution is necessary, therefore, not only because the ruling class cannot be overthrown in any other way, but also because the class overthrowing it can only in a revolution succeed in ridding itself of all the old shit and become fitted to found society anew." Karl Marx: The German Ideology, Part I: Feuerbach. Opposition of the Materialist and Idealist Outlook 1845

17. Pierre Monatte (1881 – 1960) A proof-reader by profession, he was a leader of the French CGT when it was a revolutionary syndicalist organization and, in 1909, founded its journal, La Vie Ouvrière. He was an anti-war internationalist during World War I., joined the French Communist Party in 1923 and was expelled in 1924 for opposing its bureaucratization. He then returned to revolutionary syndicalism, and in 1925 he founded La Révolution Prolétarienne, which is still being published (http://revolutionproletarienne.wordpress.com).

"Le refus de parvenir" means: "the refusal of social climbing".

# Informal economy workers and the international trade union movement: an overview [2012]

*Critical Labour Studies 8th Symposium*
*February 18 –19, 2012, University of Salford*

**What are workers in the informal economy?**

**What are informal workers? To put it simply, they are workers whose rights are not recognized and who are therefore unable to exercise those rights. What is an informal economy? Again, to put it simply, it is an economy where few social rules apply, where the strong prevail by the sole virtue of their strength because they have not met with organized opposition.**

At their origin, all trade unions were formed by informal workers, since the entire economy was informal at the time trade unions were first organized. Trade unions were, and still are, self-help organizations of workers who, through collective action, seek to regulate their wages and working conditions so as to eliminate the worst forms of exploitation, i.e. to formalize an informal situation. A "formal" economy is an economy in which the labour movement has negotiated regulated wages and conditions through a combination of Industrial and political action (by collective agreements and by law).

In an economy which is not formally organized, the social organization which is dominant comes to prevail by default. In patriarchal societies, this translates into a patriarchal organization of work relationships. It is therefore unsurprising that we find women workers numerically dominant in the informal economy, occupying the low-income, low-skill occupations.

However, historically trade unions were in most cases first organized by men and avoided tackling the causes of patriarchal exploitation of women workers, often confining their struggles to only those shop floor issues common to male and female workers. This resulted in more male workers enjoying regulated wages and working conditions while more women workers remained in the unregulated informal economy.

The effort to formalize the informal economy, which has been going on all over the world for the last 150 years or so, has been only partially successful. In terms of social relations, the economy has been "formalized" to a significant extent only in the industrialized world (mostly Western Europe, North America, Japan, Australia, New Zealand).

Elsewhere, the informal economy remained proportionally dominant and, through deregulation and privatization policies imposed by the International Financial Institutions, has actually grown at the expense of the "formal" economy (Latin America, most of sub-Saharan Africa, but also India). In some countries, where advanced mechanisms of social protection and workers' rights had been introduced in the early and middle 20th century, the economy was "de-formalized" by State violence during its last three decades (most of Latin America). In the former centrally planned economies, authoritarian formal structures have largely been replaced by an informalized economy (the successor States of the USSR and Eastern Europe) and in the remaining countries with a centrally planned economy, the informal economy is fostered by State policies behind a formal façade (China, Vietnam, Cuba). In summary, most of the world's population lives in an informal economy and even in the countries where formal arrangements have prevailed since the end of World War II, they are currently under challenge.

In most of the world, conditions for trade union activity are therefore quite comparable to those prevailing when trade unionism first started in Europe and North America in the middle 19th century, and the conditions under which trade unionism originally developed are therefore of more than historical interest.

The International Trade Union Movement

The international trade union movement originated with the First International (1864 - 1876), which included various forms of workers' organizations: political parties and propaganda groups, unions, co-operatives, mutual aid societies, etc. The Second International, which followed in 1889, like the First, also included political parties and trade unions, as well as other workers' organizations. Soon, however, the need for a clearer division of labour made itself felt. After 1900, the Second International became an organization of socialist parties and its other components gradually established their separate international organizations.

Some of the unions attending the founding congress of the International decided to establish international organizations of workers in the same trade or industry. These became known as the International Trade Secretariats (ITS), the first permanently organized form of international trade union solidarity.

The national trade union centers in different countries, some of which were not involved in the Second International (in particular the syndicalist CGT in France and the British trade unions), also felt the need for an independent international organization. As a result, a formal secretariat was set up in 1903, which became the International Federation of Trade Unions (IFTU) in 1913.

International trade unionism as such exists in a recognizable form since the last decade of the 19th century and the first decade of the 20th

In those two decades, unions in most of Europe and in North America had become mass organizations, well on the way to formalizing an informal labour force. The contrast between the formal and informal economy was not perceived in these terms but simply as an organizing issue, between organized and unorganized workers, at national and international level. However, the gender issue, which is today the crucial issue when it comes to organizing in the informal economy, was present from the beginning.

The gender issue

The labour movement, from its earliest days, had charismatic women leaders, such as Flora Tristan Moscoso (1803-1844), a social activist in France and in Peru, who wrote "L'Union Ouvrière" (The Workers' Union), where she anticipated the Communist Manifesto by calling for an international general workers' union and by stressing that the workers had to emancipate themselves by their own action, that no one else was going to do it for them, and that they had to unite internationally because society itself had become international.

Louise Michel, an anarchist leader of the Paris Commune, later deported to New Caledonia, was a beacon of revolutionary integrity. Later Rosa Luxemburg became a leader of revolutionary social-democracy and Clara Zetkin, with much the same politics, became a leader of the garment workers' international.

Unfortunately, the prominence of these outstanding leaders, among some others, did not reflect the reality on the ground.

When women workers first started to join unions they frequently had to face not only opposition from the employers and from the State (in the form of anti-labour legislation), but also opposition from their male colleagues. The early labour movement, initiated and led by men, had internalized the prevailing patriarchal values of society, regardless how radical its opposition to other aspects of the social order might have been.

With few exceptions, male workers initially viewed women as

competitors in the labour market, rejected female participation in the labour force and supported the confinement of women to the home and rearing of children. The Swiss anarchist James Guillaume, reporting on the inaugural congress of the First International, approvingly quoted a memorandum by a Paris delegate on the role of women in society, which stated: "The family is the foundation of society; the woman's place is at the domestic home; not only do we not want her to abandon it to be a delegate in a political assembly or make speeches in a club, but we would even prefer, if that were possible, that she should not leave it to take up industrial employment". This early phase has been described by Werner Thönnessen as a phase of "proletarian anti-feminism" (1).

At a later stage, when it was realized that female labour would inevitably increase, the (male) workers conceded that women had a right to work, and sought to eliminate the detrimental effect of female competition in the labour market by incorporating women in the labour movement and adopting the principle of equal pay for equal work (later: for work of equal value).

Although by that time men and women in the movement had forcefully argued for equality at all levels, and some trade union organizations had acted on such principles, discrimination against women did not disappear with these new insights. "Proletarian anti-feminism" came up in new and different forms, for example by trying to channel women's activities in the movement into social work so that other spheres of activity, where executive power was exercised, could more easily remain reserved for men.

In the 19th and early 20th century many independent women's unions were organized In North-Western Europe and North America because in many instances women workers were unable to find adequate representation in existing unions. The reasons were several: in Britain and Ireland, women were excluded from most craft unions and, as overwhelmingly unskilled workers, there was nowhere else for them to go but to create their own organizations. In other cases, as in Denmark, they were denied access even to general workers' unions and had to create their own.

Organizing informal workers was rarely an issue: the main issue was organizing women wage-workers in formal employment, although there were exceptions. One of these was the short-lived Women Workers' Federation in Switzerland. A Congress for the Protection of Home Workers met in August 1909. At that time, about half of the industrial labour force in Switzerland were home-based workers, three quarters of these women and children, in certain occupations only women. The Women Workers' Federation had made the organization of home-based workers a priority.

Verena Conzett, president of the Women Workers' Federation said that women's home work, far from being a mere supplement to the family income, was in fact in many cases the main income. Because the men were unwilling to admit that they depended on the incomes of the women, they played down the importance of home work and therefore made the organization of women home workers much more difficult.

Since men were the main reason why women were so hard to organize, Conzett concluded: "When we seek to organize these women, let us therefore begin in the first place with the men. Let us teach them, in all associations and unions, to regard homework on its own merits. Let them lose the false shame of accepting that women must contribute to the family livelihood; instead, they should enlighten the women and bring them into the organization."

Fast Forward

The political upheavals of the 20th century affected as a matter of course the international trade union movement. The Soviet Union in its early days created the Red International of Labour Unions (RILU) as a competitor to the IFTU. The RILU. was dissolved in 1937 when its existence became an obstacle to the foreign policy of the Soviet Union requiring the inclusion of Social-Democracy and, in trade union terms, of the IFTU, in "Popular Fronts".

In 1945, the IFTU was dissolved and the WWII alliance of the Western Allies and the Soviet Union was reflected in the creation of the World Federation of Trade Unions (WFTU) uniting social-democratic and communist unions, including those of the Soviet bloc.

The WFTU was a problematic construction from the beginning, because of unresolved and irreconcilable issues between the social-democratic and socialist currents and the communist current and because of the refusal of the ITSs to accept a centralized structure where they would have lost their autonomy. The onset of the Cold War collapsed this fragile edifice leading to the formation of the International Confederation of Free Trade Unions (ICFTU), by the social-democratic and North American unions, in 1949, picking up where the IFTU had left off, and leaving the WFTU as the international organization of the Soviet-dominated communist unions.

Meanwhile the Christian, mainly Catholic, unions, which had formed the International Federation of Christian Trade Unions (IFCTU) in 1920, reorganized independently after the war. After opening up to other religions (f.ex. Buddhists in South Vietnam), the IFCTU renamed itself World Confederation of Labour (WCL) in 1968.

The post-war international trade union movement was different from the pre-war movement in one significant respect: it was for the first time truly world-wide, no longer essentially European. The former British and French colonies, and others, covering most of Africa and Asia, were now independent States with their own trade union movements, and new transport and communication technologies made it possible to maintain constant contact across regions and continents.

This also meant that international trade union organizations were for the first time in close and sustained contact with economies where workers with permanent, full-time and regular employment were a small minority, and where the majority of the working class found itself in an informal economy where women were over represented.

The implication of this new situation did not register with any of the existing international trade union federations, irrespective of ideology or political affiliation. Neither the ICFTU, nor the WFTU, nor the WCL, nor the ITSs, perceived the many millions of home-based workers, street and market vendors, rag pickers, domestic workers, among others, as workers, much less as potential trade union members.

The reason, of course, is that none of their national affiliates had this perception. Even in a country like India, several trade union federations with different political allegiances fought over wage workers representing less than ten percent of the real working class, dismissing the over 90 percent of labour as being outside their scope.

The very concept of the "informal sector" or " informal economy" did not exist until it first appeared in the early 1970s in ILO documents and it did not have a significant impact on trade union policies until more than a decade later. Where the existence of an "informal sector" was acknowledged, it was assumed to be an archaic survival of earlier economic structures that would disappear as a result of economic growth in a capitalist economy.

Nor had much progress been made on the gender issue. Most of the women workers' unions which had appeared at the end of the 19th century and in the first decades of the 20th had disappeared through integration into mixed unions, and the "women's committees" that replaced them in some unions and national federations were marginalized and had neither the financial autonomy nor the political means to seriously affect union policy. The same applied at international level. Very few women occupied leading positions anywhere in the world at any but local levels.

SEWA and the First Breakthrough

What I have described here applies more or less to the three decades following WWII, which, in the industrialized world, were a period of economic growth supporting a social welfare State with few challenges, if any, to the position of trade unions in society.

This context started changing with the "second-wave feminism" of the 1960s and 1970s, in the US and Europe, also eventually in Latin America and world-wide, together with the youth revolt of the late 1960s. At the same time, the first "oil shock" of 1974 ushered in a period of permanent, structural mass unemployment in the industrialized countries, which undermined the post-war social compromise where the trade union movement had enjoyed an influential position in social policy.

The trade union movement was suddenly on the defensive on several fronts: its conservatism was challenged by labour feminists and new radical movements, at the same time as its power in society was being challenged by more aggressive business. interests backed by conservative political parties.

This was the global context at the time when the Self Employed Women's Association (SEWA) appeared in India. SEWA, based in Ahmedabad, Gujarat, grew out of the Women's Wing of the Textile Labour Association (TLA), India's oldest and largest union of textile workers founded by a woman, Anasuya Sarabhai, in 1920. The inspiration for the union came from Mahatma Gandhi, who had led a successful strike of textile workers in 1917.

The Women's Wing was established in 1954, initially to assist women belonging to the households of textile workers and its work was focused largely on vocational training and welfare activities. The scope of its activities expanded in the early 1970s when groups of informal women workers (women tailors, cart-pullers at the cloth market, head-loaders carrying loads of clothes between the wholesale and retail markets, used garment dealers) approached the union for protection.

In December 1971, to meet the demand by these women workers for an independent structure, the TLA and its

Women's Wing decided to establish the Self Employed Women's Association. The head of the Women's Wing, Ela Bhatt, became its first general secretary.

SEWA grew continuously, from an initial membership of 320 in 1972 to over 6,000 in 1981. By then, however, relations between SEWA and TLA had deteriorated. The TLA (male) leadership had become increasingly uncomfortable with an assertive women's group in its midst with its own agenda and its own views on union priorities.

In 1981, the SEWA members were expelled from the TLA over a policy conflict and SEWA became an independent union.

In 1983, SEWA was looking for support from the international trade union movement, and first approached the International Textile, Garment and Leather Workers' Federation (ITGLWF), the ITS to which the TLA was affiliated. The ITGLWF referred SEWA to the International Union of Food and Allied Workers' Association (IUF).

The IUF accepted SEWA into affiliation immediately. It rejected the objections from the Indian national trade union federations which claimed that SEWA was not a real union but a "women's NGO", that its members were not real workers because they did not have employers and that it discriminated against men because it was a women workers' organization.

This was the first time that an international trade union organization had deliberately and in full knowledge of the issues, recognized an organization of informal women workers as a union of workers and welcomed it into affiliation. Eventually SEWA also affiliated to the ITGLWF and to ICEM, with its membership in paper recycling.

The IUF at that time was itself a dissident in the international trade union movement. Many of its affiliates were small and struggling, their survival depended on the militancy and the dedication of their members and of their leadership. Its membership had a high proportion of women, particularly in the hotel and restaurant sector, but also in certain industries (fish and vegetable canning, tobacco processing). Its leadership had scant regard for the bureaucratic culture of the ICFTU and of some of the other ITSs and, although anti-communist, had no fear of socialist or other radical politics.

In the following years, the IUF supported SEWA in different ways, among others by ensuring its presence at ICFTU congresses and at the annual International Labour Conference, as part of the IUF delegation.

In 1995 and 1996 SEWA and the IUF formed the core of a broader coalition fighting for the adoption of an ILO convention for home-based workers. The Dutch national center FNV, and the secretariat of the ILO Workers' Group, then led by Guy Ryder, were supportive and the Home Work Convention (C. 177) was adopted by the International Labour Conference in 1996, by a small majority and against strong opposition from the employers.

HomeNet International, a network of home-based workers' unions and NGOs, which had been set up in 1994, also with the participation of SEWA, was part of this coalition. However, it collapsed as an international organization in 2002 over internal democracy issues. Its Asian regional affiliates survived the collapse and a new regional network in South Eastern Europe is currently under construction.

In 1997 SEWA, which by then had grown to several hundred thousand members, was instrumental in setting up WIEGO (Women in Informal Employment Globalizing and Organizing), an international network of unions and associations, academic researchers and professionals from development agencies, dedicated to advance the interests of informal workers, particularly women workers, principally through their organization into unions. This was the task of its Organization and Representation Program (ORP), which started its activities in 2000. The former IUF general secretary, who had retired from the IUF in 1997, became the first ORP director in 2000 and served in that capacity until 2002.

WIEGO, through its ORP, approached the ICFTU beginning in 2000 to explore possibilities of co-operation, but relations turned out to be difficult. The ICFTU secretariat viewed WIEGO with suspicion and hostility. This was due in part because WIEGO had stated as one of its objectives the creation of an international organization of informal workers, later amended to "international platform", but nevertheless perceived by the ICFTU as an intent to create a rival organization. In an effort to remove such fears, WIEGO then declared that it was not going to do any organizing itself, but would support organizing in the informal economy by unions, either established or new unions.

However, the problem went deeper. The ICFTU secretariat was actually in denial that workers in the informal economy had specific issues in common. Its position was that informal workers should be organized by the ITSs according to their "trade", ignoring the fact that some occupations (as in the case of home workers) cut across many "trades", and that many informal workers were moving across different occupations in their working lives.

Underlying this were of course solidly conservative and bureaucratic attitudes. It has been said that the definition of a conservative is a person who believes that nothing must ever happen for the first time. The ICFTU secretariat was not prepared to support any initiative it had not thought of itself first. The fact that new ideas and approaches were being proposed by women's organizations, represented in addition by the former IUF general secretary who was not universally popular in ICFTU circles, did not help.

At the 17th ICFTU congress held in Durban in May 2000, a group of progressive unions had come together to submit a resolution demanding that the ICFTU should make organizing in the informal economy one of its priorities. They were the FNV (Netherlands), COSATU (South Africa), KCTU (Korea) and CUT (Brazil). The congress adopted the resolution and the ICFTU secretariat had to take some action.

The action consisted in creating a "Task Force on the Informal

Economy" which met twice, once in September 2001 and another time in March 2002. WIEGO (together with SEWA as IUF delegates and, in the second meeting, StreetNet) managed to get itself invited, but the participants had been selected to make sure that the position of the ICFTU secretariat was endorsed. The WIEGO position found no support except from the FNV participant, and the Task Force was never heard from again.

Meanwhile, organizations of street and market vendors, SEWA among them, were coming together and had started to build an international network. A StreetNet office was set up in Durban, South Africa, early in 2000, work-shops were held in Africa, Asia and Latin America in 2001 and 2002 and the international co-ordinator made field trips to several countries, some of which resulted in the establishment of new organizations.

StreetNet International was formally launched in November 2002 and soon established productive working relations with Union Network International (UNI), the ITS of commercial workers (among others). StreetNet is of course also an affiliate of WIEGO. No one in the official trade union movement seemed to take notice of this development and there was no sign of opposition. After an initial set-back, the collapse of the South African Self Employed Women's Union (SEWU), one of its founders, StreetNet grew rapidly and now has forty-four affiliates in Africa, Asia, Europe and Latin America.

The ILO Recognizes that "Workers are Workers"

Also in 2002, the International Labour Conference had informal employment on its agenda. The discussion was based on an extensive report entitled: "Decent Work in the Informal Economy." A Coalition of workers' representatives, some of who were also delegates in the Workers' Group, as well as labour NGOs, coordinated by WIEGO and the Global Labour Institute (2), succeeded in significantly framing the debate in the Workers' Group and in the Tripartite Committee. The attempt of the ICFTU advisor to the Workers' Group to challenge the concept of the "informal economy" and to engage a discussion on terminology was deflected early on. The most important outcome of the discussion was the recognition of own-account workers as workers. Leah Vosko, a Canadian researcher who reported on the conference for the Coalition, wrote:

"The Conclusions concerning decent work in the informal economy note that these workers are part of the informal economy "because they lack protection, rights and representation and are trapped in poverty." This characterization is a historic move for several reasons: (1) it effectively extends the application of a range of ILO standards (certainly the core labour standards) to a new group of workers; (2) it weakens the position of employers' organizations in making claims that the own account self-employed are not workers; (3) and, it places more weight on the presence of 'dependent work' than an employment relationship per se as a threshold for providing social protection"

Vosko made another important point regarding the role of trade unions of formal workers and their international organizations as well as the role of trade unions of informal workers and, in particular, the appropriate relationship between these groups:

"Prior to the ILC, some trade unionists expressed unease, suggesting that the growing presence of democratic membership-based organizations of informal economy workers and trade unions of informal economy workers at ILO forums signalled the growth of quadripartism. In other words, many of these groups were viewed, by some, as NGOs. With the clear alliance between the Coalition and the Workers' Group at the ILC and the assertion by the ILO that 'own account workers are workers', such concerns may dissipate. Regardless, the question of the nature of the alliance between democratic membership-based organizations of informal economy workers and the international trade union movement – or the bridge between these groupings – remains. While democratic membership-based organizations of informal economy workers and trade unions of informal workers distanced themselves from the NGO movement in this discussion, thereby reinforcing tripartism in the ILO and bolstering the power of the Workers' Group, the debate over horizontal vs. vertical organizing is ongoing as is the debate about how to define representative, democratic, membership-based organizations, when it comes to informal economy workers."

Crashing the Party

The next step for SEWA and its supporters was to seek SEWA's affiliation to the ICFTU and, parallel, to constitute a group of ICFTU-affiliated national centers organizing workers in the informal economy, which had co-operated with SEWA and WIEGO previously, to advance the agenda of informal workers within the ICFTU.

This group, which was called the International Co-ordinating Committee (ICC) of unions organizing workers in the informal economy, was constituted in 2004. It held two conferences, the first in Ahmedabad, India, in December 2003 and the second in Accra, Ghana, in September 2006. The ICC core group, apart from SEWA, included the Ghana TUC, the Nigerian Labour Congress, CROC (Mexico), StreetNet International and HomeNet South East Asia.

Both conferences analyzed the situation of informal workers in the world, developed organizing strategies and raised a series of demands, addressed to public authorities and to the trade union movement. One of the demands was the establishment of a Department for the informal economy in the new international trade union confederation to be created through the merger of the ICFTU and the WCL in November 2006, and that informal economy workers' issues be included as a priority in all plans and programs of the new confederation, such as Specific Action Plans and research programs.

The ICC also regularly held side meetings at the International Labour Conference, which were well attended and raised substantial interest. .

However, the ICC only functioned as long as Pat Horn, international co-ordinator of StreetNet, also acted as ICC co-ordinator. When she withdrew from this responsibility in order to commit herself entirely to StreetNet, the ICC drastically reduced its activities. A third conference, to be held in Mexico in 2009, did not meet. The side meetings held by the ICC at the International Labour Conference continued to attract attention and were well attended but, for lack of organization, the ICC had ceased to be an effective pressure group within the international trade union movement.

On the issue of affiliation, SEWA was more successful. SEWA applied for affiliation to the ICFTU in May 2005 and its application was first examined by the ICFTU Executive Board in December 2005. In the meantime, SEWA had picked up significant additional support among ICFTU affiliates, among others the DGB, the AFL-CIO, the TUC (UK). At the EB meeting, many unions from all regions spoke up supporting SEWA's affiliation. There was just one opposition, from the INTUC general secretary, who complimented SEWA on its work but said it should join the INTUC. Sharan Burrow, then ICFTU president and presiding the meeting, supported the application. Despite this overwhelming support, the ICFTU secretariat succeeded in getting the decision postponed until the following EB meeting, pending a "fact-finding mission" to SEWA. The mission came and went, and the subsequent EB meeting, in June 2006, accepted SEWA into affiliation without opposition.

SEWA and its supporters were much less successful in translating this affiliation into policy. When the ICFTU and the WCL merged in November 2006, SEWA became automatically a member of the new International Trade Union Confederation (ITUC). and at the founding congress, Jyoti Macwan, SEWA general secretary, was elected one of the twenty-two Vice Presidents of the ITUC. That, however, was largely a symbolic achievement. The new International had neither a "department" nor a "desk" for informal workers, nor was the informal workers' agenda any part of the priorities of the new organization.

Even though the ITUC secretariat was largely identical to what it had been in the ICFTU, and such new WCL element as had been introduced in it was in no way more progressive or less bureaucratic, the continuing marginalization of informal workers could no longer be blamed just on the obstruction of the secretariat, which, after all, was now led by Sharan Burrow, who had been a SEWA ally and certainly understood the problems of informal workers and their organizations.

The problem now lies with SEWA itself, which has become a sprawling organization of 1.3 million members without adequate management structures to translate this mass into power, at least not at international level. SEWA has been a hybrid movement, a union, a women's movement and a co-operative movement, not unlike some unions of the late 19th and early 20th century. That has been a source of its strength, but if not framed in adequate structures, it can also become a source of weakness  Unless and until SEWA resolves its problem of leadership (which is now dispersed internally among several power centers), of identity (will the union identity remain dominant?) and of its priorities (reorganize in a way it can exercise power at every level of its activity) it will not be able to provide leadership in an international context. And unless SEWA can lead, the informal workers' agenda in the ITUC remains stalled.

The Next Breakthrough

The next story, which changed entirely the discussion about organizing informal workers, is that of the domestic workers. The international domestic workers' movement originated quite recently. A number of domestic workers' unions already existed, they first came together in a meeting called by IRENE (International Restructuring Network Europe), a Dutch NGO, the International Seminar on Domestic Workers (Amsterdam, November 8-10, 2006), with the support of FNV and the ICFTU and with the participation of the Asian Domestic Workers' Network and WIEGO.

This initiative eventually resulted In the creation in 2009 of the International Domestic Workers' Network (IDWN), supported by the IUF and WIEGO, which was instrumental in securing the Domestic Workers' Convention (C. 189) at the International Labour Conference of 2010. The IDWN is as much a women's movement as it is a union movement, and it derives its energy largely through the confluence of these two factors.

Thank you for your attention.

Notes

(1) Werner Thönnessen, The Emancipation of Women (The Rise and Decline of the Women's Movement in German Social Democracy 1863-1933), Pluto Press, London, 1973

(2) The Global Labour Institute, based in Geneva, is a labour service organization founded in 1997 (www.global-labour.org). It prepared a background document for the 2002 ILC called "Workers in the Informal Economy: Platform of Issues" which can be downloaded from the GLI website. The GLI is in partnership with the Global Labour Institute UK based in Manchester (http://global-labour.net), with the Global Labor Institute at Cornell University (http://www.ilr.cornell.edu/globallaborinstitute) in New York and with Center Praxis (http://www.praxiscenter.ru/about_us/english).
Postscript (December 2013)

A three-day workshop was conducted by the ITUC and SEWA in Ahmedabad from September 25 to 27, 2013. Participants were staff responsible for the informal economy at the Brussels head office and in the Latin American and African regional offices. On the first day, they visited several of SEWA's operations: organizing, the bank, the academy and the social protection division. During the conference, participants examined the ITUC policy position on the informal economy as reflected in the resolutions of its international and regional governing bodies. This was followed by presentations and discussions on the following themes:

• Overcoming obstacles to organizing workers in the informal

economy
- Social protection as an organizing drive for workers in the informal economy: What have we learned from successful experiences?
- Gaining rights and protection for workers in the informal economy – what works?
- How can the ITUC and its regional organizations promote organizing campaigns targeting workers in the informal economy?

In conclusion, it was agreed that the informal economy agenda of the ITUC should be focused on the following three key themes, which emerged from the discussions and will be put forward to the ITUC World Congress in May 2014:

1. Union growth based on organizing workers in the informal economy
2. Sustainable work, income security and social protection
3. Realizing rights of workers in the informal economy

From the reports of the workshop, it appears that the "marginalization of informal workers" in the ITUC has now come to an end and that SEWA is now in a position to lead the informal workers' agenda in the ITUC.

# Our Crisis [2013]

*This speech was held on June 19, 2013 at Saronikos (near Athens), at a meeting organized by SYRIZA and co-sponsored by the Global Labour Institute, the University of Greenwich (UK) and The Press Project.gr on the theme: Fighting Austerity: Rebuilding Unions From Below.*

Comrades,

**I want to open a discussion on our crisis, the crisis of the labour movement, because I believe that the multiple crises we are facing in society are ultimately the result of the failures of our movement, and that we cannot effectively deal with those economic, social and political crises unless we overcome our own crisis first.**

I also believe that resolving our crisis is our most direct responsibility, that it depends on us alone and that it is a task we must immediately address because time is short.

There was a time when the term "labour movement" had a precise meaning: it meant the movement of the working class with a political and an industrial wing: the party and the union, which, together with an array of auxiliary and flanking organizations, had a common aim: the emancipation of labour and the establishment of a socialist society. That, at any rate, was the dominant concept up to the second decade of the 20th century.

The present situation could not be more different. The historical alliance of the trade union movement with a mass party representing the working class has broken down. This did not happen suddenly, it was a long process, over several decades, with many lost battles, for reasons too long to go into here.

I want to focus on the outcome of this process, our present crisis, which has several basic elements.

The first is the crisis of social-democracy in Western Europe and elsewhere (India, Japan). The social-democratic labour movement emerged from World War II superficially strong, actually greatly weakened by its losses under fascism and in the war, and far more dependent on State support than it had been before the war. The socialist transformation of society was no longer on the agenda.

In the context of post-war capitalist reconstruction in Europe and Japan, and the division of the world into two power blocs led by the US and the USSR, many nominally social-democratic and labour parties abandoned their identity as class parties of labour, claimed to represent wider popular interests and adopted policies detrimental to the working class, dictated by their historical enemies.

Today, there are very few countries in Europe where relations between the trade union movement and its former historical allies are not fraught with difficulties. In effect, the trade unions have lost their political allies.

The second element is the loss of our periphery. The historical labour movement had created a powerful network of auxiliary organizations, covering most aspects of social life: culture, education, social protection, human rights, equality, a workers' press, even military self-defence. These were meant to be the building blocs of an alternative society.

Much of this was lost in the post-war period, where unions retreated to what they believed to be their core business: collective bargaining, leaving society to the State. Because the State, by its nature, cannot substitute itself to society, other social movements have occupied the space left vacant by the labour movement. In that sense, these social movements are the illegitimate children of the labour movement. We need to recognize them as our own.

The third element is the hugely destructive impact of

Stalinism. Russia had three or four years of revolution, followed by seventy years of counter-revolution. The countries of Eastern and Central Europe occupied by Russia at the end of World War II had forty years of Stalinism. Hundreds of thousands of socialists, anarchists, syndicalists, and dissident communists perished in the "purges" and in the labour camps of that regime, or were assassinated elsewhere in the world, our best people. Together with them the memory of what had been the labour movement in one fifth of the world was obliterated.

Worse yet: Stalinism corrupted and discredited the very concept of socialism, not least with the help of the conservative propaganda. Both sides colluded in this operation, the Soviet side, with its self-described "socialist countries", seeking to legitimise its system as an embodiment of historical socialism, and the conservative side, totally agreeing that the so-called "socialist countries" were indeed socialist, rather than the opposite of everything socialism had ever stood for, seeking to discredit the concept of socialism by equating it with Soviet reality.

When that regime finally collapsed under its own weight, without any workers anywhere rising in its defence, on the contrary, it left a bureaucratic ruling class recycled as a new capitalist class, as corrupt and lawless as it had ever been, and it also left a weak and disoriented labour movement, trying to find its bearings with difficulty, against enormous odds.

Before I leave this survey of the wreckage of the political movements that claimed to represent labour, I should also recall that there have always been dissidents, independent socialists, revolutionary syndicalists, who resisted. There were not many of us, but we fought and lived to fight another day, and that day is today.
I believe that we know what we now have to do. The issues are at the same time ideological, political and organizational.

Firstly: today's labour movement is essentially the trade union movement, that is what we have and that has to be our starting point. We have lost to a large extent our traditional political allies, but the trade union movement needs a political dimension. Everything we do is political.

We therefore must recover the politics which are naturally ours, taking as the sole point of departure the interests of our members, which are also the general interests of society.

Socialism remains our goal but, instructed by experience, we know that the meaning of socialism must be radical democracy: real power, democratically exercised, by real people, at every level, not by any substitutes, no vanguard parties, no so-called "progressive" authoritarians. We welcome all reliable political allies, but we cannot delegate the fight for the emancipation of labour to anyone else.

As a socialist, I would not want my party to control any trade unions. As socialists, our role should be to support the independent organizations of the working class, controlled by their members.

As socialists, we must also break with all forms of sectarianism. Those of us who are Marxists will remember what the Manifesto said: "The Communists do not form a separate party opposed to other working-class parties. They have no interest separate and apart from those of the proletariat as a whole. They do not set up any sectarian principles of their own, by which they shape and mould the proletarian movement."

Too much damage has already been done by those who place the interests of their party or their sect above the interests of the movement. They need to be left to their own isolation.

As a trade union movement, we must break with the ideology of "social partnership", which has long since been abandoned by our ruling classes. We have no "social partners", what we have is social counterparts, and that is not the same thing. Rather than lamenting the demise of "social partnership" and "social dialogue", we need to rebuild power relationships in our favour wherever possible by all means available to us.

Secondly, we need to respond to the changes in the nature of work and to reconstruct the identity of our class, the working class. In today's world, a majority of workers are in unstable, precarious, informal forms of employment, and unemployed for much of their working lives. Many are immigrants. All of them are part of our class.

Unions must develop effective structures to organize these workers. We must move beyond a narrow definition of the interests of our members and move towards class responses in new organisational forms and renewed organisations, reflecting the long-term general interest of our members and of society.

This is also an ideological and political task because it requires an inclusive approach to what we believe the working class to be and to the unions as a social movement.

Thirdly, and in the same order of ideas: we need to remain aware that women represent a huge proportion of the as yet unorganised working class, with enormous reserves of energy and courage, much of it still untapped and dormant. Despite some progress, the trade union movement remains heavily male dominated. Without a proactive policy of integrating women workers all the way to the top leadership level we deprive ourselves of an essential resource and are left fighting with one hand tied to our back.

Fourthly, there is an issue of structure. Greece, a small country like my own, has some 150 trade unions, between GSEE and ADEDY. That is far too many. Far too many general secretaries. As long as this structure dominates, it will be impossible to create a movement supported by its members alone, without State subsidies collected through taxes. What, today, is to stop the State from shutting you down, like they shut down your television, or your public hospitals?

Yours will remain a fragile and vulnerable movement unless it becomes the means through which the workers collectively rise and exercise their power. Power is not demonstrated by the ability to call 24-hour strikes. Power is demonstrated when the capitalists lose control over the State.

Comrades:

The European labour movement is today the target of an onslaught not experienced since the 1930s. This is not a passing phase. There will not be a return to what was considered normal social relations in the thirty years after the war. The project of contemporary capitalism is the destruction of the labour movement, in Europe, in North America and eventually everywhere else. Their project is the reorganisation of world society without organised labour. What they want is a society of slaves.

Greece has become the crucible of this process. Your ruling class is preparing for war. The Golden Dawn nazis are the shock troops of capitalism. You have an army that has a history of military coups whenever democracy inconvenienced your ruling class.

But you have also tremendous opportunities because everything is in flux, there is nothing to lose and everything is possible. Gramsci described the crisis of his time as: the old is dying and the new cannot be born. Our duty in our crisis is to be the midwives of the new: to make sure that the new can be born. There is nothing to stop you from rebuilding your movement to be the most powerful force in your country, as it potentially always has been and as it easily could become.

Do not look to the European trade union movement for inspiration or examples. They have nothing to teach you except how to retreat. Rely on your experience and your imagination and don't be afraid of radical solutions. In our situation, radical solutions are the realistic solutions. Is a general union for all workers imaginable in Greece? Could the GSEE and ADEDY become a single union, One Big Union?

Comrades:

We would welcome the creation of a Greek Global Labour Institute as a partner of our GLI International Network. We have created a free space for discussion and action, and this free space is expanding. We are inviting you to join. You will be joining an invisible International. We have no heavy structures, we do not seek bureaucratic hegemony. We are a network of autonomous and self-determined trade union activists working together, and working with others, with a common purpose: help rebuilding the international movement that the workers of the world need and deserve.

We recognise in you, our comrades in Syriza, the democratic and revolutionary approach which we believe to be the one our movement most needs at this time. We are here today to demonstrate our solidarity and we will stay together until every battle is won.

# The Future of the Domestic Workers' Movement [2013]

*This is a speech given at the International Domestic Workers' Federation, Founding Congress, Montevideo, October 26-28, 2013.*

Comrades,

**The subject of my speech should be the future of your movement, but who am I to tell you what your future is going to be?**

You have created your future right here, these past three days.
You have opened your own road, by walking.

I can be short because there have been many speeches and everything has already been said here about your achievement – the Federation.

One thing, though, is clear: your future is with the labour movement.

You will contribute to shape it, perhaps more than you now realize.

You have created the first international trade union federation in history that will be run entirely by women.

The gender issue is now also a class issue, but it is in fact much older and more fundamental, because it goes back to the dawn of human society.

We still live in a patriarchal society and we will not reach our goal – a society fit for all human beings to live in – until we have shaken off this burden. You have taken a huge step in that direction.

You have also created a federation of workers who until recently were not even perceived as workers.

You have demonstrated that there is no such thing as "unorganizable" workers.

Under the impact of new forms of capitalism, the working class has changed and is still changing, It has become fragmented, unsure if its identity.

The trade union movement has not kept up with these changes. Its response has been confused and weak.

Our task is now to restore the identity of all working people as a class, and to restore the trade union movement as the instrument of its emancipation.

You are part of this process, you are part of the renewal of the trade union movement.

To do this, you must stay united. Do not ever let yourselves be distracted by party political or personal issues.

Always remember: the union comes first. The union comes first, and the Federation comes first.

Today we celebrate – the hard part starts tomorrow. But you are not alone. The allies your movement has attracted will stay with you, as long as it takes, until every battle is won.

I thank you.

# About the author

Dan Gallin is Chair of the Global Labour Institute (GLI), a labour service organisation established in 1997 with a secretariat in Geneva (www.global-labour.org). From August 1960 until April 1997 Gallin worked for the International Union of Food, Agricultural, Hotel, Restaurant and Catering, Tobacco and Allied Workers' Associations (IUF), since 1968 as General Secretary. He has served as President of the International Federation of Workers' Education Associations (IFWEA) from 1992 to 2003 and has been Director of the Organization and Representation Program (ORP) of WIEGO (Women in Informal Employment Globalizing and Organizing) from June 30, 2000 to July 31, 2002. He continues to serve on the Advisory Committee of the ORP.

# LabourStart Books

**If you enjoyed this book, check out LabourStart's first three titles published in 2013:**

Campaigning Online and Winning
The Global Labour Movement: A Introduction
Firefox OS for Activists

The first two titles are also available in French.

**Order the books online from:**

http://www.labourstart.org

CPSIA information can be obtained at www.ICGtesting.com
Printed in the USA
LVOW04s1611250814

400820LV00021B/1404/P

9 781497 345614